ADVANCES IN INTERNATIONAL ACCOUNTING

Volume 3 • 1990

ADVANCES IN INTERNATIONAL ACCOUNTING

A Research Annual

Editor: KENNETH S. MOST
College of Business Administration
Florida International University

VOLUME 3 • 1990

JAI PRESS INC.

Greenwich, Connecticut *London, England*

55 Old Post Road, No. 2
Greenwich, Connecticut 06836

JAI PRESS LTD.
118 Pentonville Road
London N1 9JN
England

ISBN: 1-55938-078-0

Manufactured in the United States of America

CONTENTS

PART III. FOREIGN CURRENCY TRANSLATION

PART IV. CROSS-CULTURAL STUDIES

LIST OF CONTRIBUTORS

Mahmood Abdelsalam — College of Administrative Sciences, King Saud University, Saudi Arabia

Ahmed Belkaoui — Department of Accounting, University of Illinois at Chicago, United States

Kathleen R. Bindon — School of Accountancy, University of Alabama, United States

Robert Bloom — Department of Accounting, John Carroll University, United States

Gurprit Chhatwal — Department of Accounting, Rutgers University, United States

Eugene E. Comiskey — College of Management, Georgia Institute of Technology, United States

Timothy S. Doupnik — Division of Accounting, University of South Carolina, United States

Thomas G. Evans — Bowling Green State University, United States

M. Ali Fekrat — School of Business, Georgetown University, United States

Ahmad Hosseini — Department of Accounting, University of Detroit, United States

Bikki Jaggi — Department of Accounting, Rutgers University, United States

Robert J. Kirsch — Department of Accounting, Bowling Green State University, United States

W. Daryl Lindsay — College of Commerce, University of Saskatchewan, Canada

M.R. Mathews — Department of Accountancy, Massey University, New Zealand

Kenneth S. Most — School of Accounting, Florida International University, United States

Charles W. Mulford — College of Management, Georgia Institute of Technology, United States

Ahmed Naciri — Departement des Sciences Comptables, University of Quebec at Montreal, Canada

Gordian A. Ndubizu — Department of Accounting, Drexel University, United States

Hossein Shalchi — School of Management, University of Michigan-Flint, United States

M.H.B. Perera
Department of Accountancy
Massey University
New Zealand

Dick van Offeren
Faculty of Economics-Business
University of Amsterdam
The Netherlands

INTRODUCTION

We welcome contributors to this volume from the Arab world and from New Zealand. The first three volumes of *Advances in International Accounting* reported research from all parts of the world except South America, and I will continue to try and attract scholars from that region to expose their work here.

Two research areas have been added to this volume—international auditing and cross-cultural studies. A survey of accounting and auditing periodicals reveals that international auditing research is just beginning. Several recent publications discuss international auditing standards, a topic which has been well explored since Stamp and Moonitz directed their attention to it in 1979. The more "international" problem, however, is auditing across national frontiers; the first paper in this volume identifies a number of situations that demonstrate how extensive and critical this problem is. The two papers on cross-cultural studies represent an attempt to transfer research questions and methods to accounting from other fields which examine international issues comparatively. Attention is directed to the role of environmental factors in accounting system differences by Mueller in his 1967 *International Accounting*. Since then a number of accounting researchers have done cross-cultural studies without, it appears, any awareness of related studies in the social science literature on management, sociology, education, and so on. This is similar to energy research ignoring Einstein's laws of thermodynamics.

There is a broader issue, however, and that is to demonstrate how culture affects the kinds of decisions that result in differences between accounting practices. Someone once said that all psychological explanations are true and irrelevant, and the same may also apply to culture. In the United States, we witness daily the arrival of immigrants from the most diverse cultures who, with few exceptions, assimilate quickly the culture of their adopted country without strain. At the same time, Japan provides an illustration of a country that has embraced accounting practices from several foreign cultures as an act of policy and without any accompanying changes in the environment. This is the essence of a research question: Given that we expect environmental factors to affect accounting practices, do they, and if so, how?

I do not apologize for publishing more reports on foreign currency translation, which remains, with consolidation, among the most intractable accounting problems. I would like to receive more country studies (particularly from South America), and additions to the literature on international government accounting and auditing. Finally, I repeat my challenge to taxation scholars to send me some comparative studies to supplement the extensive literature on the foreign provisions of the U.S. tax code.

Kenneth S. Most
Editor

PART I

INTERNATIONAL AUDITING STANDARDS

INTERNATIONAL AUDITING PROBLEMS

Kenneth S. Most

ABSTRACT

The International Federation of Accountants (IFAC) has issued International Auditing guidelines dealing with basic philosophical and some practical aspects of auditing that are assumed relevant throughout the world. They do not cover international auditing, however, and to this extent they appear to be misnamed. A survey of international business and international finance reveals that, in addition to the special problems of auditing multinationals, a number of peculiarly international forms of transactions and other events present auditing problems that have not been investigated. They are here presented in some detail as an indication of the scope of the work facing international auditing standard-setters.

INTRODUCTION

The International Federation of Accountants (IFAC), was formed in 1977 as the last act of the International Coordination Committee of the Accountancy Profession, an informal body whose main responsibility had been the organization of international congresses of accountants.[1] It has the same

Advances in International Accounting, Vol. 3, pages 3-21.

ISBN: 1-55938-078-0

membership as the International Accounting Standards Committee, and has assumed responsibility for the harmonization of auditing practices, accounting education, professional ethics and other aspects of accounting and auditing throughout the world. Its International Auditing Practices Committee (IAPC) had issued some thirty International Auditing Guidelines (IAGs) through 1988.

In spite of the name, however, there is nothing international about these IAGs. They deal with the same subject matter as the generally accepted U.S. auditing standards (GAAS), often in the same terms, and contain philosophical and sometimes practical propositions that should be applicable to all audits that have as their objective the issuance of an opinion on financial statements. They do not deal with the important subject of international auditing practice, which has emerged as a large part of public accounting since World War II.

International auditing has two dimensions. One aspect relates to the audit of multinational corporations, whose operations by definition transcend the boundaries of nation states; the United Nations call them, for this reason, "transnationals." Auditing and international accounting textbooks usually include a discussion, albeit superficial, of the issues raised during an international audit engagement. Suffice to say, the existence of research problems in the audit of multinationals has been recognized, even though little research in the field has been undertaken. In this area, as in auditing generally, the researcher is handicapped by the high degree of secrecy associated with audit engagements.

In addition to auditing multinationals, and other entities doing business in more than one jurisdiction, an auditor may be faced with international transactions and other events of a financial, production, marketing, or other functional nature while auditing an entity that does not meet the criteria of a multinational corporation. Because auditors are not exposed to such situations in academic programs, and because training programs, with the exception of those of the largest international public accounting firms, fail to discuss them, they present a high profile for accounting research. Such research could well be performed under the sponsorship of IFAC.

Preliminary exploratory research has identified a number of types of international transactions and other events and circumstances that are primarily international in nature, and which, therefore, represent areas of interest to international auditing researchers.

INTERNATIONAL CASH MANAGEMENT

Cash management has become a complex activity as a result of high interest rates, the proliferation of financial intermediaries, and the growth of communications based on electronic technology: today, float is a household word. The same factors influence international cash management, amplified by volatile foreign currency markets, differential rates of inflation, remittance restrictions, geopolitical factors, and global rather than domestic competition. The auditor's function is difficult in a domestic setting, and becomes alarmingly so when offshore transfers are encountered, often involving use of CHIPS (New York) and CHAPS (London), electronic payment systems using automated interfaces between banks.

The natural tendency for a treasurer obliged to function in an international environment is to try to "internationalize" the principles and methods that have been found to work domestically. However, domestic cash management cannot simply be projected into an international arena. First, financial services and support systems that exist in the United States, for example, are not available in other countries, yet those other countries may have superior facilities that are unknown at home. As paymaster to a British military unit operating in all four zones of a partitioned postwar Germany, I did the job in several difficult ways before discovering the convenience of the German postal checking system, which at that time had no counterpart in the United Kingdom.

Some practices that are unknown in Canada or the United States have important audit implications. Value dating is used in some countries for much the same purpose as assigning float. Value dates decided and assigned by banks dictate when a transaction is completed and the funds are available, or begin to earn interest. They are also used by banks for calculating compensation for services. In some countries dates are assigned by law; in France, for example, a paid cheque must be debited to a customer's account on the date it was drawn, and not on the date when it is presented for payment.

Second, traditional sources of information used for determining credit, predicting interest and inflation rates and identifying opportunities to issue securities or place funds at interest, rarely suffice for international cash management. Treasurers must develop a new information system, and operate on a different real time scale than that to which they are accustomed.

Third, and perhaps most important, treasurers must operate with knowledge of the applicable laws and regulations in all the jurisdictions in which they will do business. The potential problems in international cash management are limitless given the many different ways in which governments control their foreign exchange reserves, foreign currency exchange rates, and domestic interest rates, and even use the banking system to limit imports and promote exports. Measures to inhibit the drug trade also have an impact. Not the least of the problems is the ever-present temptation—and frequent opportunity—to bypass the legal framework [see Securities and Exchange Commission, 1985]. Thus, global balance reporting, a necessary ingredient in international cash management, may be fraught with concealed dangers. One of the audit implications of strict control over the monetary system is that companies operating in such environments may use as many as 30 different banks, some of which permit overdrafts.

Finally, such mundane issues as accounting policies and computer systems sometimes work against the interests of international cash management. The critical distinction between collected and available balances, on the one hand, and book or ledger balances, on the other, brought together within company-wide data processing routines that require foreign currency translation at predetermined rates, can result in the cash manager trading with his company rather than with the outside world.

An understanding of the wire transfer of funds between banks throughout the world is crucial to dealing with international cash management. In the United States, the average daily transaction volume per bank over the Fedwire alone is estimated to represent 20% of total bank assets; at some large banks, daily volume sometimes exceeds the institution's total assets. Federal Reserve Bank members transfer funds over Fedwire by means of a credit transfer system. Other transfer mechanisms exist, of which the Society for Worldwide Interbank Financial Telecommunications (SWIFT) is the largest international system. There were over 45 million Fedwire transactions of this kind during 1985 [Comptroller of the Currency, 1977].

The wire transfer of money is one of the "end points" through which criminals can convert the proceeds of fraud or embezzlement to their own use, and very rapidly at that. Other mechanisms include credits to accounts, cheques issued or certified by the bank, tellers' and other cash funds, and items of value received or delivered. The most publicized case so far was that of Mark Rifkin who in 1978 used his knowledge of the wireroom operations of the Pacific National Bank to steal $10 million (*Wall Street Journal*). Other cases have been reported in the Fraud Bulletin distributed to auditors by the Bank Administration Institute, but it is believed that many banks maintain silence on the subject. It should be noted that error is even more likely than fraud in the use of wire transfers, as the missing $10 million from the Sultan of Brunei in the U.S. Irangate scandal demonstrated.

The only guidance available to auditors in this complex area is AICPA's *Industry Audit Guide–Banks* [1968/1983]. Chapter 22 concerns the international department of a bank and foreign currency transactions, but lacks any discussion of the issues previously enumerated. For example, it states that "the operations of an international department may include processing cable and mail transfers of funds," but the absence of further discussion leads us to assume that the procedures for verifying domestic transfers are adequate for international ones. The relevant internal control question is: Are the duties of origination, testing, processing, and balancing of wire transfer requests segregated?

The issues involved in wire transfers are also encountered in the practice known as "netting," used by large companies with many intracorporate cross-border flows. With netting, there is no settlement of international transactions at the invoice date. Instead, on a prearranged date the parties to transactions report their values to a central treasury department responsible for effecting settlement. This department converts all receivables and payables to a common currency, and nets intercountry flows into one receipt or payment for each subsidiary. One step beyond this is the reinvoicing center, a separate legal entity established to facilitate treasury control and minimize foreign exchange risk exposure. This center eliminates the need for subsidiaries to undertake dealings in foreign currencies for intracorporate cash flows.

Strict government control of capital markets and foreign exchange presents additional problems—a typical example of a social issue that calls for accounting and auditing responses. A multinational's funds in Colombia, for example, will typically be "blocked" from repatriation. Such funds are exposed to devaluation risks, which may be quantified as, say, 3% per month, with a maximum downside potential of 50% over 12 months. This situation creates great pressures to find methods to transfer money out of Colombia, and a number of strategies have been developed for this purpose.

One of these is the use of countertrade. Countertrade is a generic term that covers several different types of transactions involving nonmonetary exchange. Barter is the best known, but many complex and esoteric forms are encountered, including offsets, buybacks, compensation deals, switches, counterpurchase agreements, and even three-cornered transactions that utilize hedging. According to observers, countertrade today accounts for about 60% of world trade, and presents an interesting example of a business development that has been ignored by accounting standard-setters and textbook writers alike. Accounting Principles Board Opinion No. 29, "Accounting for Non-monetary Transactions," although relevant, was clearly written with something else in mind. Domestic barter presents valuation and other problems to auditors, particularly where it involves stock in one or more companies as part of the exchange. However, even an apparently straightforward international case, where the Colombian subsidiary of a multinational corporation purchases stock in a Colombian company using blocked pesos, then transfers ownership of the shares to the U.S. parent, for sale in the United States to repatriate funds, raises legal issues that are difficult to resolve in terms of future loss contingencies. Other countertrade transactions utilize multiple exchanges—Brazilian orange juice for South African wine for trucks manufactured in Canada, and so on—leading to problems of value and ownership that challenge the auditor's knowledge of international laws, customs, and markets.

Consider also an international stock swap, in which domestic currency is exchanged for stock in a company registered in another country. Because stock is defined as a "good," such a purchase would not be illegal in a blocked currency environment, as would a currency swap. The method requires two multinationals; for example, Colombian subsidiaries where one deals primarily in pesos and the other in dollars. The peso-rich company declares a peso dividend, payable to the Colombian account of its parent (Parent A). Parent A uses the pesos to buy nonvoting, nondividend-paying stock in the subsidiary of the dollar-rich parent (Subsidiary B). Parent B pays dollars for nonvoting, nondividend-paying treasury stock of Parent A. The parents and subsidiaries then arrange a stock swap, whereby the two parents end up owning their own (or an affiliate's) stock. Such transactions involve currency brokers and investment bankers in both the domestic and parent countries.

Apart from the possibilities of countertrade, however, cash managers in such an environment will likely engage in as many deals as possible, large or small, that result in losses less than the opportunity cost of holding the blocked currency. The possibility of losing control of corporate assets is strong. Another strategy, that of increasing local purchases, may produce inventory and other asset historical costs that are above economic values.

Beyond the valuation issue, loss contingencies obviously represent another major problem area. In the AWACs case, the U.K. government decided to buy the AWACs early warning defense system, but required the manufacturer to agree to an initial 130% offset purchase commitment, only 10% of which related directly to work on AWACs itself [*Countertrade*, 1987]. Another auditing issue is the physical count of inventory: an example is that of an airline which acquires fuel in a foreign country under a countertrade transaction. Some of the fuel is used on the flight back to the home base, and some remains as a residual in the tanks of the aircraft. The accountant may find it difficult to verify the quantity purchased and the quantity remaining.

Returning to the cash transfer issue, an article in the *Wall Street Journal* (1987) drew attention to problems created by delays in wire transfers, which are on the rise, and the associated cash management risks. It would seem that all auditors could use fairly detailed auditing guides covering the different forms of international cash transactions, which would require regular updating as new techniques, institutions, and procedures appeared on the international business scene.

INTERNATIONAL BANKING

Bank failures are a heavy burden on the economy of the country in which they occur. Not only do financial losses create direct hardships for shareholders and depositors, and even governments, but the impact of these failures necessarily has a multiplier effect that is felt throughout the community. Moreover, such failures undermine the fragile credibility that is the foundation of all free economies, ultimately leading to social discontent and disorder, and even revolution.

There have been a number of indications in recent years that banks find it difficult to operate in the international arena. They have suffered billion-dollar losses on foreign loans, multimillion dollar losses speculating in foreign currencies, and countless millions from simple employee fraud facilitated by transactions across national borders. It is hard to say how much of this represents bad business decisions, and how much is the consequence of weak management controls that could have been strengthened by better internal and external auditing. However, the quality of management is one of the factors that auditing standards require auditors to evaluate in probing for evidence of illegality, fraud, and errors in accounting records; it appears that some auditors may have been less than vigilant in this respect.

The problem has been aggravated by the aggressive thrust of banks to internationalize their operations over the past 40 years. In part, this has been a response to the needs of their customers, in particular, the multinationals. However, banks themselves have participated in the transformation of money markets from a domestic to a world scale, commencing, perhaps, with the birth of the eurocurrency market after World War II. They have also perceived an opportunity to avoid federal and state regulation, including income taxes, by conducting much of their business offshore. For U.S. banks, international transactions between nonresidents that are conducted offshore are exempt from Federal Reserve Board Regulations D and Q (reserve requirements and interest rate restrictions). For all of these reasons, small countries such as Bermuda, the Bahamas, the Cayman Islands, the Netherlands Antilles, and Panama replaced traditional offshore banking centers such as Tangiers and Kuwait, both of which ceased to be useful for such purpose. (Liechtenstein still serves the same purposes, although it is in this respect really a part of Switzerland.) It is noteworthy that the U.S. Internal Revenue Service has found it difficult to trace bank transactions involving these offshore tax havens, and it may be inferred that auditors encounter similar problems.

To complicate matters, it is often unnecessary to establish an offshore subsidiary in order to obtain some of the benefits of doing so, and a bank may create an international banking facility (IBF) simply by segregating a set of asset and liability accounts on the books of the parent. One advantage of this is that banks are thereby able to minimize foreign exchange risk exposure. An illustration of the auditing problem was provided in 1977 when the Corporate Tax bureau of New York State Finance and Taxation Department began a large-scale audit of banking operations, to determine the extent to which so-called international operations were subject to state and local income taxes. Since that time, New York has enacted legislation to permit closer regulation of IBFs.

Another issue arises out of the relative ease with which banks and other investors can obtain control over banks in other countries. In some cases these acquisitions can be regarded as legitimate business ventures, and many of the largest and most respected banks have expanded overseas by means of such acquisitions. But the way is also open to those with less socially desirable motives, and some instances of money laundering, looting and other illegal activities have already come to light. There is a constant danger of a large-scale operation that siphons off a bank's assets to a place where they can be held and used with impunity.

The situation usually encountered following such acquisitions can be illustrated by the case of a Japanese bank that purchases a U.S. bank for the purpose of doing business in the North American continent, including Canada. The Canadian Business Corporation Act provides that a corporation may borrow money unless the articles, bylaws, or unanimous shareholder agreement restrict the power to borrow. Lenders, therefore, need assurances that such restrictions do not exist. There are Canadian income tax provisions that must be known before decisions concerning interest rates and disposition of assets pledged as security can be made. Canada has tax treaties with both Japan and the United States, either or both of which may apply. If a case goes to court, the Canadian Currency and Exchange Act requires money judgments in Canadian currency. Many U.S. banks still calculate interest using a 360-day year, whereas by law and custom Canadian interest calculations use a 365-day year. Japanese interest rates are expressed on a daily basis.

An interesting point concerning auditing is the increasing use of the ECU (European currency unit) as a unit of account. As currency exchange rates became unstable, use of the ECU exploded, and today over 1,000 banks in 30 countries are active in the ECU market. Financial statements expressed in ECU's are now being published. It would seem that accountants should know more about ECUs and other international currencies, including the Special Drawing Rights or SDRs of the International Monetary Fund.

INTERNATIONAL LETTERS OF CREDIT

The letter of credit has become the preferred instrument of international trade. Financing of import-export operations by means of letters of credit is one of the most important services provided by international banks. It has been estimated that half of world trade is based on letters of credit. International transactions are more complex than domestic trades, and letters of credit present additional opportunities for fraud, misrepresentation, and error. Thus, on one hand, there are the usual problems of establishing credit worthiness and ensuring that the terms of the transaction are respected; on the other, problems of language, culture, different legal systems, politics, geographic distance, and the interposition of two or more additional parties vastly increase the risks of international trade using letters of credit.

A letter of credit is an instrument issued by a bank, whereby the bank substitutes its credit for that of a buying party to a transaction. The bank's credit is both good and well-known, and is thus superior to that of the buying party involved. The instrument guarantees payment to the seller of a specified sum of money on proof that (s)he has complied with a specified set of conditions. If the buyer deposits money with the bank at the time the letter of credit is opened it acts as a kind of escrow. The letter of credit is quite separate and distinct from the transaction in respect of which it is established, and protects both buyer and seller. The buyer knows that payment will not be made until all the conditions have been complied with. The seller knows that (s)he will be paid as soon as the terms of the letter have been met.

A distinction must be made between revocable and irrevocable letters of credit. The former, as the name implies, may be revoked at any time, and are used mainly to ease the process of financing production and obtaining export permits and other documents. In the present discussion, however, commercial letters of credit consist of irrevocable letters of credit. The name implies that they may not be revoked within the period during which they are valid, and for this reason they are in general use in international trade, although the revocation of irrevocable letters of credit is not unknown. The July 30, 1987 *Wall Street Journal* reported the case of a Texas bootmaker who accepted two letters of credit before delivering more than $1 million in merchandise, the customer stopped payment and the company was in court trying to collect.

Letters of credit were first used by Finnish importers of Brazilian coffee in 1840. In less than a century, they were standardized internationally and the mercantile laws of the leading trading nations interpreted them consistently. A standardized letter of credit form may be made subject to the Uniform Customs and Practice for Documentary Credits of the International Chamber of Commerce. Nevertheless, other laws may affect their function. The central bank of a country with foreign exchange controls may forbid payment; quotas may prevent the conditions from being met; any contact with Israel, Israelis, an Israeli ship, or even a vessel carrying a cargo to Israel may provide an Arab bank with an opportunity to withhold payment.

There is no real distinction between an import or export letter of credit. A documentary letter of credit requires that the beneficiary's draft be accompanied by specified documents; a "clean" letter of credit only requires a draft. This type of trade financing is becoming quite common, and is also known as a standby letter of credit. A letter of credit may provide for payment at sight or after a stated period of time. A revolving letter of credit may be renewed, for example, where several shipments are to be made. A letter of credit may provide for payment in any currency, may specify the bank through which it must be negotiated, and may also permit transferability if the words "or transferee" are added after the beneficiary's name [see FASB Statement No. 5, for the sole mention of letters of credit in GAAP].

Banking Problems With Letters of Credit

The letter of credit is quite separate and distinct from the contract for purchase or sale in respect of which it has been issued. Such a documentary credit normally involves four parties: the applicant (buyer), the issuing bank, the beneficiary (seller), and the negotiating bank, usually a corespondent of the issuing bank in the seller's country. An irrevocable letter of credit may be confirmed, in which case the negotiating bank undertakes to honor the seller's draft, or unconfirmed, in which case it merely advises the exporter that the credit has been opened. Under a red clause credit the seller can obtain an advance from the negotiating (correspondent) bank, in order to finance the manufacture of the goods.

Every letter of credit is different, and there are no precedents to be followed; the conditions enumerated in the letter must be met exactly before the paying bank can collect from its customer. Thus, error is a more likely occurrence than fraud, especially when payment to the seller is made by a negotiating bank in one country with recourse to the issuing bank in another country for repayment.

One obvious source of error is that letters of credit are issued in the language of the country of the issuing bank, which may not be the language of the country of the negotiating bank, or of either buyer or seller. The letter of credit may contain a host of technical specifications concerning the goods, their method of transportation and insurance, how they are to be loaded and stored on board the ship or aircraft, how they are to be landed and warehoused, and so on. Sometimes, the exact meaning of the letter of credit, or of the documents evidencing the shipment, cannot be determined, and the negotiating bank may need to go to some lengths to have them translated by a translator who knows the technical terms involved and refuse payment until the question has been resolved. In practice, the letter of credit will often be returned to the customer who opened the credit, perhaps unknown to the other party to the transaction.

Another source of misunderstanding is the amendment to a letter of credit. Such amendments should be in writing and signed by all parties, but a bank's customer may find it necessary to file an amendment by telephone in order to secure execution of the contract.

Error is more easily discovered than fraud, usually perpetrated by the seller, the beneficiary of the letter of credit. All parties to the letter of credit deal in documents, not in goods, and discrepancies must be resolved on the basis of the documents alone. The negotiating bank does not normally inspect the shipment itself, or even see the containers, and the letter of credit merely provides that, if a shipment can be documented that apparently complies with the terms and conditions of the letter of credit, the seller will be paid. Between the time the bank pays the beneficiary and the time it is reimbursed, the bank assumes title to the goods.

In this case, the goods are collateral for the advance receivable by the bank. The value of this collateral depends upon the marketability of the goods, and the more specific they are, the greater the risk. The author is familiar with a transaction in which an aluminum plant was imported into the United States under a letter of credit, and payment depended upon the performance of the plant in the period following its installation. Banks will normally require documents accompanying the goods to be in negotiable form, and proof of insurance.

Case Involving a Bank Letter of Credit

The Barckus Toy Co. Inc. of Baltimore purchased a quantity of toys from Fon Ton Ltd. in Hong Kong, under an irrevocable letter of credit from Marley Bank Inc. in Baltimore. When Fon Ton presented the documents to Far East Bank Ltd. in Hong Kong for collection of the amount due under the letter of credit the bank discovered:

- A discrepancy between the written and typed money amounts in the letter of credit. The money amount was $20,000 higher than the written amount, and Fon Ton's draft was for the higher amount.
- Shipment was made on a vessel sailing for San Francisco, and then overland to Baltimore, instead of an Atlantic port as specified in the letter of credit.

When Far East Bank contacted Marley Bank, it was discovered that:

- The file contained a pro forma invoice showing the lower amount in the letter of credit.
- The file also contained a handwritten memorandum of a telephone call from Barckus, agreeing to shipment via San Francisco, but giving the name and date of sailing of a different vessel than the one actually used.
- The file did not contain any evidence, such as a copy of a Barckus corporate resolution, that the person who signed the application for the letter of credit was duly authorized to do so.
- The letter of credit showed the word "approx." following the written amount, which was the amount that had been charged to the customer's account and credited to an account for liabilities under letters of credit outstanding. This meant that the credit could be drawn on the face value plus or minus 10%. The bank's policy was to book such credits at the highest level of liability.

Finally, another problem arises in countries with critical shortages of foreign currency, such as those of Latin America. In most of these countries, imports are categorized by priorities, and reserves allocated accordingly. Commercial banks that finance international trade must apply to the central bank of the country, to obtain a guarantee that the funds will be available to pay the letters of credit they issue. Even after such guarantees have been given, however, domestic political unrest or foreign policy considerations may cause the country's government to restrict payment to imports of oil, arms, and medicines. If the letter of credit is for automobile parts, for example, and a correspondent bank in the exporting country has confirmed the letter of credit the latter will have to pay the exporter on receipt of documentary proof that the terms of the letter of credit have been complied with. The issuing bank remains liable under the letter, and may develop foreign exchange exposure problems as a result of this situation.

Accounting Problems of Letters of Credit

There are number of accounting and auditing problems associated with letters of credit. The prevailing practice of banks in the United States, the United Kingdom, Canada and several other countries is not to record or report guarantees undertaken by correspondent banks on behalf of issuing banks. A number of other countries (France, Germany, Italy) require banks to record and report as assets and liabilities, both guarantees and the corresponding assets representing the liabilities to them of issuing banks.

In this connection, FASB *SFAS 5,* "Accounting for Contingencies," requires commercial banks only to disclose standby letter of credit obligations. Such loss contingencies having the characteristic of a guarantee should be disclosed even if the possibility of loss is remote. However, this provision does not cover any other type of letter of credit.

The accounting and auditing problems go well beyond this issue. For example, with any letter of credit, a bank will want to ensure that:

- assets and liabilities are fairly stated in the general ledger;
- documents and records are properly safeguarded;
- applications and authorizations are made by the proper officers;
- payments are effected in accordance with specified terms and conditions;
- fees are assessed, collected and recorded in accordance with the bank's policies and procedures;
- the forms and procedures of the Uniform Commercial Code, the Uniform Customs and Practices of the International Chamber of Commerce, and the applicable regulations have been followed; and
- up-to-date information on the progress of the letter of credit toward payment is maintained on file.

From the viewpoint of the seller, it is important to recall that should any one of the terms of the letter be contravened, the security afforded by the letter is lost. If the seller has accepted contract provisions specifying that documents such as acceptance and progress reports must be signed by the buyer, refusal by the buyer to sign such reports effectively blocks the credit. If the buyer has stipulated that a document must be notarized by a consular official, it is important to ensure that a consul of that country will be available at the proper time. All such factors affect the accounting for the transaction, and the valuation of an account receivable or an item of inventory.

From the viewpoint of the buyer, the application for and issue of a letter of credit means incurring a liability, with or without a corresponding asset. The matter is out of the buyer's hands, unlike a purchase order that may be cancelled, or for which delivery may be refused. The buyer may not stop payment on an irrevocable letter of credit, as might be done with a cheque, and should the issuing bank refuse payment and be faced with a lawsuit, it will look to the buyer for indemnity. However, if the buyer can establish egregious fraud on the part of the seller, and satisfy general standards for injunctive relief, (s)he may apply to the court to enjoin the issuing bank from making payment.

INSURANCE PROBLEMS

International Insurance and Reinsurance

The field of international insurance provides a striking illustration of past and potential future frauds arising out of the reinsurance and transportation aspects of international business.

The name Lloyds of London conjures up an image of integrity that has been carefully nurtured during the 300-year history of the international insurance market. The market is made by syndicates of "names," wealthy individuals who provide the capital for the underwriters to write insurance contracts on a variety of risks. The liability of the names is unlimited, one of the factors underlying confidence in the market. Since World War II, the number of names and the value of insurance have increased dramatically, providing ample opportunity for abuse of the system by unscrupulous underwriters. The most obvious method for perpetrating fraud is for the underwriter to channel premiums through a labyrinth of offshore companies and brokers, the ultimate destination being a company owned by the underwriter, possibly the managing agent for a syndicate of innocent names. Either the underwriter would benefit from the interest earned on the premium money, or, in the worst case, it would simply be converted to his own use.

An example of this was provided by the so-called Fidentia affair, in which at least £6.2 million were allegedly misappropriated over a 13-year period, only to resurface, through reinsurance contracts, in a Bermudan insurance company named Fidentia that was owned by the two underwriters responsible for the money. In the Savonita affair, a claim was made for 301 supposedly fire-damaged automobiles unloaded from the MV Savonita, which were subsequently sold in Italy for nearly their full value. The so-called PCW affair involved a well-known Lloyds underwriter who set up his own agency and then sold it to a company (Minet) for £2 million. The underwriter and a colleague continued to operate the agency. Gossip on Lime Street, where Lloyds is housed, prompted the insurer's governing council to look into a reinsurance contract which remitted £800,000 to a secret bank account in Geneva, Switzerland. More serious discrepancies were uncovered by one of the Big Eight public accounting firms investigating reinsurance contracts placed by syndicates controlled by a Lloyds broker acquired by an American insurance company. In this case, the auditors discovered that some $55 million had been misappropriated by managers of the broker. The investigation led to the PCW principals, and Minet subsequently discovered that about £40 million was missing, much of it channelled to offshore compannies controlled by Minet's managers.

These and other scandals resulted in the appointment of a prominent London chartered accountant as the chief executive of Lloyds, with a mandate to institute controls that would prevent such looting. The Lloyds Act of 1982 was passed by Parliament to provide tighter controls on the market, without changing its traditional structure of self-regulation. The opportunity for fraudulent conversion is always present, however, and only a rigorous audit requirement can serve to reduce its incidence by ensuring speedy discovery and prosecution.

It should not be assumed that such problems are peculiar to the London insurance market. The *Wall Street Journal* reported that American Express Company had settled SEC charges of improperly accounting for certain reinsurance transactions and overstating profit by $54 million in 1981 and $40 million in 1982. These charges arose out of practices whereby an insurance subsidiary of American Express made payments to another insurance concern that were supposed to be premium payments but were actually deposits, reclaimed in subsequent years. In this case, the money did not disappear, but the potential for loss arising out of the transactions was unmistakable.

The Captive Insurance Company

New opportunities for fraud and misrepresentation have presented themselves as more and more companies outside the insurance field have set up their own "captive" insurance companies offshore. This is a clear example of how a social problem becomes an accounting problem, and ultimately an auditing problem.

For a variety of reasons—for example, mismanagement, poor investment returns, civil suits resulting in punitive court awards, and fraud on the part of insured persons the insurance industry has proved incapable of performing its social function. Particularly in North America, individuals, businesses, professional firms, and even governments are finding it impossible to obtain coverage for the usual risks, or are able to purchase such coverage only at prohibitive rates. For this reason, self-insurance is, in many cases, the only practical way to convert risks into costs.

The conventional methods of self-insurance, however, face certain obstacles. From the accounting point of view, FASB *SFAS 5* effectively prevents conversion of a risk into a cost in financial reports. The "premium" is not tax deductible. Internally, the funds that should be segregated for the payment of losses are not protected from predatory managers, who fight against placing the money on deposit at, say, eight percent interest when it could be invested in business operations that may possibly return many times that amount.

The logical solution to this problem would be for the self-insuring entity to establish its own "captive" insurance company, which might not provide any accounting or tax advantages but would at least permit the premiums to be protected, and possibly establish relationships with other insurance companies leading to reinsurance contracts. Some wholly-owned ("pure") captives have been set up, but they face considerable obstacles in the form of state regulations and licencing provisions that must be complied with, and often result in great expense. These difficulties could be mitigated somewhat by making the captive "impure," by permitting it to insure others than the parent, or by establishing homogeneous captives for groups of companies in the same industry, or non-homogeneous captives willing to admit anyone who will pay the fee.

During the past few years, however, a number of offshore jurisdictions have grasped the opportunity to help companies establish captives that will provide accounting and tax advantages to the insured companies, and also help them avoid the regulatory and licencing costs that affect captives formed in major industrial countries. For example, Barbados can provide advantages to U.S. companies because of its income tax treaty with the United States, and help them avoid some or all of the federal excise tax on insurance premiums. To encourage them to take advantage of this situation, the Barbados Exempt Insurance Act was passed in 1983 to enable companies to carry on insurance business from within the country, essentially free of regulation and with minimal—in some cases, non-existent—capitalization. The fee for filing an application for a licence to carry on the business of exempt insurance is currently $B500.00, while the annual renewal costs $B5,000.00.

The June 10, 1986 *Wall Street Journal* reported that 66 United States corporations, most of them at the top of the *Fortune* 500 list, had invested $395 million in a new offshore company for the purpose of providing substantial liability coverage to each of the principals. The corporations formed a Cayman Islands holding company as the parent of a Barbados-based insurance company. Corporations that were not members of the investor group will also be able to buy coverage from this insurance company. The report stated that these companies "are based outside the United States to avoid U.S. securities and insurance regulation and U.S. taxes." Presumably, the formation of the holding company in the Cayman Islands also related to the secrecy factor.

It may be observed that captives are managed by insurance brokers who are remunerated by commissions on premium income, and who often receive warrants to buy some of the captive's stock. Fees are also paid to investment firms that manage the captive's investments. The situation is fraught with opportunities for fraud and misrepresentation through concealment of information, aggravated by the fact that one of the motives for forming such companies is to avoid regulations that were designed to reduce opportunities for fraud and misrepresentation.

FOREIGN TRADE ZONES

A foreign or "free" trade zone is a secure area where goods can be imported from abroad and reexported without becoming subject to domestic customs regulations, tariffs or duties. In some cases, these goods may be imported to the domestic market at reduced tariffs. The practice is of considerable antiquity; the first known free port specifically designed to promote trade was established by the Romans on the Aegean island of Delos. In modern times, the prototype of the free trade zone was the free port of Hamburg in Germany, created in 1888.

The success of European foreign trade zones prompted the United States Congress to pass the Foreign Trade Zones Act of 1934, and the Boggs Amendment of 1950, which authorized manufacturing in such zones. This Act provided for authority to operate them as public utilities by qualified corporations under authority granted by the Foreign Trade Zones Board. There were 155 U.S. foreign trade zones in 1984, and 427 throughout the world, and it is estimated that about 10% of world trade utilizes such a zone in one way or another. The volume of trade conducted through foreign trade zones is expected to double by 1990.

The advantages of foreign trade zones to importers are:

- reduced cash outflows through exemption from or postponement of duties;
- exemption from customs inspection, appraisal and classification, which simplifies paperwork and speeds handling;
- reduced insurance and financing costs, because value does not include duties;
- opportunity to hold limited quota merchandise pending reopening of a quota, or convert inventory into non-quota goods;

- lower import duty on manufactured goods than the sum of the duties on the imported components, and possible avoidance of quota limitations; and
- elimination of duties on goods that are damaged in transit, spoil, or experience shrinking or evaporation while in the zone.

A typical modern zone is the Miami Free Zone in Florida, occupying 50 acres near Miami International Airport. It offers tenants such in-house services as:

- full-time U.S. Customs personnel during working hours;
- security around the clock covering merchandise and personnel access;
- computerized visitor/employee security control;
- bonded cartment for direct export, and other related import/export services; and
- periodic warehouse inventory inspections to ensure compliance with Customs regulations.

It is apparent that a foreign trade zone is simply a shell that contains the operations of a number of individual enterprises, large and small. The critical element is a system of accountability, to control the flow of information about these operations. Accountability rests with the customs service of the country in which the zone is located. In the United States, U.S. Customs controls the movement of goods to the foreign trade zone, approves and supervises the operations performed upon the goods, and controls the movement of the resulting goods out of the zone. A customs officer does this personally, and businesses operating in the zone reimburse the officer's salary and expenses. However, the inventory control system is the key element in the proper functioning of the zone.

Historically, such an inventory control system was maintained and operated by U.S. Customs, and individual businesses could keep separate inventory records, manual or computerized. The growth in number and size of foreign trade zones impaired the ability of U.S. Customs to discharge this function satisfactorily, and on September 3, 1976 it established a procedure for a foreign trade zone business operator to establish its own inventory records and control under Customs supervision. The AICS system of the Miami Foreign Trade Zone is an example of a system that must maintain an audit trail for U.S. Customs, provide accurate and timely reports for use in spot-checking inventories, identify shortages and surpluses, account for or permit the derivation of the output of given inputs, and provide the information necessary for invoicing, entering, classifying, and appraising the goods upon entry to the U.S. Domestic market.

Besides the conventional accounting problems of costing and inventory control, U.S. Customs now faces the sampling and other problems of auditing inventories that are kept by business firms. On-site physical inspection has been drastically reduced, and even discontinued. At the Miami Foreign Trade Zone, Customs only keeps copies of the documents produced by the AICS. The bond that foreign trade zone business operators must post with the Customs is to cover any lost customs duties resulting from misplaced or misappropriated goods wthin the zone; it does not constitute a security for damage caused by fraudulent activity. The consequences of misusing a foreign trade zone for say, narcotics trafficking, are well known in Miami, but there are also ample opportunities for fraud and error in relation to legitimate merchandise.

Thus, an aspect of international trade requiring strict governmental control is expanding vigorously at a time when public expenditures are being cut back. The Miami Foreign Trade Zone is unlikely to be atypical, and the role of the local Customs Service is equally critical in other U.S. zones and in other countries. The possibility of fraud and/or defalcation exists in relation to any goods purportedly stored in such a zone. AICPA has promulgated auditing standards that deal specifically with goods held in public warehouses (AU Section 90—Public Warehouse Controls and Auditing Procedures for Goods Held) and provide a basic framework for domestic audits. There is no question that such an auditing standard for foreign trade zonse and other similar (bonded) warehouses is needed, andwould best be promulgated internationally.

CONCLUSION

The need to develop standards for the audit of multinational clients has been recognized by public accounting firms, some of which have written their own manuals of standard operating procedures for this type of audit situation. These manuals rarely contain detailed guides for the audit of international business transactions, but are concerned primarily with relations between the firm's home office and its overseas offices and field staffs, and with other auditors that may be involved. Auditing methodologies differ between firms [Cushing and Loebbecke, 1986], and there is little doubt that such differences are even greater where international auditing is concerned. It is reasonable to suppose that interfirm cooperation would improve the quality of such audits, especially because many, if not most, foreign subsidiaries of multinationals are not audited by the firm that audits the parent.

This study has also drawn attention to a range of auditing problems that transcend national boundaries, regardless of whether the entity is a multinational corporation. Some arise out of the growth in international business that has taken place since World War II, others out of the globalization of financial markets, a phenomenon that has its own dynamic, and others out of a deliberate effort to escape the costs and difficulties of operating in a regulated environment. The list of international auditing problems presented here is not exhaustive, particularly because the discovery of such problems was not part of a formal research project. It is suggested, however, that those identified are sufficiently important to require urgent atention, and eventually the publication of a series of accounting and auditing guidelines.

Both of these tasks are particularly appropriate for the International Auditing Practices Committee of the International Federation of Accountants. The IAPC is at a disadvantage in moving toward its goal of establishing a universal level of auditing standards, compared to the national professional associations that are its members. Only the national bodies can determine such issues as the nature and scope of the audit, the rights and duties of auditors, their educational and professional qualifications, and the problems of independence and objectivity. Audit techniques, such as those aimed at verification of assets and revenues, can only be dealt with satisfactorily within the context of a named jurisdiction. On the other hand, the description and flow-charting of such issues as international cash movements, the identification of required controls, and determination of the points of the system which should be tested, are best dealt with by accountants from different countries working in collaboration.

NOTE

1. The "C" IFAC has no significance; it was put there to avoid the possibility of confusion with the International Football Association (IFA).

REFERENCES

American Institute of Certified Public Accountants, *Industry Audit Guide–Banks* [New York: AICPA, 1968/1983].

Comptroller of the Currency, *Handbook for National Bank Examiners* [Washington, D.C.: Comptroller of the Currency, 1977].

Connor, J.E., "Enhancing Public Confidence in the Accounting Profession," *Journal of Accountancy* [July 1986], p. 82.

Countertrade and Barter [April/May 1987].

Cushing, B.E., and J.K. Loebbecke, "Comparison of Audit Methodologies of Large Accounting Firms," *Studies in Accounting Research No. 26* [Sarasota, FL: AAA, 1986].

Financial Accounting Standards Board, *Statement of Financial Accounting Standards No. 5*, "Accounting for Contingencies" [FASB, March 1975].

Securities and Exchange Commission, *Accounting Series Release No. 292* [April 3, 1985].

PART II

COUNTRY STUDIES

THE USE OF CORPORATE FINANCIAL REPORTS BY INVESTORS IN SAUDI ARABIA

Mahmoud Abdelsalam

ABSTRACT

This paper provides indicators of the investor's level of use and understanding of the accounting information contained in the corporate financial reports for the Investors in the Kingdom of Saudi Arabia (KSA), when they are making investment decisions related to buying, holding or selling common stock. The paper focuses on: (a) the review of earlier studies on the subject in the United States, United Kingdom, and other countries; (b) Saudi investors' views on the importance of financial statements and important sections in the annual report; (c) the source of financial information when Saudi investors are making investment decisions; (d) the comparison of the results of the study in Saudi Arabia with other studies in the United States, United Kingdom, New Zealand, and Australia.

Advances in International Accounting, Vol. 3, pages 25-39.

ISBN: 1-55938-078-0

INTRODUCTION

Accountants have always believed for the most part in the usefulness of corporate financial reports for individual investors as well as for firms and financial analysts. However, few studies have been undertaken to see just how important those investors find the financial reports themselves, and specifically what information in those reports the investors value. Those studies that have been performed in the form of investor surveys yield mixed results among several countries including the United States, United Kingdom, and Australia. Even within the United States, the results are not clear, although American investors do not seem to reply murh on financial reports. Because the Saudi market is relatively new, and because the financial reports are required to be not only distributed but also published in local newspapers, Saudi accountants must assume these reports contain useful information.

The usefulness of the reports is not at issue here. Rather, the questions here are whether investors individually use the reports, and on what information in those financial reports do they most heavily rely. This paper discusses the investor characteristics in Saudi Arabia and reconciles the resultus of prior studies. First, some of the previous studies on investor use of financial reports, will be described. Second, the methodology is explained and the attributes of the investors studies are discussed. Third, the results of the survey are described and then compared to prior studies.

RELATED RESEARCH AND HYPOTHESIS

Two decades ago some questions arose about who needs financial reports, what information they need, and whether corporate financial reports were useful to investors. To answer these questions a number of investor surveys were conducted in the United States [e.g., Epstein, 1975; Baker and Haslem, 1973; Chang and Most, 1977], the United Kingdom [Lee and Tweedie, 1976], New Zealand [Wilton and Tabb, 1978], and Australia [Winfield, 1978]. Table 1 shows the main findings of some of these earlier studies.

It seems that in the United States the individual investors rely heavily on stockbrokers, but not so much themselves on published financial statements. However, in the United Kingdom and Australia these financial reports act as an important source of information. Given these results, what might on investor survey of Saudi Arabia add to accounting knowledge? Saudi Arabia has two attributes that the countries of the previous studies do not: (1) it has a very new market, regulated only in 1984, and (2) this market is heavily influenced by its government.

The government owns shares in about one-third of the corporations, and guarantees a minimum profit for about one-sixth of the rest. Given this kind

Table 1. The Main Findings of the Earlier Studies

Earlier Studies	*The Main Findings*
Epstein (United States)	• 15% of individual investors rely on corporate financial reports as a source of investment information • 48.8% rely on stockbrokers' advice
Baker and Haslem (United States)	• 7.9% of investors depend on financial statements • 46.8% rely on stockbrokers
Lee and Tweedie (United Kingdom)	• Financial reports are considered an important source of information for investment decisions to the sample of individual shareholders in the United Kingdom
Winfield (Australia)	• 70.5% of investors use annual reports • 55.8% rely on the financial press
Chang and Most (United States, United Kingdom, and New Zealand)	• Financial reports represent information useful for investment decisions in the United States, United Kingdom, and New Zealand

of economy, a study of investor use in Saudi Arabia should contrast with surveys in the United States and United Kingdom for the following reasons. Investors in new markets probably have different uses for financial information than do those in long established markets: the new market has fewer "other" scources of financial information, and different knowledge may negate some of the traditional needs for financial reports. When a firm has a guaranteed minimum profit the investors do not worry so much about the firm's financial condition.

This paper studies the hypothesis that Saudi investors do use financial statements as an important source of market information. It also looks at the specific financial items that investors find most useful, and compares these results to those of prior studies. The following section describes the research methods and investors.

THE RESEARCH SURVEY IN SAUDI ARABIA

Since 1970, individuals have been able to invest their resources in Saudi corporations in four main economic sectors: financial, industrial, agricultural, and commercial. Although they did so through brokers, the early market was mostly informal. Eventually the Ministry of Commerce issued regulations to control and supervise Saudi companies in order to safeguard the public interest and protect private funds. Furthermore, stock regulations were officially issued

Table 2. Number of Questionnaires Delivered and Responses to the Survey*

	Number of Questionnaires Delivered	*Number of Responses*	*Percentage*
Share Register Department in Saudi corporations	100	72	72.0
Stock Trade Department in Saudi commercial banks	250	139	55.6
Saudi Businessmen List	50	20	40.0
Total	400	231	57.7

Note: * This survey to Saudi investors started on August 1986 and ended February 1987, and includes the major areas of Saudi Arabia (Riyadh, Jeddah, Dhahran, Ahsa, and Qasim).

to control the Saudi stock market through share departments in Saudi commercial banks. These included the requirement that financial statements be both issued to stockholders before each annual general meeting and published in local newspapers. At the present time there are more than 40 Saudi corporations, with 330 million shares and 38 billion Saudi Riyals (SR) invested (1 SR = $.267 American).

To find out whether the owners of those 330 million shares actually use the financial reports sent them, a questionnaire based on earlier studies in the United States and other countries was prepared. The motive behind this study, as a first survey in Saudi Arabia, was to indicate the use of corporate financial reports by Saudi investors when they were making investment decisions related to buying, holding, or selling stocks in Saudi Arabia. The questionnaire was divided into two parts. The first part aimed to indicate the investment characteristics of the Saudi investors. The second part aimed to indicate the investors' views on which sources of information they most heavily relied and on the importance of specific sections in the annual reports.

These questionnaires were distributed to Saudi investors through the Share Register department in Saudi corporations, the Stock Trade Department in Saudi commercial banks, and to other investors selected randomly from a list of Saudi businessmen in the Chamber of Commerce Consul. Table 2 shows the distribution of the questionnaire and the investor responses to the survey. The overall response rate was over 50%.

The aim of this section is to study the economic characteristics of the investor in Saudi Arabia; the kinds of corporations in which the Saudis invest (banking, industry, electricity, real estate, and so forth) the number of shares owned, in whose name shares are registered, investors' annual incomes, the reasoning behind buying or selling the shares, and whether the investors read the corporate financial reports and attend the annual general meetings. Tables 3-10 show these investor characteristics with regard to the 231 respondents to the survey.

Table 3. Types of Corporation in Which Saudis Invest

Corporations	*Number of Responses*	*Percentage*	*Ranking*
Bank	158	68.4	1
Cement	116	50.1	5
Electricity	121	52.4	4
Industrial	126	54.5	3
Transportation	115	49.8	6
Real Estate	62	26.8	8
Hotels	70	30.3	7
Agriculture	151	65.4	2

Table 4. Number of Shares Owned by Saudi Investors

Number of Shares	*Number of Responses*	*Percentage*	*Ranking*
Fewer than 100 shares	27	11.7	4
100 to 499 shares	53	22.9	2
500 to 999 shares	52	22.5	3
1000 or more shares	97	42.0	1

Table 5. Share Registration by Saudi Investors

Share Ownership	*Number of Responses*	*Percentage*	*Ranking*
Investor's Name	79	34.2	2
Investor's and His Family's Name	139	60.2	1
Others	13	5.6	3

The corporations in which the 231 respondents invested is indicated in Table 3. Because of the high dividends per share (15%-20%), 68.4% of the Saudi shareholders invest in the financial sector (e.g., banking); 65.4% of the sample invest in agricultural corporations, which many believe have high growth potential. However, only 26.8% and 30.3% invest in real estate and hotels, respectively.

Table 4 shows the number of shares each respondent owns. Forty-two percent of the Saudi investors own more than 1000 shares and only 11.7% own fewer than 100 shares; a big portion of stock shares in Saudi Arabia are owned by big shareholders.

Table 5 indicates in whose name(s) these shares are registered: 60.2% of Saudi investors buy the stock shares under their families' names as well as their own,

Table 6. The Annual Income of The Sample of Saudi Investors

Annual Incomes (1 Saudi Riyal = $.267)	*Number of Responses*	*Percentage*	*Ranking*
Under 120,000 SR	74	32.0	1
120,000-299,000 SR	63	27.3	2
300,000-499,999 SR	51	22.1	3
500,000 or more SR	41	17.7	4

Table 7. Reason for Buying the Shares of the Corporation

Reason for Buying Shares	*Number of Responses*	*Percentage*	*Ranking*
Profit Achieved	142	61.5	1
High Dividend Per Share	109	47.2	3
Government Subsidized	85	36.8	4
Saudi and Non-Saudi Corporation	14	6.1	5
Future of the Corporation	138	59.7	2

Table 8. Reason for Selling Shares of the Corporation

Reason for Selling Shares	*Number of Responses*	*Percentage*	*Ranking*
No Profit Achieved	107	46.3	1
Low dividend Per Share	93	40.3	2
Not Government Subsidized	55	23.8	4
Economic Situation of the Company	92	39.8	3

and 34.2% buy the shares under their names alone. Table 6 deals with the respective wealth of the stockholders; that is, it breaks down the sample by incomes. Thirty-two percent of the respondents earn under 120,000 SR per year. Only 17.7% earn 500,000 SR or more.

Given this data, it would seem likely that stockholders invest in order to earn some extra income or profit. Table 7 shows five reasons for purchasing shares in Saudi corporations as well as the investors' responses to these reasons: 61.5% buy stock shares for the profits achieved, whereas 59.7% are interested in the future of the companies. However, only about one-third of the shareholders buy shares because of the guaranteed minimum profit (government subsidization).

While all investors buy the shares, some have sold shares and all must think about why they would sell. Table 8 indicates four reasons why stockholders

Table 9. Reading Corporate Financial Reports by Saudi Investors

	Number of Responses	*Percentage*
Read Financial Reports	197	85.3
Does Not Read Financial Reports	33	14.3

Table 10. Attending the Corporate Annual General Meeting by Saudi Investors

	Number of Responses	*Percentage*
Attend the Corporate General Meeting	104	45.0
Does Not Attend the General Meeting	126	54.5

would sell their shares; the majority (46.3%) claimed it is because no profit was achieved, whereas 40.3% would have sold the shares because the dividend per share was insufficient. These are not surprising results given their annual incomes and original reasons for buying. However, now come the two characteristics related to the main part of this study; that is, the use of the financial reports for making investment decisions.

Table 9 indicates whether or not the respondents read the annual reports, and Table 10 reports if they attend the annual meeting for which those financial statements were prepared. According to this survey, 85.3% of Saudi investors read the corporate financial reports when they are making economic decisions related to buying or selling stock shares; only about 45% attend the corporate general meeting to discuss the corporate financial reports.

Thus, one sees a 'representative' stockholder as: owning at least 1,000 shares in bank stocks under his family name; earning under 120,000 SR per year; buying the shares specifically to earn a profit; selling the shares if the profit were not achieved, reading the financial reports to make these decisions; and not attending the annual general meeting. Having discussed the investor survey and the characteristics of the respondents, this paper can now turn to the questions dealing specifically with the hypotheses of investor use of financial statements. The results are discussed in the following section.

RESULTS AND COMPARISON WITH EARLIER STUDIES

After giving information about themselves and their investment decisions, the Saudi investors were asked what their sources of information were when making decisions related to buying, holding, or selling common stock. Their

Table 11. Sources of Information by Saudi Investors When Buying or Selling Common Stock Shares

Sources of Information	*Number of Responses*	*Pecentage*	*Ranking*
Financial reports	156	67.5	1
Newspaper	120	51.9	2
Stock brokers	80	34.6	4
Personal expectations	97	42.0	3
Advice from friends	56	24.2	5
Rumors from the market	28	12.1	7
Advice from the bank	50	21.6	6
Others	18	7.8	8

Table 12. Saudis Views on the Importance of Sections of the Annual Report

	Number of Responses	*Percentage*	*Ranking*
Income statement	71	30.7	4
Profit and loss account	181	78.4	1
Balance sheet	109	47.2	2
Statement of changes in financial position	72	31.2	3
Statement source and application of funds	40	17.3	6
Director's report	25	10.8	7
Auditor's report	64	27.7	5
Others	11	4.8	8

responses to these questions are given in Table 11. According to this survey, 67.5% of Saudi investors depend on corporate financial reports when buying or selling common stock shares. Also, the ranking of responses shows the secondary source of information is the newspaper. Remember that annual financial statements as well as weekly stock information are published in local papers.

Given that financial reports are an important source of information overall, the next question is what section(s) of these statements is (are) most useful for investment decisions. Table 12 shows the responses to this question. This table lists sections of the annual reports along with the number of positive responses and their percentage of overall responses. These sections are then ranked 1 through 8 according to highest through lowest percentages. One can see that 78.4% of the respondents consider the profit and loss account the most important section in the financial report. According to the response ranking, the balance sheet and statement of changes in financial position are the two next most important sections. Interestingly, the income statement itself ranks only fourth.

Table 13. Information Contained in Financial Statements

	Number of Responses	Percentage	Ranking
Total expenditures	76	32.9	4
Total revenues	91	39.4	3
Owners' equity	137	59.3	2
Profits	184	79.7	1
Debtors	20	8.7	6
Creditors	36	15.6	5
Others	14	6.1	7

Table 14. The Other Information Needed by Saudi Investors

Information	Number of Responses	Percentage	Ranking
Directors of the company	133	57.6	1
Sales in past years	98	42.4	4
Financial policy of the company	110	47.6	3
General economic conditions	111	48.1	2
Share book value	58	25.1	5
Other	12	5.2	6

Apart from the sections of the financial statements, the Saudi investors were asked what financial information concerned them when they were buying, holding, or selling common stock shares. These responses are shown in Table 13. Here seven types of information such as total expenditures, debtors, and creditors are mentioned along with number and percentage of responses and ranking. Here 79.7% of the sample of Saudi investors indicate that profit is the important item contained in the financial statements. Owners' equity and total revenues are the second and third most important, respectively. Given the characteristics of the investor in the previous section, it makes sense that they would look first to profits and to the profit and loss accounts.

Apart from specific items in the financial statements, the Saudi investors were asked what other information they needed when buying, holding, or selling common shares. Table 14 shows that 57.6% of the respondents need more information related to management and directors of the company before they make market transactions. Also, they need more information about general economic conditions and the financial policy of the company. Past sales and share book value are also specifically mentioned, but the first three again related to the ability to earn profits and, therefore, come as no surprise.

Finally, the Saudi investors were asked to what degree of importance was selected information when they were making investment decisions. The scale for judging the selected information runs from very important to not very important. Table 15 lists 9 items and the number and percentage of responses for each in the 'very important' and 'important' classifications. The top three very important preselected items are the future of the company, the directors, and the expected dividend per share, while the top three important items are last year's sales, last year's dividend, and expected profits and sales (these two tied for third place). Note that these are all related to investors' hopes for increased incomes, which fits with the rest of the survey. The two items ranking close to last in both categories are liquidity of the company and accounting policies, neither of which has much to do with investor earnings.

With all this information from the questionnaires now collated, the results of the study in Saudi Arabia can be compared with the results of prior studies in the United States and other countries. The relative importance of the sources of information for investors in Saudi Arabia are compared with two American surveys [Baker and Haslem, 1973; Chang and Most, 1981], two Australian studies [Chenhall and Juchau, 1977; Winfield, 1978], and one from New Zealand. Eleven sources and their percentage of responses and relative ranking for each survey are given in Table 16.

As previously discussed, the two most important sources of financial information to Saudi investors are financial reports and newspapers. This matches the Chang and Most [1981] study in the United States and the Winfield [1978] survey in Australia. Similarly, financial reports and newspapers rank in the top three sources for both Chenhall and Juchau [1977] and Wilton and Tabb [1978]. Even in the Baker and Haslem [1973] survey, where financial statements rank only fifth, the primary source is stockbrokers, who themselves rely heavily on financial statements. The Chang and Most study, which was later than and more extensive than the Baker and Haslem study, indicates the American investors do rely on financial reports. The anomalous results of the Baker and Haslem study probably arose because their sample was mainly composed of large and institutional investors. Rumors from the market and advice from friends rank low in all the studies. Thus, the financial reports are an important source of information to investors overall.

Table 17 compares the Saudis views on the most important sections in these financial statements with other studies; in particular, Lee and Tweedie [1976] in the United Kingdom, Wilton and Tabb [1978] in New Zealand, and Winfield [1978] in Australia. In all but Winfield, where it ranks second behind the chairman's report, the profit and loss account is considered the most important part of the financial statements. Things such as the auditor's report, statistical data, and the historical operating summary are of little importance. This indicates that among individual investors all over, it is the hope of earning profits that most influences their investment decisions. The source of this information is primarily the financial statements.

Table 15. Importance of Selected Information by Saudi Investors

	Very Important Information			*Important Information*		
Information	*Number of Responses*	*Percentage*	*Ranking*	*Number of Responses*	*Percentage*	*Ranking*
Future of the company	174	75.3	1	52	22.5	8
Directors of the company	137	59.3	2	77	33.3	5
Expected amount of sales in next year	105	45.5	5	95	41.1	3
Expected profits	18	51.1	4	95	41.1	3
Expected dividend per share	120	51.9	3	83	35.9	4
Dividend per share in last years	85	36.8	7	96	41.6	2
Amount of sales in last years	86	37.2	8	100	43.3	1
Liquidity of the company	91	39.4	6	75	32.5	6
Accounting policies	85	36.8	7	71	30.7	7

Table 16. Comparison of the Source of Financial Information by Saudi Investors With Other Studies

Source of Information	Saudi Investors		Baker and Haslem (United States)		Chang and Most (United States)		Chenhall and Juchau (Australia)		Winfield (Australia)		Wilton and Tabb (New Zealand)	
	Percent	*Rank*	*Percent*	*Rank*	*Percent*	*Rank*	*Percent*	*Rank*	*Percent*	*Rank*	*Percent*	*Rank*
Financial reports	67.5	1	7.9	5	46.8	1	30	1	70.5	1	39.5	3
Newspaper	51.9	2	14.8	3	38.0	2	16.6	3	55.8	2	57.0	1
Stock brokers	34.6	4	46.8	1	33.3	3	27.5	2	34.8	3	51.8	2
Published statements by company directors	—	—	—	—	—	—	—	—	—	—	26.3	4
Personal expectations	42.0	3	—	—	—	—	—	—	—	—	—	—
Proxy statements	—	—	—	—	16.6	5	—	—	—	—	—	—
Advice from friends	24.2	5	9.7	4	13.1	6	3.2	6	19.7	4	8.7	6
Rumors from the market	12.1	7	5.2	6	7.8	7	15.1	4	—	—	3.7	7
Advice from the bank	21.6	6	—	—	—	—	—	—	—	—	—	—
Advisory services	—	—	15.6	2	32.1	4	7.6	5	—	—	14.1	5
Others	7.8	8	—	—	—	—	—	—	19.1	5	—	—

Table 17. Comparison of Saudis Views on the Important Sections in Financial Reports with Other Studies

Sections in Financial Reports	*Saudi Investors*		*Lee and Tweedy (United Kingdom)*		*Wilton and Tabb (New Zealand)*		*Winfield (Australia)*	
	Percent	*Rank*	*Percent*	*Rank*	*Percent*	*Rank*	*Percent*	*Rank*
Income statements, or	30.7	4	—	—	—	—	—	—
Profit and loss account	78.4	1	52.8	1	58.8	1	41.0	2
Balance Sheet	47.2	2	42.0	3	51.5	2	41.1	2
Statement of changes in financial position	31.2	3	—	—	—	—	—	—
Statement of sources and application of funds	17.3	6	—	—	—	—	28.5	3
Director's report	10.8	7	—	—	29.1	4	—	—
Auditor's report	17.7	5	—	—	10.3	7	—	—
Others	4.8	8	—	—	—	—	—	—
Chairman's report	—	—	44.3	2	40.0	3	56.4	1
Notes to accounts	—	—	—	—	20.0	5	—	—
Statistical data	—	—	—	—	16.4	6	—	—
Financial highlights	—	—	—	—	—	—	26.3	4
Historical operating summary	—	—	—	—	—	—	18.9	5

CONCLUSION

The investor survey in Saudi Arabia indicates that Saudi investors in domestic corporations rely on the corporate financial reports when making decisions related to buying, holding, or selling common stock. Furthermore, studying the responses to this questionnaire shows the following: First, investors feel that the financial reports represent information useful to investment decisions in Saudi Arabia. Second, the profit and loss account and the balance sheet are the most important sections in the Saudi corporate financial reports. This result emphasizes the importance of earnings and financial position for the investors. Third, Saudi investors want more information when they are buying or selling common stocks, such as management and directors of the firms, general economic conditions, and the financial policies of the companies. These again emphasize investor interest in income and earnings potential.

Finally, there are many similarities between the results of the Saudi investor survey and the surveys in other countries such as the United States, United Kingdom, New Zealand, and Australia. These include the reliance on financial statements for decision making, and the use of the profit figure as an important decision criterion. Thus, while individual investors all over do find the financial statements a useful source of information, they look only to the simple bottom line to make investment decisions, and not to the complex and detailed sections such as notes to the accounts or even the income statement itself. This is, however, the first investor survey in Saudi Arabia, and it is hoped that the results will be useful to accountants and preparers of financial statements as well as to those analyzing investment decisions.

REFERENCES

Abdelsalam, M., "The Influence of Economic Growth in Saudi Arabia on Accounting and the Accountant," Accounting Seminar series at the University of California [Berkeley, 1988].

———, "Improving the Quality of Corporate Financial Disclosure in Developing Countries: Saudi Arabia As a Case Study," paper presented at the AAA Western Region Meeting, Las Vegas [May 4-6, 1989].

Abdelsalam, M., and D. Satin, "Oil Revenues As a Predictor of Corporate Earnings in Saudi Arabia," paper presented at the Annual Conference on Business Forecasting, Bethesda [1988].

Anderson, R., "The Usefulness of Accounting and Other Information Disclosed in Corporate Annual Reports to Institutional Investors in Australia," *Accounting and Business Research* [Autumn 1981], pp. 259-265.

Briston, R.J., "The Private Shareholder and the Corporate Report," *The Accountant's Magazine* [December 1977], pp. 504-507.

Chang, L.S., and K.S. Most, "An International Comparison of Investor Uses of Financial Statements," *The International Journal of Accounting Education and Research* [Fall 1981], pp. 43-60.

_______, *The Perceived Usefulness of Financial Statements for Investors' Decisions* [University of Florida, 1985].

Chenhall, and J.R. Juchau, "Investor Information Needs: An Australian Study," *Accounting and Business Research* [Spring 1977], pp. 11-119.

Epstein, M.J., "The Usefulness of Annual Reports to Corporate Shareholders" [California State University, Los Angeles, 1975].

Hines, R.D., "The Usefulness of annual Reports: The Anomaly Between the Efficient Markets Hypothesis and Shareholder Surveys," *Accounting and Business Research* [Autumn 1982], pp. 296-309.

Kent, B.H., and J.A. Haslem, "Information Needs of Individual Investors," *Journal of Accountancy* [November 1973], pp. 64-69.

Lee, T.A., and D.P. Tweedie, "The Private Shareholder: His Sources of Financial Information and His Understanding of Reporting Practices," *Accounting and Business Research* [Autumn 1976], pp. 304-314.

_______, "Accounting Information: An Investigation of Private Shareholder Usage," *Accounting and Business Research* [Autumn 1975], pp. 280-291.

Wilton, R.L., and J.B. Tabb, "An Investigation Into Private Shareholder Usage of Financial Statements in New Zealand," *International Journal of Accounting Education and Research* [May 1978].

Winfield, R.R., *Shareholder Opinion of Published Financial Statements* [1978].

ECONOMIC CONSEQUENCES IN CANADIAN ACCOUNTING STANDARD SETTING:

A TEACHING TOOL

Robert Bloom and M. Ahmed Naciri

ABSTRACT

This paper deals with classroom coverage of the recent development of "economic consequences" as a criterion for evaluating Canadian accounting standards. Our focus is on the following issues as examples: research and development, leases, foreign currency translation, and the Petroleum Incentives Program (PIP) grants. An analysis of the accounting standard for each issue is provided, including a consideration of the possible economic consequences of changes in the standard. Also furnished is a review of empirical research on the informational content of changes in methods of accounting for research and development, leases, foreign currency translation, the investment tax credit, and PIP grants. We emphasize the nature of changes in accounting standards including cash flow effects and agency costs. Above all, this paper is concerned with the influence of economic consequences in accounting standard setting, stressing the dynamic nature of formulating standards and the economic impact of standards on various parties.

Advances in International Accounting, Vol. 3, pages 41-59.

ISBN: 1-55938-078-0

ACCOUNTING STANDARDS AND "ECONOMIC CONSEQUENCES"

"Economic consequences" may be defined as the impact of accounting standards on preparers and users of financial reports as well as the public at large. The concept of economic consequences includes all economic ramifications associated with the standard in question such as effects on the prices of the firm's securities, on its cost of capital, and on its debt covenants. The issue of "economic consequences" has become a factor in accounting policy decisions, which are concerned with the selection of accounting methods and the extent and nature of supplementary disclosure. Policy decisions are made by the Accounting Standards Committee (AcSC) of the Canadian Institute of Chartered Accountants (CICA) as well as individual accounting firms and business corporations. Formulation of policies on the part of the AcSC is influenced at least in part by interests who lobby on their own behalf.

The subject of economic consequences has changed the accounting policy-making process. No longer are different accounting policies or standards supported or denounced solely because of conformity or lack of conformity to the measurement of such concepts as economic income and wealth. Those criteria have not been helpful in evaluating alternative standards. Today, accounting standards or proposed standards are assessed in part on their perceived economic consequences, which follows an open admission in the policy-making process that preparers and users of financial reports are motivated by self-interest. While changes in accounting standards generally do not have significant direct cash flow effects on income tax payments, such changes may well have significant indirect cash flow effects (agency costs). Economic consequences have thus become a factor in the standard-setting process.

Accordingly, accounting students should be aware of these consequences and the role they play in the establishment of accounting standards. Coverage of this subject in the intermediate courses and beyond is desirable. In discussing accounting standards, the subject of economic consequences should be raised in the classroom. Emphasis ought to be placed on the economic and political factors that influence the development of accounting standards—including the need for compromises in the standard-setting process. In so doing, our students should gain a greater appreciation for the controversial nature of standard setting and achieve a better understanding of the standards per se.

While the Financial Accounting Standards Board (FASB) in the United States has openly admitted that it is significantly influenced by the perceived economic and political consequences of proposed standards as well as the economic impact of standards that have been adopted [Financial Accounting Foundation Structure Committee, 1977], there did not appear to be as much overt concern about economic and political consequences on the part of AcSC according to a study for the Clarkson-Gordon symposium in 1981; that study was based on empirical data from the late 1970s, and unfortunately there is no published current study of this kind [Waterhouse, 1982]. In all fairness, however, Waterhouse conducted his study several years ago, so perhaps the current AcSC members if interviewed today would express more concern about the economic and political impact of standard setting. Furthermore, as A.W. Hopkins, one of the paper's discussants points out, asking decision makers how they make decisions is a weak form of research into the decision process.

AcSC holds no open meetings or public hearings whatsoever, and there is no public call for AcSC to do so. Neither does AcSC presently indicate in each accounting standard the number of committee members who voted for, and the number who dissented from, the standard or the reasons for dissenting votes. Additionally, AcSC makes very limited use of external task forces and circulates exposure drafts to the public only upon request, placing considerable reliance on the confidential associates of each committee member in the standard-setting process.

By contrast, the FASB has responded to the issue of economic and political consequences by establishing "due process" procedures, creating an atmosphere of openness in standard-setting. Additionally, the FASB has commissioned several research studies on the economic impact of such standards as research and development, leasing, foreign currency translation, and inflation accounting. Further, the FASB holds all its meetings open to the public and indicates in the standards the members who voted for each standard as well as those who dissented and their reasons for doing so. For most projects, an external task force is appointed by the FASB. Finally, the FASB circulates publicly all its discussion memorandums as well as exposure drafts on each issue under consideration. AcSC circulates only exposure drafts, through CICA.

In Canada, as a matter of fact, economic and political consequences occurred subsequent to the issuance by the CICA of accounting recommendations for leases, foreign currency translation, and of guidelines for the Petroleum Incentives Program (PIP) grants. Yet standard setters in Canada do not seem to perceive their role as a political activity, and potential economic consequences do not appear to weigh heavily on their minds. However, there may well be several reasons for the lack of outward emphasis by AcSC on such consequences. First, AcSC may conceivably wish to maintain a sense of autonomy, to insulate itself from political pressures and lobbyists, and to rely on its collective professional judgment. Second, Canadians as opposed to Americans are more apt to accept the authority of the standard-setting body—the CICA's AcSC—as legitimate, and are less inclined to act in an adversarial manner, and take their complaints to the government. Third, Canadian standards are generally formulated and instituted some time after the corresponding American standards have been issued, and AcSC may well be averse to going against a standard that has alreadly been established in the United States, economic consequences notwithstanding. Fourth, many large Canadian companies are American-owned, thus falling under the jurisdiction of the U.S. Securities and Exchange Commission, and, therefore, apply U.S. accounting standards in external financial reporting. The now-defunct U.S. Accounting Principles Board (APB) attempted to skirt the issue of economic and political consequences—to no avail. The inability of the APB to deal with economic consequences was a key factor that led to its downfall according to Zeff [1978, p. 60].

To the extent that such consequences become more pronounced in policymaking, AcSC may well have to change its ways. Instead of maintaining a veil of secrecy in its standard-setting process, AcSC should be opening up this process, by widely circulating discussion memorandums on projects under study, not just exposure drafts as it currently does, and also by conducting public hearings. Furthermore, AcSC ought to place more emphasis on commissioning research to be used in the standard-setting process.

Hopkins, another discussant of the Waterhouse paper, takes a countervailing position on this matter [Waterhouse, 1982, p. 143]:

> More open discussion...will increase the political nature of the standard-setting process in Canada. The present confidential system with extensive use of associates provides an opportunity for diverse views from a large cross-section of individuals. It facilitates freedom of discussion and reduces the political aspects of the process.

According to the previously-cited Waterhouse study, AcSC members did not appear to be concerned about research, or a conceptual framework, as a point of departure for establishing standards. On the contrary, AcSC members interviewed in the Waterhouse study asserted that their own professional judgment and practical experience were the foundations for formulating standards. AcSC members further maintained that there is an overriding emphasis on logic and "economic reality" (whatever that term means, since they have not defined it) in the process of setting standards.

The significance of the subject of economic consequences in financial reporting has been largely based on the assumption of naive users of financial reports and inefficient capital markets. It should be emphasized that in general the expected economic consequences that managers and other interested parties often attribute to accounting policy controversies are "much ado about nothing" apart from agency factors to be considered below [Beaver, 1973]. In an efficient capital market, stock prices act as if they fully reflect all information in a rapid and unbiased manner. The term "efficiency" refers to the market's speed of processing information. The efficient market hypothesis has been characterized in terms of three forms: (1) the "weak" form indicates that stock prices fully reflect the information contained in past stock prices; (2) the "semistrong" form indicates that stock prices fully reflect all publicly available information; and (3) the "strong" form indicates that stock prices fully reflect all information, including inside information. The semistrong form is most applicable to financial accounting. Many empirical studies have supported the semistrong form, and demonstrate that the market prices of common stocks are based on their underlying economic substance rather than the cosmetic effects of accounting methods used in financial reporting [for analyses of such studies, see Beaver, 1981, pp. 150-158].

Most changes in accounting methods appear to be cosmetic, having no economic substance and no significant direct effects on the cash flows of the firm. The idea that expensing research and development (R&D) costs would discourage corporate expenditure on this activity generally reflects a belief that capital markets are inefficient and functionally fixated by bottom-line income figures (i.e., they attach relevance to income differences that stem from cosmetic changes in accounting methods), when in fact a change from capitalizing to expensing R&D (or vice versa) should have no direct cash flow effects on the firm. That capitalization of leases as opposed to expensing them would serve to increase the cost of capital of a firm, and be a disincentive to leasing appears to be counterintuitive, for a switch from one approach to another has no significant direct cash effect. However, reflecting financing on the face of, rather than off, the balance sheet, in particular, can affect the debt ratios of the firm and thus its conformity to existing debt covenants. A violation of a debt covenant or contract may produce indirect cash flow effects, which may or may not engender security market responses. Thus, how leases are treated in accounting could well have economic consequences. The idea that changes in foreign exchange rates generate accounting gains and losses, and therefore managers face higher costs of capital and lower stock prices, is also contrary to the efficient market hypothesis. That government subsidies in the form of PIP grants or investment tax credits should be accounted for as immediate benefits in the period received rather than a reduction in the fixed asset cost, to be subsequently amortized, is yet another case of misperceived economic consequences, since neither method should affect the cash flows of the firm significantly apart from effects on its existing contracts. Additionally, debates over whether to include accounting data on the face of, or in the footnotes to, the financial statements generally miss the point that full disclosure, regardless of its geography, is required.

It appears, therefore, that accounting policy changes, even seemingly cosmetic policy changes, conceivably may have significant direct or indirect cash flow effects. Disclosure-oriented standards, which affect the nature and extent of disclosures (e.g., "new" types of data, disaggregation of data) should have direct cash effects and thus impact security prices. Even a switch from one accounting depreciation method to another may have economic consequences in terms of any economic substance the switch may have—for example, a change in the rate of obsolescence of the depreciable asset. Such changes could affect users', competitors', and regulators' perceptions of the firm's performance and wealth. While that has not apparently been the case with current cost and inflation-accounting data, there may be intervening factors to explain this phenomenon—for example, the uncertainty and subjectivity of the new data conveyed. Additionally, as previously stated, seemingly cosmetic changes in accounting methods conceivably may affect contracts and bond indentures that the firm has previously signed, calling for maintenance of particular debt-equity ratios, and thus have indirect cash flow effects. Moreover, changes in accounting methods can affect management compensation plans and regulatory commission actions. Zimmerman [1980, p. 114] sets forth a positive theory of accounting to explain management's choice of accounting policies, on which a growing body of supportive and unsupportive empirical research has thus far been performed:

> [A]ccounting numbers affect the firm's cash flows and hence stock prices by altering agency costs (which include bookkeeping costs), taxes, the effects of regulation, and political costs (e.g., antitrust, price controls, etc.). That is, changes in accounting procedures (e.g., switching from accelerated to straightline depreciation for financial accounting only) affect the firm's net cash flows beyond the bookkeeping costs of making the changes. In particular, the firm's net cash flows are affected if the accounting change alters the numbers in debt and management compensation contracts, the firm's revenues if it is a regulated utility, and the costs incurred by the firm from increased government investigative and regulatory activities if the change increases government scrutiny of the firm.

See Kelly [1983] for a comprehensive analysis of agency theory and financial reporting.

Agency theory is a framework for considering why management lobbies for, and, if allowed to do so, adopts particular alternative accounting methods or policies in financial reporting. Management is viewed as rational and wealth-maximizing, and the firm is examined in terms of its agency contracts with management, investors, and creditors. Managers do not necessarily act in the stockholders' and bondholders' best interests. In addition, management may be bonded to protect the stockholders' and bondholders' interests. Moreover, monitoring expenses may well be incurred to keep management under control.

In light of empirical findings on the positive theory of accounting, which deals with the reasons for choosing alternative accounting policies, perhaps much of the empirical research on stock market reactions to accounting changes should be redone. It should be emphasized, however, that positive theory does *not* conflict with the efficient market hypothesis. Nevertheless, if seemingly cosmetic accounting changes were not actually cosmetic because of agency factors, stock prices might react to such changes. Indeed, the choice of accounting methods can affect transaction costs, and thus have indirect effects on the cash flows of the firm. Such transaction costs constitute the present value of renegotiation costs that would be spent in the event of changes in accounting standards, whereas the agency costs include the restrictiveness stemming from using GAAP in covenants and the dysfunctional effects on subsequent investment and financing decisions in order to maintain the ratios set forth in the covenants [Thornton and Bryant, 1984].

All decisions regarding accounting policy choices should have real, not imagined, economic consequences, or else there is no justifiable reason for the choice or change. Beaver [1981, pp. 50-51] observed the following real economic consequences of financial information, which seem to be consistent with the implications of the efficient market hypothesis and agency theory:

1. Financial information can affect the distribution of wealth among investors. This consequence involves issues of equity or fairness. Differential access to the information may permit more informed investors to increase their wealth at the expense of the less informed.
2. Financial information can affect the aggregate level of risk incurred and can affect the distribution of the risk among the constituencies.
3. Financial information can affect the rate of capital formation in the economy with a resulting reallocation of society's wealth between consumption and investment.
4. Financial information can also affect how investment is allocated among firms. Disclosure may alter investors' beliefs about the relative rewards and risks associated with particular securities.
5. Financial information can affect the amount of resources devoted to the production, certification, dissemination, processing, analysis, and interpretation of disclosures.
6. Financial information involves the use of resources in the development, compliance, enforcement, and litigation of disclosure rules.

What follows are analyses of four reporting issues—research and development, leases, foreign currency translation, and the PIP grants, the controversy underlying each issue, and empirical research, albeit almost exclusively from American studies, on the effects of changes in accounting for each subject area and economic consequences. Based on the efficient market hypothesis, changes in accounting for these items should generally have no effect on stock prices, absent any real economic substance. On the other hand, agency factors may serve to impart economic subtance to the switch in accounting methods, and the change could have significant, indirect cash flow effects.

This material can be used by instructors selectively in the intermediate and upper-level courses, undergraduate and graduate, with a view to emphasizing the role of economic consequences in standard setting and the dynamic nature of the standard-setting process. The extent of coverage of the economic consequences may well depend on the sophistication of the class. For example, graduate accounting concentrators should be expected to read various studies on the economic consequences of particular standards, including efficient market and agency research papers.

RESEARCH AND DEVELOPMENT

FASB *Statement No. 2* (*FAS 2*) calls for the expensing of research and development (R&D) costs. Prior to the issuance of this statement in 1974, companies had the option of either immediately expensing R&D costs or first capitalizing, and subsequently amortizing, them. The FASB issued this statement to improve comparability with respect to R&D in financial reporting. In light of the uncertainty associated with the future benefits from R&D costs, the FASB decided to call for their immediate expensing. Prior to *FAS 2,* the majority of firms expensed R&D even though a significant percentage used the deferral and subsequent amortization approach.

The corresponding Canadian standard, issued in 1978, calls for expensing of research costs but allows for capitalization of particular development costs to the extent of their expected recoverability through sales or use, in contrast to *FAS 2.* According to Section 3450 of the CICA *Handbook,* development costs are to be deferred and subsequently amortized if all of the following criteria are satisfied (par. 21):

A. the product or process is clearly defined and the costs attributable thereto can be identified;
B. the technical feasibility of the product or process has been established;
C. the management of the enterprise has indicated its intention to produce and market, or use, the product or process;
D. the future market for the product or process is clearly defined or, if it is to be used internally rather than sold, its usefulness to the enterprise has been established; and
E. adequate resources exist, or are expected to be available, to complete the project.

However, most R&D costs are to be expensed immediately in the Canadian standard, following *FAS 2.* Both the American and Canadian versions of this standard are concerned with the uncertainty associated with the future value of R&D expenditures.

Vigeland [1981] examined the stock market reaction to *FAS 2* and found no significant stock price effects. Horwitz and Kolodny [1980] empirically evaluated and rejected the hypothesis that *FAS 2* had no effect on the amount and variability of privately-funded R&D expenditures. In particular, the

FASB's expense-all standard engendered a cutback in R&D expenditures by small high-tech companies that had used the deferred approach prior to *FAS 2*. It was the small firms that were primarily affected by the R&D standard. Horwitz and Kolodny asserted that changes in the methods of reporting R&D may affect the firm's adherence to provisions in its contracts (e.g., bond indentures, management compensation agreements), which represent economic consequences due to agency factors. The reduction in R&D costs, according to Horwitz and Kolodny, can also be attributable to perceived or actual inefficiencies in capital markets, stock exchange listing requirements, and government contract assessment practices, all of which constitute economic consequences. There is no published Canadian study on the economic impact of Section 3450 of the *Handbook*.

LEASING

The first time that lease financing was formally recognized by the accounting profession was in 1949, when *Accounting Research Bulletin* (*ARB*) *No. 38,* "Disclosure of Long-Term Leases in Financial Statements," a general and broad statement was issued. *ARB 38* asserted that a lessee's material equity in the leased property justified capitalization of the lease. *Accounting Research Study No. 4* (1962) adopted a legal orientation towards leasing, arguing that the creation of legal property rights called for capitalization. In APB *Opinion No. 5* (1964), emphasis was placed on the notion of material equity and noncancellability as requirements for capitalization. APB *Opinion No. 31* (1973) required footnote disclosure of information tantamount to capitalization of leases. From the viewpoint of the lessor, *APB Opinion No. 7* (1966) provided different, asymmetrical criteria for the lessor vis-à-vis the lessee to reflect a capital lease—that is, a sales-type lease. APB *Opinion No. 27* (1972) dealt with sales-type and direct-financing leases.

Finally, by the end of 1976, the FASB issued *Statement No. 13,* "Accounting for Leases" (*FAS 13*), which specified criteria for classifying leases as capital or operating. Two basic methods of reporting lease financing are:

1. The lease is considered to be an installment purchase, and therefore the present value of minimum payments should be reported as part of the long-term debt of the lessee.
2. The lease is considered to be an operating lease, and therefore only the periodic payments on the lease contract are reported on the income statement.

FAS 13 was drafted as a guide to lease reporting in order to standardize the capitalization of leases that are in substance purchases of property. The major issue in lease accounting is whether the risks and rewards of ownership have been transferred from the lessor to the lessee. If so, the lessor and the lessee should be treating the agreement as a sale and a purchase, respectively. All leases that fail to meet the capitalization criteria are considered to be operating in nature. One of the most arbitrary standards, *FAS 13* specifies criteria that have some logical purpose even though the particular percentage criteria—the 75 and 90 percent rules—are arbitrary. The intent was to promote capitalization of leases. The Canadian standard on leasing, Section 3065 (1978), closely parallels its American counterpart.

The FASB has issued a number of interpretations of *FAS 13*. Nevertheless, the lease accounting dilemma is still unsettled today. Because the alternative reporting methods affect various financial ratios, the firm's ability to borrow and to fulfill current debt obligations could be impaired. Those are economic consequences of lease accounting due to agency factors.

With regard to empirical research on lease accounting, Wilcox [1971] argues that the probability of corporate failure increases as the proportion of the expected cash inflows of the borrower due to debtholders increases. The findings of Dietrich and Kaplan [1982] as well as Foster [1978] have supported this argument. Abdel-khalik and El-Sheshai [1977] as well as Stephens [1980], among others, confirm that the debt-to-equity ratio is used by lenders when assessing loans. Palmon and Kwatinetz [1980] demonstrate that lease capitalization reporting requirements produce a material increase in the debt-to-equity ratio of the firm, and hence loan officers should be affected in their decision to grant credit in a way favorable to firms that do not capitalize leases. Firms have various incentives to influence their reported debt-to-equity ratios by managing the terms of their lease agreements. According to Palmon and Kwatinetz [1980], leasing companies have circumvented *FAS 13* by devising lease contracts so as to avoid capitalization. This makes the establishment of capitalization criteria a perplexing task.

Like many FASB standards, *FAS 13* has generated considerable controversy in the accounting and financial communities. In fact, many firms that had essentially capital leases which were reported off the balance sheet prior to *FAS 13* were required to capitalize them, substantially increasing their debt-to-equity ratios as a consequence. This increase in the debt-to-equity ratio according to Hamada [1972] serves to increase the risk of the firm. However, given the efficient market hypothesis, lease financing reported either way (the capital or operating approach) has the same economic effect on the firm apart from agency considerations. In view of this situation, many researchers have attempted to examine the real economic consequences of reporting leases.

In contrast to the results of Ro [1978], which indicate that disclosure of lease information under the Securities and Exchange Commission (SEC)'s *Accounting Series Release* (*ASR*) *No. 147* (1973) is associated with changes in market prices, Abdel-khalik, Thompson, and Taylor [1981] as well as

Bowman [1980] found that stock prices behave as though financial leases were equivalent to any other form of debt, and the method of reporting them has no effect. In other words, the specific geography of lease accounting disclosure does not matter. Thornton's [1982] study in a Canadian context also showed no significant, permanent reactions of stock prices to lease capitalization. Additionally, Thornton examined a sample of firms with respect to the transitional provision in the CICA pronouncement on leasing, Section 3065, allowing leasees to capitalize leases either retroactively or prospectively as long as the proforma effect of retroactive treatment, that is, the present value of lease obligations, is footnoted. Firms selecting the "prospective" option had larger increases in their debt-equity ratios, which was not surprising, since such firms "would be more likely to face...costs relating to bond covenant problems, costs that might be mitigated somewhat by the selection of the [prospective] accounting policy" [Thornton, 1982]. It was also found that retroactive implementation of the lease pronouncement would not have changed significantly the ranking of sample firms, either in total or by industry, in terms of debt-equity ratios [Thornton, 1982]. It should be noted that this is the only published Canadian empirical evidence on economic consequences that we are aware of to date.

The aggregate-level studies notwithstanding, there is insufficient research evidence on the impact of lease disclosures on share prices at the individual level. It seems, however, that the majority of loan officers and analysts have evaluated companies that did not capitalize leases in more favorable terms. This is evident from the studies by Dopuch and Ronen [1973], and Abdel-khalik, Thompson, and Taylor [1981]. By contrast, Wilkins and Zimmer [1983, p. 749] suggest "that lenders' credit evaluations and decisions are affected only by 'real' levels of leverage of loan applicants and not by whether the applicants' debt financing is by term loan or financial lease."

FOREIGN CURRENCY TRANSLATION

The issue of foreign currency translation was first considered in 1931 and later in 1934 when the Special Committee on Accounting Procedures of the American Institute of Accountants (called the American Institute of Certified Public Accountants since 1957) issued *Bulletin No. 92,* "Foreign Exchange Losses," and *Bulletin No. 117,* 'Memorandum on Accounting for Foreign Exchange Gains." The position expressed then was the basis for *Accounting Research Bulletin* (*ARB*) No. 4, issued in 1939, calling for the application of the current-noncurrent method, whereby current assets and current liabilities are translated at current exchange rates, while non-current balance sheet items are translated at historical exchange rates. Ten years later, following the devaluations of many European currencies after World War II, the American

Institute published a memorandum in 1949 on the subject titled "Accounting Problems Arising from Devaluation of Foreign Currencies." In 1953, the Institute issued *ARB No. 43,* which incorporated *ARB No. 4.* Chapter 12 of *ARB No. 43,* as modified by paragraph 18 of *APB Opinion No. 6,* became the authoritative pronouncement concerning foreign currency accounting for more than twenty years. Chapter 12 called for translations based on the current-noncurrent method and the immediate recognition of all exchange losses; exchange gains were to be credited to income if realized and preferably deferred otherwise.

In 1960, the National Association of Accountants published a research report titled *Management Accounting Problems in Foreign Operations,* which described the current-noncurrent method as irrelevant, and recommended as a replacement the monetary-nonmonetary method. The latter approach is different from the current-noncurrent method with respect to inventories, long-term receivables, and long-term payables. The monetary-nonmonetary approach was given official recognition in 1965 when the Accounting Principles Board issued *Opinion No. 6.* In 1975, however, the FASB issued *Statement No. 8,* calling for uniform procedures to report the foreign currency position of multinational corporations. *FAS 8* required the temporal method, which differs from the monetary-nonmonetary method only in minor particulars. The temporal method reflects monetary assets and monetary liabilities at current exchange rates, and nonmonetary items at the appropriate historical exchange rates, in order to preserve GAAP and historical costing. The paper exchange adjustments—or gains and losses—are reflected in income using this approach. The application of this method, however, caused the following economic consequences:

- volatile reported earnings (due largely to translation of nonmonetary amounts at historical rates), and
- accounting figures that did not reflect economic realities in regard to foreign exchange rate changes.

In attempting to rectify these problems, FASB *Statement No. 52* (1981) adopted the following objectives for translations:

- to provide information that is generally compatible with the expected economic effects of a change in the exchange rate on the cash flow and equity of the enterprise, and
- to reflect in consolidated statements the financial results and relationships of the individual consolidated entities as measured in their functional currencies in conformity with GAAP.

The approach that was adopted is referred to as the functional currency approach, that is, using the currency of the primary economic environment for the foreign operation in question. However, it is not necessarily obvious which currency is the functional one for a particular foreign operation. Under *FAS 52* the current rate approach is to be used, which means translation of all functional currency assets and liabilities into dollars at the current exchange rate. The problem of volatile earnings under *FAS 8* is treated in *FAS 52* by reporting the translation adjustments (i.e., the so-called "gains" and "losses") in shareholders' equity, as a so-called "valuation adjustment."

Canadian pronouncements on foreign currency translation have been essentially the same as the corresponding American standards, apart from differences in the use of terminology. In fact, the Canadian Institute of Chartered Accountants (CICA) issued a standard prescribing the temporal method of translation (1978), essentially the same as *FAS 8,* which was so controversial that the CICA suspended Section 1650 in the CICA *Handbook* [1979]. In 1983, a new Section 1650 was issued which is basically the same as *FAS 52.*

Research studies conducted on foreign currency translation have dealt mainly with *FAS 8*. The studies are concerned with the effects of this statement on management practices and stock prices. Evans, Folks, and Jilling [1978] found the financing and/or investment policies of various companies have been affected by the accounting provisions set forth in *FAS 8*. In that study, about 25 percent of the respondents asserted that *FAS 8* occasionally caused them to refrain from investing overseas, and the same percentage of respondents said that they have reconsidered their dividend policy in light of *FAS 8*. The findings of studies dealing with the impact of *FAS 8* on stock prices have generally supported the belief that its initial implementation did not affect stock prices significantly. According to Dukes [1978], Fredrickson and Mogus [1978], as well as Shank, Dillard, and Murdock [1979], the issuance and implementation of *FAS 8* had no measurable impact on market prices. Dukes [1978], however, found that from 1975 to 1976 the performance of firms having substantial foreign operations was inferior to those of comparable risk with fewer foreign operations. Shank et al. also concluded that multinationals were generally affected negatively following the issuance of *FAS 8*. Dukes and Shank et al. have advised, however, that this negative effect could be attributed to various economic factors other than *FAS 8*. Naciri [1983] argues that the change in the accounting standard in October 1975, in turn, may have changed the way multinationals manage their exchange risk, and thus may have created special situations in which the managers undertook various operations whose sole purpose was to offset the accounting impact of *FAS 8,* that is, by smoothing or following suboptimal strategies, such as tactics to refrain from undertaking desirable foreign investment projects. Any multinational that undertakes smoothing policies and/or suboptimal strategies may well suffer a decrease in its stock market price.

PIP GRANTS

As part of Canada's National Energy Program (NEP), in 1981 the federal government inaugurated the Petroleum Incentive Program (PIP) in order to provide grants or subsidies to Canadian-owned companies to stimulate the exploration for oil and gas. AcSC has viewed such grants as a form of governmental assistance, which is the subject of Section 3800 (1975) of the CICA *Handbook* [par. 25-6]:

> Government assistance towards the acquisition of fixed assets should be either: (a) deducted from the related fixed assets with any depreciation calculated on the net amount; or (b) deferred and amortized to income on the same basis as the related depreciable fixed assets are depreciated.

Thus, the *Handbook* calls for amortization of the benefits of the PIP grants over the life of the exploration expenditures. A draft of an AcSC guideline on accounting for PIP grants in conformity with Section 3800 of the *Handbook* was prepared and circulated in 1981. The guideline was subsequently instituted in 1982 despite considerable political opposition.

Many Canadian oil companies wanted to show the PIP grants as immediate income benefits to the extent of their payments of a then newly-introduced Petroleum and Gas Revenue Tax of 8 percent on currently-used oil and gas wells, which was enacted to finance the PIP grants. The oil companies were apprehensive about market perceptions of lower net income if the government grant approach were applied, apparently revealing a belief in inefficient, functionally-fixated capital markets or a concern with the "agency" consequences of using this conservative rule. Yet auditors could not sanction the "offset" policy while the CICA recommended the "grant" approach. Oil executives took their case to the federal government, but that proved to be an exercise in futility. The federal government had seriously threatened the CICA with an amendment to the Canada Business Corporation Act (CBCA) (1975) in order to permit oil companies to use the offset accounting approach for PIP grants. However, the CICA refused to succumb to political pressure, and the federal government decided in the end not to amend the CBCA.

It should be noted that AcSC subsequently confirmed its position on the PIP grants in issuing its standard on the Investment Tax Credit, Section 3805 of the *Handbook*. Section 3805 calls for accounting for the investment tax credit by a cost reduction or deferral approach [par. 12-13, 1985]. Under the tax approach, the benefits to be received from the tax credit are amortized over the useful life of the qualified depreciable property. Investment tax credits related to the acquisition of assets are to be either [par. 13]:

(a) deducted from the related assets with any depreciation or amortization calculated on the net amount; or
(b) deferred and amortized to income on the same basis as the related assets.

Kaplan and Roll [1972] studied the impact of changes in methods of accounting for the investment tax credit, which is similar in nature to the PIP grants, from the deferral to the flow-through approach, the latter viewing the investment credit as current-period income or a tax savings versus the former approach considering the credit to be a long-term benefit that pertains to the life of the "investment" in question. Kaplan and Roll found no significant effects on stock prices, other than temporary changes around the date of the announcement of the switch in accounting methods. Selection of the flow-through or the deferral method of accounting for investment tax credits or PIP grants should not affect stock prices, assuming that adequate data is furnished in the financial reports to enable users to make adjustments from one method to another. Regardless of the method used for the PIP grants—Section 3800's grant approach or the "offset" approach—there would be no significant direct impact on cash flows of the firm even though there would be a significant effect on its net income.

Cheung [forthcoming] provides empirical research evidence on the economic consequences, including stock price effects, of the PIP grant controversy in Canada. Cheung hypothesizes that the PIP accounting guideline had economic consequences in view of firms' contracting costs, monitoring costs, and political costs. This guideline, it is argued, would constrain firms already encumbered with covenants. "Additionally, real operating effects are...hypothesized to be a possibility given the extensive use of contracting in risk sharing in the industry. On the other hand, firms with high political visibility are expected to benefit" from this conservative rule, thus discouraging regulators from focusing their attention on the performance of these firms [pp. 17-18]. "The results indicate significant associations between abnormal [security] returns and proxies for contracting and monitoring costs and for political visibility, thus lending support to the claim that the rule had an adverse impact on financial flexibility" [p. 1].

CONCLUDING COMMENTS

Claims of economic consequences of accounting policy changes appear to reflect misconceptions about the way in which preparers and users of financial reports act, resulting in costly and unwarranted expenditures of resources. By and large, the various capital market studies concerned with particular accounting policy changes have demonstrated that the market as a whole is not fooled by accounting artifacts, though corporate managers are hardly convinced of that. However, the idea that most accounting policy changes constitute "much ado about nothing" must be qualified particularly when the firm has existing debt covenants and other contracts that stipulate the maintenance of certain ratios such as debt-equity and liquidity. An otherwise cosmetic accounting policy change of this kind could propel the firm into technical default, causing significant transaction costs on the part of the firm in order to modify its covenants and contracts. Furthermore, changes in accounting policies can affect management compensation plans and regulatory commission actions. Thus, while cosmetic changes in accounting policy do not have significant direct cash flow effects on the firm, they could in various circumstances have significant indirect cash flow effects.

The effects of economic and political factors on financial reporting cannot be neglected by standard-setting bodies. Standard setters ought to be concerned with how the stock markets, competition, regulatory authorities, unions, among other parties, may conceivably react to the information conveyed and the benefits versus costs of conveying this information. In large part, such factors serve to explain the history of accounting policy changes [Zeff, 1982].

The question might be asked: Why has the subject of 'economic consequences' been neglected thus far in our accounting courses? Zeff [1979] provides the following answer:

> A recognition of 'economic consequences' considerations ... could well open the discussion to imponderables that would frustrate students who would prefer the security of a definitive answer.

All too many accounting majors have a low threshold for uncertainty and ambiguity, and have gravitated into accounting programs in search of closure.

In response to the question—Why should we emphasize "economic consequences" in our intermediate and upper-level accounting courses?—Zeff [1979] argues that:

> they constitute an indispensable element in the explanation of the forces at work in today's accounting environment. ... An essential part of the education of any future professional—whether in law, economics, diplomacy, or accounting—is how change actually occurs, and how it has shaped the contours of professional practice and behavior.

Standard-setting bodies have been confronted with all too many political battles in recent years among different interest groups, having different points of view. Therefore, accounting students ought to be aware of the economic consequences and the role they play in the establishment of accounting standards. The subject of economic consequences should be taught in our curricula. To pursue this recommendation a step further, we should place more emphasis on the political and social aspects of the standard-setting process.

> [S]tandard setters will be wise to make an assessment of the likely economic consequences of a proposed standard if they are to avoid creating unnecessary trouble for themselves and for the community after the standard is issued. Thus it makes no sense at all to produce a standard one of the principal effects of which will be to induce businesses to arrange their affairs so as to eliminate the influence of the standard. It cannot be too strongly emphasized that the principal task of accountants is to measure what has been done and the effects thereof. It is essential that accounting standards should not permit a company to conceal from outsiders the economic consequences to the company of actions that it has taken. Standards must not allow history to be rewritten. Nor must they compel businessmen to engage in artificial transactions [*Corporate Reporting,* 1980].

REFERENCES

Abdel-Khalik, A.R., R.B. Thompson, and R.E. Taylor, "The Impact of Reporting Leases Off the Balance Sheet on Bond Risk Premiums: Two Exploratory Studies" in *Economic Consequences of Accounting Standards: Selected Papers* [FASB, 1978].

________, The Economic Effects on Leases of FASB *Statement No. 13:* "Accounting for Leases" [FASB, 1981].

Abdel-Khalik, A.R. and K.M. El-Sheshai, "Information Choice and Utilization in an Experiment on Default Prediction," *Journal of Banking and Finance* [June 1977].

Altman, E., R.G. Haldeman, and P. Narayana, "ZETA Analysis: A New Model to Identify Bankruptcy Risk of Corporations," *Journal of Banking and Finance* [June 1977].

Ball, R., "Changes in Accounting Techniques and Stock Prices," *Empirical Research in Accounting: 1972. Supplement to Journal of Accounting Research,* pp. 1-38.

Beaver, W.H., *Financial Reporting: An Accounting Revolution* [Prentice-Hall, 1981].

Beaver, W.H., "What Should be the FASB's Objectives?" *The Journal of Accountancy* [August 1973].

Bowman, R.G., "The Debt Equivalence of Leases: An Empirical Investigation," *The Accounting Review* [April 1980].

Canadian Institute of Chartered Accountants, *Handbook* [CICA, 1975].

Cheung, J.K., "The PIP Grant Controversy in Canada: A Study of the Economic Consequences of Accounting Standards," *Journal of Business Finance and Accounting* [forthcoming].

Corporate Reporting: Its Future Evolution [CICA, 1980].

Crandall, R.H., "Government Intervention—the PIP Grant Accounting Controversy," *Cost and Management* [September-October, 1983].

Dhaliwal, D.S., and A.A. Schepanski, "On the Use of Positive Economic Theory to Explain the Choice of Accounting Methods to Financial Accounting Students," *Journal of Accounting Education* [Fall 1984].

Dietrich, J.R., and R.S. Kaplan, "Empirical Analysis of the Commercial Loan Classification Decision," *The Accounting Review* [January 1982].

Dopuch, N., and J. Ronen, "The Effects of Alternative Inventory Valuation Methods—An Experimental Study," *Journal of Accounting Research* [Autumn 1973].

Dukes, R.E., *An Empirical Investigation of the Effects of Statement of Financial Accounting Standards No. 8* [FASB, 1978].

Evans, T.G., W.R. Folks, and M. Jilling, *The Impact of Statement No. 8 on the Foreign Exchange Risk Management Practices of American Multinationals: An Economic Impact Study* [FASB, 1978].

Financial Accounting Foundation Structure Committee, *Structure of Establishing Financial Accounting Standards* [FASB, 1977].

Fogelson, J.H., "The Impact of Changes in Accounting Principles on Restrictive Covenants in Credit Agreements and Indentures," *The Business Lawyer* [January 1978].

Foster, G., *Financial Statement Analysis* [Prentice-Hall, 1978].

Fredrikson, E.B., and T. Mogus, "FASB 8 and Returns on Equities: An Empirical Examination," Working Paper No. 78-9, School of Management, Syracuse University [April 1978].

Goshay, R., *Statement of Financial Accounting Standards No. 5: Impact on Corporate Risk and Insurance Management* [FASB, 1978].

Hamada, R.S., "The Effect of the Firm's Capital Structure on the Systematic Risk of Common Stocks," *Journal of Finance* [May 1972].

Holthausen, R., "Evidence on the Effect of Bond Covenants and Management Compensation Contracts on the Choice of Accounting Techniques: The Case of the Depreciation Switch-Back," *Journal of Accounting and Economics* [March 1981].

Horwitz, B., and R. Kolodny, "The Economic Effects of Involuntary Uniformity in the Financial Reporting of R & D Expenditures," *Studies on Economic Consequences of Financial and Managerial Information: Effects on Corporate Incentives and Decisions. Supplement to Journal of Accounting Research* [1980].

Horwitz, B., and R. Kolodny, "The FASB, the SEC, and R & D," *The Bell Journal of Economics* [Spring 1981].

Kaplan, R., and R. Roll, "Investor Evaluation of Accounting Information: Some Empirical Evidence," *Journal of Business* [April 1972].

Kelly, L., "The Development of a Positive Theory of Corporate Management's Role in External Financial Reporting," *Journal of Accounting Literature* [Spring 1983].

Naciri, A., "Empirical Evidence of the Economic Effects of Accounting Standards: The Case of FAS 8," unpublished manuscript, Université du Quebec a Montreal [1983].

Palmon, D., and M. Kwatinetz, "The Significant Role Interpretation Plays in the Implementation of SFAS No. 13," *Journal of Accounting, Auditing, and Finance* [Spring 1980].

Ro, B.T., "The Disclosure of Capitalized Lease Information and Stock Prices," *Journal of Accounting Research* [Autumn 1978].

Shank, J.K., J.F. Dillard, and R.J. Murdock, *Assessing the Economic Impact of FASB 8* [Financial Executives Research Foundation, June 1979].

Solomons, D., "The Politicization of Accounting," *The Journal of Accountancy* [November 1978].

Stephens, R.G., *Uses of Financial Information in Bank Lending Decisions* [University of Michigan, 1980].

Thornton, D.B., "Economic Consequences of Lease Capitalization in Canada: Implications for Standard Setting," in *Research to Support Standard Setting in Financial Accounting: A Canadian Perspective,* edited by S. Basu and J.A. Milburn [Clarkson Gordon Foundation, 1982].

Thornton, D.B., and M.J. Bryant, "Gaap Vs. Tap (Tailored Accounting Principles) in Lending Agreements: Theory and Canadian Evidence," unpublished manuscript [1984].

Vigeland, R., "The Market Reaction to Statement of Financial Accounting Standards No. 2," *The Accounting Review* [April 1981].

Waterhouse, J., "A Descriptive Analysis of Selected Aspects of the Canadian Accounting Standard Setting Process," in *Research to Support Standard Setting in Financial Accounting: A Canadian Perspective,* edited by S. Basu and J.A. Milburn [Clarkson Gordon Foundation, 1982].

Watts, R., and J.L. Zimmerman, "Towards a Positive Theory of the Determination of Accounting Standards," *The Accounting Review* [January 1978].

Wilcox, J.W., "A Simple Theory of Financial Ratios as Predictors of Failure," *Journal of Accounting Research* [Autumn 1971].

Wilkins, T., and I. Zimmer, "The Effect of Leasing and Different Methods of Accounting For Leases on Credit Evaluation," *The Accounting Review* [October 1983].

Zeff, S.A., "The Rise of Economic Consequences," *The Journal of Accountancy* [December 1978].

________, "'Intermediate' and 'Advanced' Accounting: The Role of 'Economic Consequences,'" *The Accounting Review* [July 1979].

________, "Towards a Fundamental Rethinking of the Role of the 'Intermediate' Course in the Accounting Curriculum," in *The Impact of Rule-Making on Intermediate Financial Accounting Textbooks,* edited by D.L. Jensen [Ohio State University, 1982].

Zimmerman, J.L., "Positive Research in Accounting," in *Perspectives on Research,* edited by R.D. Nair and T.H. Williams [University of Wisconsin-Madison, 1980].

INVESTMENT DECISIONS AND EQUITY ACCOUNTING STANDARDS: THE CASES OF SINGAPORE AND MALAYSIA

Eugene E. Comiskey and Charles W. Mulford

ABSTRACT

The ownership percentage criterion of 20% has gained widespread international acceptance for purposes of determining whether application of the equity method is in order. Accounting standards in Singapore and Malaysia both employ a 20% benchmark. Research on U.S. firms has indicated that a 20% ownership criterion influences the extent-of-holding dimension of firm investment decisions. The purpose of this paper is to determine whether a similar conclusion can be reached with respect to Singaporean and Malaysian investor firms. Annual reports are surveyed to judge the importance of 20% ownership in defining associated companies. Then, the profitability and risk characteristics of investees in which investment positions are just under 20% (cost method used) are contrasted with those of investees in which the investment positions are just over 20% (equity method used). The results reveal that in Singapore and Malaysia 20% ownership is a key feature in defining associated companies for purposes of application of the equity method. Moreover, the 20% criterion appears to influence investment decisions by causing firms to take those ownership positions which yield more desirable reported results. The implication is that the behavioral effect of the 20%

Advances in International Accounting, Vol. 3, pages 61-70.

ISBN: 1-55938-078-0

ownership criterion is not solely a U.S. phenomenon but plays an important role internationally in investment decision making. This suggests that any revisions of accounting standards for associated companies should consider elimination of any reference to an arbitrary ownership percentage benchmark. Reliance could, instead, be placed upon a more conceptual decision rule which emphasizes the possession of significant influence without regard to size of share holding.

INTRODUCTION

There is presently widespread international application of a 20% ownership criterion for application of the equity method. For example, the United States and Great Britain both employ a 20% ownership benchmark.[1] In Singapore and Malaysia, accounting principles based on International Accounting Standard No. 3 (*IAS 3*), *Consolidated Financial Statements* [1976] also use a 20% ownership criterion. A similar 20% measure is proposed in International Accounting Standard Exposure Draft 28: *Accounting for Investments in Associates and Joint Ventures* [1986].

Significant influence over the investee is presumed, usually calling for application of the equity method, when a voting stock interest becomes 20% or greater. The cost method is appropriate when a voting stock interest falls below 20% and there is absence of significant influence. Under the equity method, an investor recognizes its proportionate share of investee earnings and losses. In contrast, under the cost method, an investment is carried at cost to the investor and income is recorded only when a dividend is declared by the investee.

Ownership positions are taken in other firms for a variety of reasons. For example, an investment might be made in an effort to ensure the supply of a strategic input, to expand or diversify in a related or unrelated industry or simply to take advantage of an income or capital gain opportunity. Presumably, the size of the ownership position taken is primarily a function of these and other factors which will affect cash flows directly, and not the 20% accounting standard.

However, Comiskey and Mulford [1986] found evidence which suggests that the 20% accounting standard does affect the ownership positions taken by investor firms. Examining a distribution of 1,225 investment positions in 1982, comprised primarily of U.S. companies, they identified a statistically significant concentration of positions just under and just over 20%. A graph of this ownership percentage distribution is provided in Figure 1.[2]

The marked downward slope depicted in Figure 1 indicates an inverse relationship between the number of investor firms and ownership percentage. As ownership percentage increases, fewer investor firms are either willing or able to commit the resources required by such an investment position. Investors

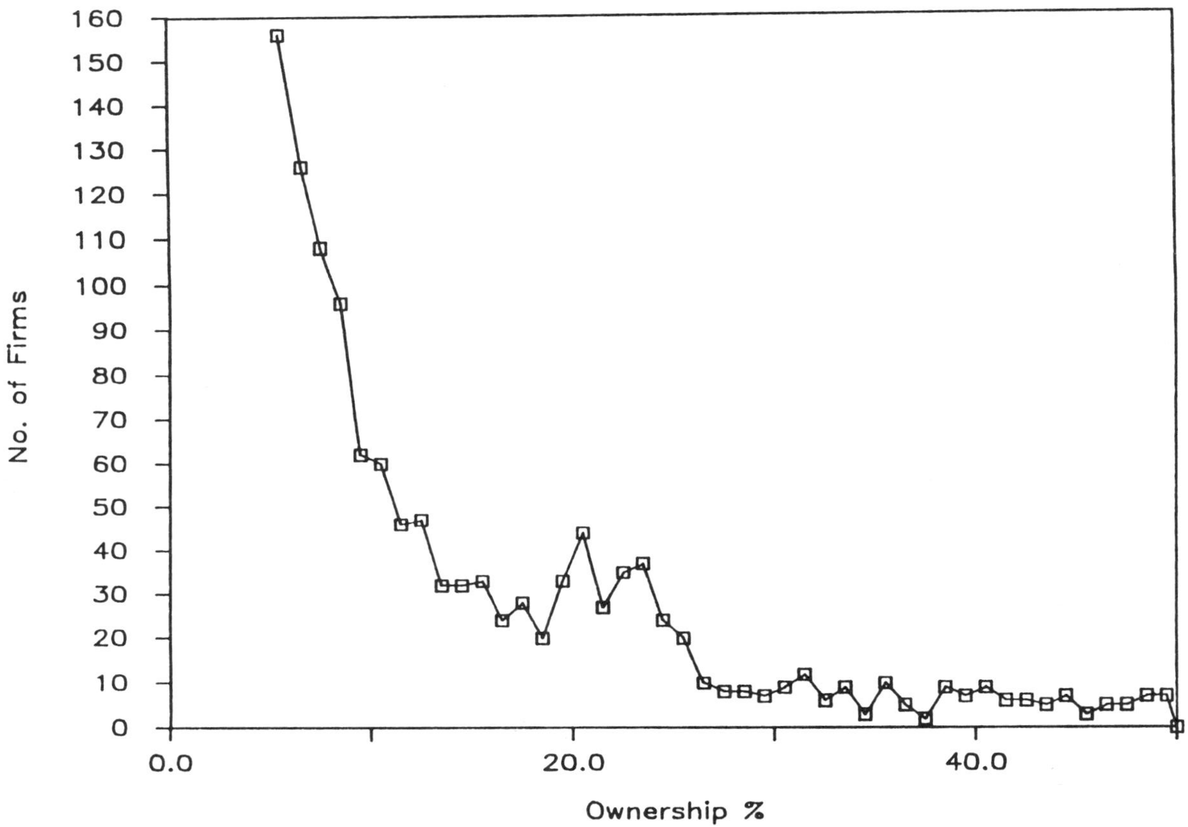

Figure 1. Ownership Percentage of Distribution: United States

are apparently balancing the perceived benefits of investment with their cost. The heavy concentration of investment positions around 20%, however, runs contrary to the downward slope of the graph. This collection of investment positions around 20% suggests that investor firms are taking ownership positions which enable them to either marginally qualify for, or marginally avoid, the equity method.

To test the hypothesis that the 20% accounting standard led to the frequent positioning of investments at just under, or just over 20%, the authors contrasted certain key characteristics of the 19 to 19.99% investees (cost method) with the 20 to 20.99% investees (equity method). It was found that the cost method investees reported net losses significantly more often and were more risky than the equity method investees. Investor firm managements were apparently, at least in part, taking ownership positions which provided the most favorable *reported* results given the requirements of the 20% accounting standard. The importance of reported results to management is readily apparent when such contractual agreements as bonus compensation plans tied to reported earnings and debt covenants based upon financial statement ratios are considered. In the presence of such agreements, managements can be expected to utilize features of investment policy (i.e., ownership positions) to achieve desired effects on accounting measures of earnings and financial position.

In concept, the 20% accounting standard should be decision-neutral; that is, it should allow investment decisions to be based primarily upon business and financial considerations. However, the Comiskey and Mulford [1986] findings indicate that the standard does influence the size of holding dimension of investment decisions in the United States. Investment decisions made subject to this constraint may produce less firm value than decisions arrived at in its absence. Thus, the implication is that, rather than providing neutral guidance to managements in the reporting of investment results, the 20% accounting standard is influencing investment behavior.

The present study explores whether Singaporean and Malaysian investor firms apply the 20% accounting standard as rigidly and place as heavy an emphasis on reported results in making investment decisions as do firms in the United States. More specifically, the study surveys a sample of Singaporean and Malaysian annual reports to determine the extent to which the ownership position of 20% is employed in defining investee firms as associated companies, resulting in use of the equity method. In addition, an ownership percentage distribution of Singaporean and Malaysian firms is contrasted with the Comiskey and Mulford [1986] U.S. distribution. Finally, profitability and risk characteristics of investee firms positioned just under and just over 20% are examined.

Widespread application of the 20% criterion coupled with evidence that managements are placing a heavy emphasis on reported results in making investment decisions would indicate that, consistent with the United States, the 20% accounting standard is providing non-neutral guidance to managements in the reporting of investment results. The implication would be that the 20% ownership criterion is playing an important role internationally in investment decision making.

ANNUAL REPORT SURVEY

Annual reports were requested of the 200 Singaporean and Malaysian firms identified in *Daiwa's Companies Handbook* [1984]. Reports for 100 companies were received: 48 Singaporean and 52 Malaysian firms. For each company, the footnotes which accompany the financial statements were examined to determine the firm's policy regarding its definition of associated companies.

Accounting standards in both Singapore and Malaysia have adopted, with few changes, the definition of associated companies contained in *IAS 3*. *IAS 3* defines an associated company as an investee company that is not a subsidiary and in which the investor (a) has a substantial voting power interest; (b) has the power to exercise significant influence over the financial and operating policies of the investee; and (c) intends to retain its interest as a long-term investment. *IAS 3* indicates that an investor may exert significant influence over the financial and operating policies of the investees in several ways: board representation and participation in policy decisions, material intercompany transactions, and interchange of managerial personnel. *IAS 3* does state, however, that if the investor holds less than 20% of the voting power of the investee, it should be presumed that the investor does not have the power to exercise significant influence, unless such power can be clearly demonstrated.

In examining the Singaporean and Malaysian company accounting policies regarding associated companies, it was noted that the provisions of *IAS 3* were followed with few exceptions. Of particular note was, consistent with the United States, a heavy emphasis on 20% ownership in defining significant influence. Representative of the accounting policies employed is that of Apollo Enterprises Limited, which states: "An associated company is defined as a company, not being a subsidiary, in which the company has a long-term interest of not less than 20% of the equity and in whose financial and operating policy decisions, the company exercises significant influence" [1984, p. 31].

Of the 34 Singaporean and Malaysian firms which disclosed an accounting policy regarding associated companies, only five Singaporean and two Malaysian companies did not specifically mention application of the 20% ownership criterion. Four of the five Singaporean companies were banks, and did not use the equity method. Interestingly, the fifth firm, United Engineers Limited, disclosed the following policy regarding associated companies: "The Group treats as associated companies those active trading companies in which

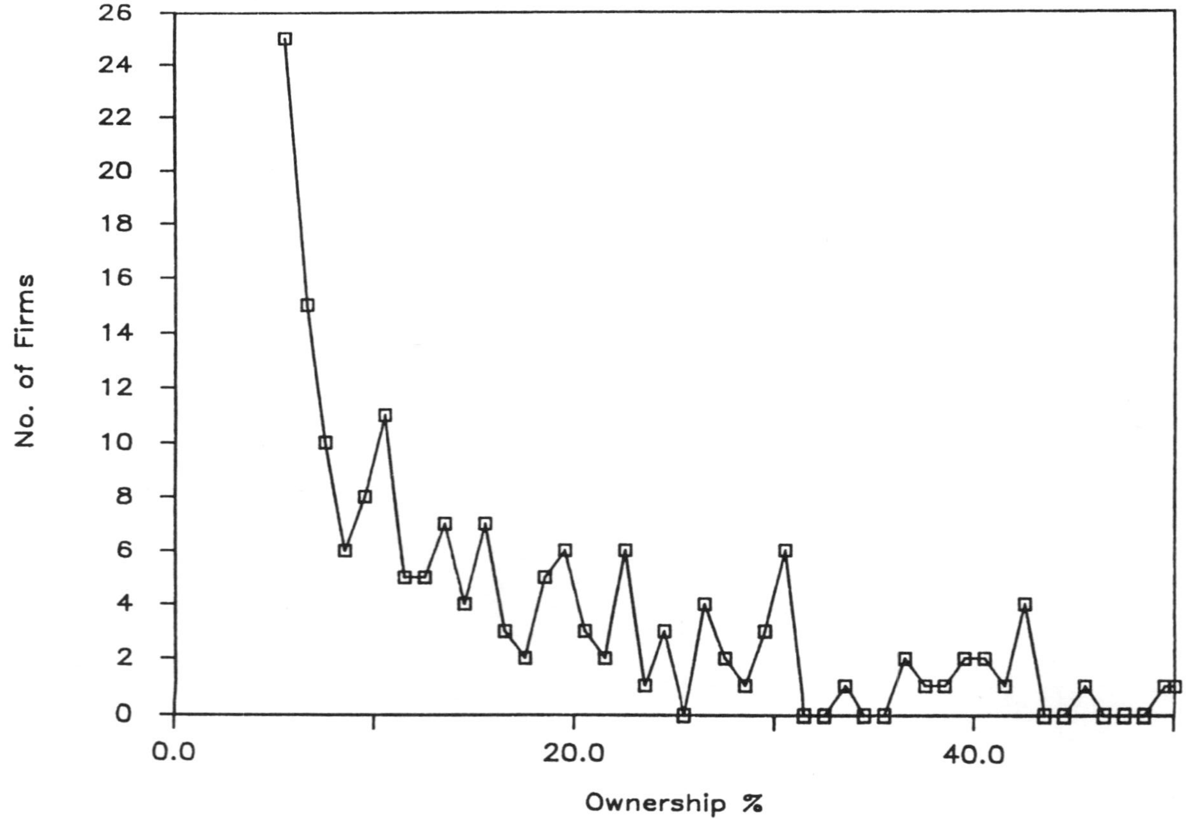

Figure 2. Ownership Percentage Distribution: Singapore and Malaysia

it has a long-term equity interest of between 19% and 50% and has board representation" [1984, p. 13]. Both of the Malaysian firms, Malayan United Industries and Tronoh Mines Malaysia, did not indicate a specific ownership interest. Rather, they noted simply that an investee was considered an associated company when the investor was in a position to exercise significant influence.

Having reviewed the accounting policies regarding associated companies for 100 Singaporean and Malaysian firms, it becomes apparent that, as in the United States, the 20% ownership criterion is employed with few exceptions. Whether this wide application of the 20% criterion has an effect on management investment decisions regarding the size of ownership positions taken is the focus of the next two sections.

OWNERSHIP PERCENTAGE DISTRIBUTION

The annual reports described in the previous section were used to construct a combined ownership percentage distribution for the Singaporean and Malaysian firms. For purposes of constructing this distribution, each firm was viewed as a potential investee. The "Substantial Shareholders" section of the reports was used to identify corporate investors, subject to the 20% accounting standard, with holdings of between 5% and 50% inclusive. A total of 167 investment positions were identified. Figure 2 presents a graph of this ownership percentage distribution.

In Figure 2, the downward slope so evident with the U.S. ownership percentage distribution (as seen in Figure 1) is present. The heightened variability of the graph, when compared with Figure 1, is presumably the result of a smaller sample size.

Figure 2 presents no evidence of an unusual concentration of investing firms around 20% like that noted in Figure 1. Accordingly, the graph provides no preliminary evidence of investor firms taking ownership positions which would either allow them to marginally qualify for, or marginally avoid, the equity method.

CHARACTERISTICS OF INVESTEES

A total of 21 investees was identified in which investment holdings were either marginally under 20% (17 to 19.99%, the cost method investees) or marginally over 20% (20 to 22.99%, the equity method investees). The cost method investees were contrasted with the equity method investees on dimensions of profitability and risk. Profitability was defined as mean return on stockholders' equity (ROE).[3] Risk was defined as the coefficient of variation of net income (CV). Both statistics were computed using data available in *Daiwa's Companies*

Handbook [1984]. Three years of data (1981, 1982, and 1983) were available for this purpose.

If the 20% ownership criterion is influencing the investment decisions of Singaporean and Malyasian managements, then the equity method investees would be expected to be more profitable and less risky than the cost method investees. Applying the equity method to a more profitable investee would have a more favorable impact than if the investee were less profitable. Moreover, if a less profitable cost method investee is viewed as more likely to report a net loss, applying the cost method to such an investee would provide the investor with a shield from the negative consequences on their reported results of such a loss. The cost method provides a similar shield when an investee exhibits a more variable income stream.

The data indicate that the Singaporean and Malaysian equity method investees were more profitable and less risky than were the cost method firms. Mean (median) ROE was 14.9% (17.0%) for the equity method investees and 12.3% (13.0%) for the cost method investees. Mean (median) CV was .43 (.34) and .56 (.50) for the equity method and cost method investees, respectively. The nonparametric Mann-Whitney U test indicates that differences between the equity method and cost method investees were statistically significant at the .06 level for both profitability and risk. These results indicate that reported results have played an important role in the ownership positions taken by Singaporean and Malyasian investor firms. The 20% ownership criterion has influenced the investment decisions made by these firms.

It can be argued that, even in the absence of the 20% accounting standard, investors would take larger investment positions in investees that are perceived to be more profitable or less risky. This could provide an alternative explanation for the results observed here. Such an explanation is considered unlikely since differences in the ownership percentage ranges examined are so small (i.e., 17 to 19.99% and 20 to 22.99%).

However, to validate the results against this alternative explanation, an additional statistical test was performed. The profitability (ROE) and risk (CV) of investees grouped above and below three other ownership positions were examined. The benchmarks selected—10%, 30%, and 40%—do not include the 20% equity-accounting threshold. If the previous findings that 20 to 22.99% investees are more profitable and less risky than 17 to 19.99% investees were not a result of the 20% accounting standard, then similar findings should be obtained for investees positioned around 10%, 30%, and 40%. The results are presented in Table 1. For ease of comparison, Table 1 repeats the results for the 20% ownership position benchmark.

The results presented in Table 1 validate the previous findings. Only in the 20% ownership position benchmark case were investees positioned just above the benchmark significantly more profitable than investees positioned just below it. With respect to risk, in only one other case besides 20% (namely,

Table 1. A Comparison of Investees on Dimensions of Profitability and Risk

Ownership Position (%)		*Profitability*[1]			*Risk*[2]		
Benchmark	*Below Benchmark* / *Above Benchmark*	*Mean*	*Median*	*Sig.*[3]	*Mean*	*Median*	*Sig.*[4]
10	7-9.99	12.4	13.5	NS	.49	.49	NS
	10-19.99	12.4	7.4		.55	.52	
20	17-19.99	12.3	13.0	.06	.56	.50	.06
	20-22.99	14.9	17.0		.43	.34	
30	27-29.99	14.5	14.1	NS	.77	.78	.02
	30-32.99	14.2	14.3		.32	.32	
40	37-39.99	12.8	8.3	NS	.51	.35	NS
	40-42.99	9.0	7.3		.45	.26	

Notes: [1] Return on Stockholders' Equity (ROE).

[2] Coefficient of Variation of Net Income (CV).

[3] Using the Mann-Whitney U test, Above Benchmark investees exhibited a higher median ROE than Below Benchmark investees at the significance level indicated. NS indicates that Above Benchmark investees did not exhibit a higher median ROE at the .10 significance level than Below Benchmark investees.

[4] Using the Mann-Whitney U test, Above Benchmark investees exhibited a lower median CV than Below Benchmark investees at the significance level indicated. NS indicates that Above Benchmark investees did not exhibit a lower median CV at the .10 significance level.

the 30% ownership case) were investees positioned just above the benchmark significantly less risky than investees positioned just below it. Based on these findings, the results documented for the 20% benchmark cannot be attributed to the identification of a positive association between ownership position and profitability or a negative association between ownership position and risk. Another explanatory factor, hypothesized here to the 20% accounting standard, is influencing the investment positions taken.

CONCLUSIONS

Internationally, the ownership position of 20% is an important factor in determining whether application of the equity method is in order. Recent research in the United States indicates that the existence of this 20% ownership criterion has influenced management investment decisions. The results of the present study indicate that investor firms in Singapore and Malaysia, like firms in the United States, are also influenced by the existence of a 20% accounting standard. Investees accounted for under the equity method were found to be more profitable and less risky than cost method investees.

In the United States, the Financial Accounting Standards Board is presently reconsidering accounting and reporting guidelines for consolidations and the equity method. Similarly, the International Accounting Standards Committee is deliberating accounting for investments in associates and joint ventures. Considering the results presented in the present study, as well as in Comiskey and Mulford [1986], both standard setting bodies may want to consider eliminating reference to an arbitrary owernship percentage benchmark for purposes of applying the equity method. The choice of cost versus equity could turn, for example, simply upon whether or not the investor possesses significant influence.

NOTES

1. In the United States, the relevant accounting standards are Accounting Principles Board Opinion No. 18: *The Equity Method of Accounting for Investments in Common Stock* [1971], and Financial Accounting Standards Board Interpretation No. 35: *Criteria for Applying the Equity Method of Accounting for Investments in Common Stock* [1981]. In Great Britain, the relevant principle is Statement of Standard Accounting Practice No. 1: *Accounting for the Results of Associated Companies* [1971, revised effective 1982].
2. Reproduced from Comiskey and Mulford [1986] with permission.
3. Comiskey and Mulford [1986] defined profitability as reported net earnings. A nonprofitable firm was one which reported a net loss. Interestingly, in the present study, none of the 21 firms identified as cost method or equity method investees reported a net loss for a three year study period. Accordingly, ROE was adopted as an alternative profitability measure. Investees with a higher ROE provide more income per dollar invested for investors to report. Higher ROE investees are also less likely candidates for reporting net losses.

REFERENCES

Accounting Principles Board, *APB Opinion No. 18:* "The Equity Method of Accounting for Investments in Common Stock" [AICPA, 1971].

Apollo Enterprises Limited, *Annual Report* [1984].

Comiskey, E., and C. Mulford, "Investment Decisions and the Equity Accounting Standard," *The Accounting Review* [July 1986], pp. 519-525.

Daiwa's Companies Handbook: 200 Singapore and Malaysia Stocks [Daiwa Singapore Limited, 1984].

Financial Accounting Standards Board, *FASB Interpretation No. 35,* "Criteria for Applying the Equity Method of Accounting for Investments in Common Stock" [FASB, 1981].

Institute of Chartered Accountants in England and Wales, *Statement of Standard Accounting Practice No. 1,* "Accounting for the Results of Associated Companies" [Institute of Chartered Accountants in England and Wales, 1971 (amended in 1974, revised in 1982)].

International Accounting Standards Committee, *International Accounting Standard No. 3,* "Consolidated Financial Statements" [IASC, 1976].

________. *International Accounting Standard Exposure Draft 28,* "Accounting for Investments in Associated and Joint Ventures" [IASC, 1986].

United Engineers Limited, *Annual Report* [1984].

AN INVESTIGATION OF THE IMPACT OF CONTEXTUAL FACTORS ON CANADIAN BANKERS' PERCEPTIONS OF AUDITORS' ABILITY TO RESIST MANAGEMENT PRESSURE

Daryl Lindsay

ABSTRACT

Critics allege that auditors often comply with the accounting treatment preferred by client management when a difference of opinion on matters of accounting principles or practices, or financial statement disclosure, arises during an audit engagement. The objective of this study is to investigate factors that may influence bankers to conclude that such compliant behavior may occur. A repeated measures experiment was conducted using 55 commercial account managers as subjects. Analysis of variance results show the nature of the accounting issue, as well as three contextual factors: the size of the audit firm, the nature of the competitive environment for audit firms, and the degree to which the audit firm also provides non-audit services to the audit client, as being four important factors.

Advances in International Accounting, Vol. 3, pages 71-85.

ISBN: 1-55938-078-0

INTRODUCTION

A Canadian auditor when formulating his audit opinion is required by the CICA Handbook to "exercise his professional judgment as to the appropriateness of the selection and application of principles to the particular circumstances of an enterprise and to the overall effect on financial statements of separate decisions made in their preparation" [Canadian Institute of Chartered Accountants (CICA), Handbook, Section 5400.13]. Incorrect exercise of such a judgment, as evident in the recently concluded hearing into the Calgroup Graphics Corporation Ltd. affair by the Professional Conduct Committee of the Institute of Chartered Accountants of Ontario, can have dire consequences for the audit professional. In that instance, the audit was found to be deficient in that the auditors did not properly adhere to either generally accepted auditing standards (inappropriate reliance on management representations) or to generally accepted accounting principles (accounted for a transaction as a purchase rather than as a reverse takeover). The Committee recognized that exercising professional judgement in applying GAAP could lead to this transaction being accounted for in either way [Williamson and Carmona, 1988, p. 8]. Why do such problems arise and how might reasonably knowledgeable users of financial statements assess such a judgment?

In a recent address to the Auditing Section of the American Accounting Association, the Chief Accountant of the Enforcement Division of the Securities and Exchange Commission observed: "The essence of professionalism in accounting is the ability to exercise an independent judgment, even when that judgment runs counter to the client's wishes, and especially where the judgment cannot be supported by a clear statement in the literature" [Sack, 1987, p. 2]. John Twigg [1987, pp. 1, 2] quoted Dan McDonald of Simon Fraser University in his presentation to the Commission to Study the Public's Expectations of Audits (Macdonald Commission) as having said: "the wide menu of options offered under generally accepted accounting principles enables publicly traded and other companies to choose a financial presentation that does not fairly present their position but still receives the auditor's signature." These observations imply that the required judgments may be more difficult to exercise when the technical accounting standards are either nonexistent or flexible, and may result in less than fair presentation. Such concerns on the part of the Canadian public led to the formation of the aforementioned Macdonald Commission.

Audit environment factors, in addition to nonexistent or flexible accounting standards, have been identified as issues which may be leading the public to question the ability of auditors to take a strong independent stance when a disagreement arises between auditor and client regarding the appropriateness of a management proposed accounting treatment. For instance, Patricia Chisholm, a financial columnist, in commenting on the Professional Conduct

Committee inquiry into the Calgroup affair, observed that auditors are accused of improperly complying with client demands in that they are essentially failing to adhere to generally accepted accounting principles. She attributes this complaint behavior, in part, to the strong competition for audits and the resulting price cuts which have pressured auditors both to cut corners and to deliver the kinds of financial statements desired by client management [Chisholm, 1988, pp. 3, 4]. Corcoran questioned the ability of an auditor to maintain his independence when providing a wide range of non-audit services to management and at the same time having to cope with "generally accepted accounting principles that are vague, inconclusive and open to interpretation" [Corcoran, 1986, pp. 1, 2]. The Reverend Desmond Kimmitt, the first public governor of the Board of Governors of the Canadian Institute of Chartered Accountants, suggested that factors such as the highly competitive environment and the receipt of an increasing proportion of fee income from the provision of non-audit services to audit clients is causing the public to question auditor independence [Kimmitt, 1985].

Some Canadian accounting academics also have questioned whether auditors will be perceived as being able to maintain their independence in an environment which has the potential for reducing the ability of auditors to resist attempts by client management to influence audit opinion formulation [Amernic and Aranya, 1981; Lindsay et al., 1987]. A task force created by the Canadian Academic Accounting Association to provide input to the Macdonald Commission raised concerns regarding the impact of: provision of non-audit services to audit clients, competition among audit firms to retain existing or to attract new clients, and opinion shopping, on the ability of auditors to maintain their independence [The Canadian Academic Accounting Association (CAAA) Task Force on the Expectations Gap, 1986]. Similarly, Blazouske questioned whether fierce competition among accounting firms for both audit clients and the related provision of non-audit services would erode the ability of an audit firm to operate independently of client management when issuing an audit report [Blazouske, 1986]. A common theme to these observations is the question of whether an auditor will be able or be perceived as being able to exercise the independent professional judgment required by the CICA Handbook under the identified environmental conditions.

The purpose of this paper is to present empirical data regarding bankers' perceptions of the ability of an auditor to resist client management pressure to comply when a significant conflict arises over the treatment of a material accounting issue. Specifically, the study investigates how the nature of the accounting issue as well as three environmental factors (provision of non-audit services, extent of competition among audit firms, and the size of the audit firm) are perceived by bankers to affect the ability of an auditor to resist management pressure. The paper is organized as follows. The second section describes the rationale underlying each hypothesis. The third section overviews the research methodology. The fourth section describes the results and their interpretation, and the final section provides the conclusions.

HYPOTHESIS RATIONALE

Nature of the Accounting Issue

In this section, the nature of the accounting issue will be differentiated based on whether the technical accounting standards of the profession (CICA Handbook) specify the appropriate treatment of a particular issue or are relatively silent as to what the appropriate treatment should be in the circumstances. Concerns have been raised that the resolution of differences of opinion between an auditor and client management on any matter of accounting principles or practices, or financial disclosure may result in less than fair treatment when the auditor is unable to draw upon official pronouncements to support his otherwise correct opinion. For instance, the staff of the Ontario Securities Commission (OSC) in its submission to the Macdonald Commission expressed concern about the number of important accounting issues for which the technical standards of the profession are either nonexistent or too general to be of practical value. The chairman and the chief accountant of the Ontario Securities Commission, in discussing the concerns raised by their staff, conclude: "There is no escaping it—auditors must strongly assert their independence and exercise sound professional judgment in assessing any proposed financial presentation" [Beck and Cherry, 1987, p. 42]. They thought that some accountants and auditors either were ignoring the spirit of the standards or were taking the position that "anything goes" when the standards in Canada were otherwise silent. Ann Shortell, a financial columnist, expressed similar sentiments when she suggested that in practice some auditors just take managements' word for it when the standards are too general or absent [Shortell, 1986].

Two accounting issues were selected to assess the extent to which the nature of the accounting issue affected bankers' perceptions of the ability of auditors' to resist management's pressure to comply with a proposed accounting treatment. A disagreement over the appropriate treatment of a material subsequent event was chosen to represent a precisely treated accounting issue because Section 3820.10 of the CICA Handbook clearly specifies the generally accepted accounting treatment. On the other hand, a dispute over the appropriate treatment of a material unrecorded liability was selected to represent a situation where the technical standards of the Canadian accounting profession are relatively silent. Each issue was clearly described to the participants and they were informed as to whether or not the CICA Handbook precisely dealt with the issue. The following hypothesis was used to test the effect of the nature of the accounting issue:

H_1. Bankers will perceive that management is more likely to obtain its preferred accounting treatment in a conflict with an audit firm when the accounting issue is not dealt with precisely by technical standards, as opposed to the situation where the accounting issue is dealt with precisely by technical standards.

Non-Audit Services

For the purpose of this paper, the term *non-audit services* will be used in its more limited sense to mean management advisory services. That is, it is not considered to include activities such as the provision of tax services. Although the provision of non-audit services to audit clients has been the subject of considerable research over the past two decades in the United States [Schulte, 1965; Titard, 1971; Hartley and Ross, 1972; Lavin, 1976; Shockley, 1981; Knapp, 1985] and has been of concern to Congressional committees (Metcalf and Dingell) over a similar period of time, it has received only limited attention by Canadian researchers [Dermer, Evans, and Pick, 1971; Lindsay, Rennie, Murphy, and Silvester, 1987]. Lindsay et al. [1987, p. 187] found that a relatively large minority (41.6%) of Canadian bankers were concerned that the performance of management advisory services for audit clients might lead to loss of independence. Apparently these bankers perceive the auditor who performs MAS for an audit client as likely to become more dependent on that client because he may fear the loss of fees generated by those services and, therefore, in order to protect those fees may be more inclined to accept management's preferred accounting treatment when a disagreement arises. An editorial in the February 1987 issue of *Bottom Line* [p. 3] provides some additional evidence as to the current degree of concern in Canada. The editorial identified the question of whether auditor independence could be ensured when an audit firm provided both audit and MAS to the same client as being one of three common themes addressed in a series of submissions to the Macdonald Commission.

In order to capture the banker concerns identified in the Lindsay et al. [1987] study, the following non-audit service scenario originally developed by Knapp [1985] was used to depict a not atypical MAS situation:

> Allied's [client] auditors are also currently working on a large management consulting project involving Allied's cost accounting system. The consulting engagement will most likely not be completed for another twelve months. The total fee for this project is expected to be equal to approximately 40 percent of the current year's audit fee.

The alternative scenario was that the audit firm was not to be providing any advisory services to the client in the ensuing twelve months.

The following hypothesis was used to test the bankers' reactions to the provision/non-provision of management advisory services:

H_2. Bankers will perceive that management is more likely to obtain its preferred accounting treatment in a conflict with an audit firm when the firm provides a significant amount of non-audit service to the client as opposed to providing no such service.

Competition

Canadian academicians and practitioners have expressed concerns that when an audit firm has a disagreement with client management over the treatment of an accounting issue it may be less willing to resist management pressure to comply when a highly competitive market for audit services exists. For instance, the task force of the Canadian Academic Accounting Association in its submission to the Macdonald Commission said:

> In addition increasing competition among auditing firms seems to be causing clients to view the audit as a commodity. ... Such management attitudes can also lead to opinion shopping when management shops around for the most compliant auditor. Eventually such competitive pressures could lead to "low balling" (charging unreasonably low fees with the possibility that an audit of poor quality or an incomplete audit will be performed) and loss of objectivity on the part of the auditor [Canadian Academic Accounting Association, 1986, p. 17].

Arthur Johnson, a financial columnist with the *Toronto Globe and Mail,* quoted David Smith, Executive Vice-President of the Certified General Accountants Association of Ontario, as having stated:

> fierce price competition among audit firms poses a real danger to the independence of auditors. Audit fees are being negotiated as loss leaders to solicit other business for accounting firms. Obviously, there are only so many (audit) appointments to go around.
>
> When an auditor disagrees with management about an item on a financial statement, he does have the option of saying so, providing what is called a "qualified statement."
>
> But ... there is a very large concern on the part of management of a corporation to ensure that their audited statements are not qualified [Johnson, 1985, p. B3].

Two alternative scenarios, consistent with Knapp [1985], were presented to bankers for their deliberations. In one of the scenarios, the immediate audit market within which Allied's (client) auditors compete was depicted as being composed of a number of large auditing firms that were aggressively pursuing practice development (expansion) programs. Otherwise, the other major auditing firms in the immediate area in which Allied's auditing firm operates were described as not being aggressive competitors. The extent to which competition affected the perceptions of bankers was tested by the following hypothesis:

H_3. Bankers will perceive that management is more likely to obtain its preferred accounting treatment in a conflict with an audit firm when the market in which the audit firm operates is characterized by a high, rather than low, level of competition.

Audit-firm Size

Traditionally, underwriters in Canada have insisted, for reasons of perceived public confidence, on having the name of one of the large public accounting firms associated with a prospectus [Canadian Institute of Chartered Accountants, 1978, p. 56]. This practice is not inconsistent with the suggestions of Mautz and Sharaf [1961] who thought a large firm would not be as economically dependent as a small firm on any one client, or with the views of Hartley and Ross [1972] who suggested that the impact of losing a client and its MAS revenue would not be as great for a large firm as for a smaller firm. In a Canadian study, Amernic and Aranya [1981] found public accountants in large firms to be perceived as being more independent than those in small firms. Since all their subjects were public accountants, we have no evidence as to whether bankers concur with their perceptions. We do know from the Lindsay et al. [1987] study that there were significant differences of opinion between bankers and public accountants in eleven out of fifteen situations and that in nine of these situations bankers were more concerned than the public accountants about auditor independence [Lindsay et al., 1987, p. 187].

Two scenarios were developed to examine whether bankers perceived smaller (rather than larger) audit firms to be more likely to comply with client management preferences when a disagreement arose over an accounting issue. The audit firms in the study were depicted as being either one of the largest national CA firms in Canada or as being a local one-office CA firm with a staff of fifty professionals. The following hypothesis was used to test the effect of audit-firm size on the perceptions of bankers:

> **H_4.** Bankers will perceive that management is more likely to obtain its preferred accounting treatment in a conflict with an audit firm when the audit firm is a small firm rather than a large firm.

Although numerous interactions among these four independent variables might be hypothesized, the decision was made to only formally test for main effects. However, information is provided regarding first-order interactions. The next section of paper contains an overview of the research methodology employed.

RESEARCH METHODOLOGY

Study Participants

The Executive Director of the Institute of Canadian Bankers was contacted initially to request the participation of a subgroup (commercial account

	Treatment Level	
	1	*2*
Accounting Issue	Materiality dispute	Disclosure dispute
Non-audit Service	40 percent of audit fee	None
Competition	Aggressive	Not aggressive
Audit-firm Size	Local	Large national

Figure 1. Treatment Levels of Independent Variables

managers/loan officers) of its membership. Participation of members of this group was requested because they had raised concerns previously about auditor independence [Lindsay et al., 1987], a member of the group was the second public representative appointed to the Board of Governors of the Canadian Institute of Chartered Accountants, and they are considered to represent reasonably informed financial statement users. Members of this group should understand the importance of audit firm independence and the significance of audit firm-client management conflict.[1] The Executive Director, through his Advisory Committee, identified five schedule "A" and one schedule "B" banks that were willing to supply participants for the study. Eighty sets of research instruments were sent to members of these banks.[2]

Fifty-five (68.75%) of the eighty bankers initially contacted returned usable responses. Forty-four were considered to be early responders and the other eleven were deemed to be late responders. The respondents had a mean length of experience as a commercial account manager of 8.3 years with a minimum of 1 year, a maximum of 25 years, and a median of 7 years. Twenty-one had 10 or more years of experience.

Experimental Procedures

The experiment was a full-factorial, repeated measures analysis of variance design with four independent variables, each of which had two treatment levels as shown in Figure 1. Analysis of variance was chosen due to its efficiency in dealing with categorical data and its ability to reveal interactions between/among the independent variables.

Two versions of the research instrument were used to determine whether an order effect influenced the bankers' responses. Each version had a different random ordering of the cases and the independent variables within each case. The bankers were provided with the following constant information regarding the audit client (Allied Manufacturing): publicly-owned, listed on the Toronto Stock Exchange, and in quite good overall financial condition (all of the company's solvency and profitability ratios compared favorably to industry averages and net income had shown a modest but steady growth pattern over the last five years).

An example of one scenario is presented in the Appendix. The bankers were required to record the likelihood that the dispute depicted would be resolved in favor of the alternative desired by client management, rather than the auditor, in each of the sixteen cases. Bankers had all 16 cases available simultaneously and their responses were recorded on a 7-point, equal-interval Likert scale. Consistent with the recommendation by Torgerson [1958, pp. 66-68], only the two endpoints on the scale were labeled. To minimize the bias due to changes in the bankers' psychological scales as they progressed through the cases, the bankers were informed that any number of cases could be assigned a given number on the scale and were encouraged to alter any response to earlier cases if they should change their minds while completing the instrument.

RESULTS

Overall Analysis

The overall analysis of variance (ANOVA) results are presented in Table 1. Each of the four main effects (A, N, C, and S) was highly significant at a .01 level and in the predicted direction. In addition, order and response, and the interactions between these two factors and the nature of the accounting issue were found to be significant at at least a .05 level. The absolute and relative omega-square statistic for all effects found to be significant by the F statistics is presented in Table 2.[3] In addition, the means for the treatment levels of each independent variable are presented in Table 3.

The empirical results support all four hypotheses. However, the effect of the nature of the accounting issue was much greater than the effect of any of the other variables as demonstrated by both the percentage of explained variance (54.4) reported in Table 2 and as indicated by the much greater difference in means (4.38:3.06) presented in Table 3. The bankers, consistent with the member quoted in note 1, also identified the size of the audit firm as being an important factor in assessing how an accounting dispute might be resolved. The percentage of variance (25.1) explained and the difference in means (4.17:3.27) are much greater than for the non-audit services and competition factors.

The empirical results strongly support the rationale underlying the first hypothesis that an audit firm might be perceived to be less able to resist client-management pressure in a conflict situation involving an accounting issue which requires the exercise of considerable judgment than in a situation where the accounting treatment is reasonably clearly specified by generally accepted accounting principles. The implications for accounting standard setters appear to be clear.

Table 1. Analysis of Variance for All Main Effects and First-Order Interactions

	SS	*df*	*MS*	*F*	*p*
Main Effects					
A Accounting Issue	382.3	1	382.3	170.4	.000
N Non-audit Services	37.6	1	37.6	16.8	.000
C Competition	55.0	1	55.0	24.5	.000
S Audit-firm Size	178.2	1	178.2	79.4	.000
O Order	21.1	1	21.1	9.4	.002
R Response	25.5	1	25.5	11.4	.001
Interactions					
AN	4.7	1	4.7	2.1	.150
AC	3.8	1	3.8	1.7	.192
AS	7.6	1	7.6	3.4	.065
AO	15.7	1	15.7	7.0	.008
AR	9.5	1	9.5	4.2	.040
NC	3.6	1	3.6	1.6	.208
NS	0.0	1	0.0	0.0	.928
NO	1.5	1	1.5	0.7	.420
NR	0.0	1	0.0	0.0	.989
CS	0.8	1	0.8	0.3	.559
CO	0.3	1	0.3	0.2	.695
CR	0.6	1	0.6	0.3	.615
SO	5.5	1	5.5	2.5	.118
SR	3.6	1	3.6	1.6	.209
OR	2.7	1	2.7	1.2	.271

Note: Repeated measures ANOVA designs use the mean square associated with the specific treatment subject interaction as the *F*-ratio denominator. None of the second or higher order interactions were significant at a .01 level.

Table 2. Variance Explained by Significant Effects for All Banker Responses

Effect	*F*	W^2	*Relative* W^2
Accounting Issue	170.4	0.143	0.544
Non-audit Services	16.8	0.013	0.049
Competition	24.5	0.020	0.076
Audit-firm Size	79.4	0.066	0.251
Order	9.4	0.007	0.027
Response	11.4	0.009	0.034
Accounting Issue-Order interaction	7.0	0.005	0.019
Accounting Issue-Response interaction	4.2	—	—
		0.263	1.000

Table 3. Means for Treatment Levels of Independent Variables

	Treatment Level	
	*1**	*2*
Accounting Issue	4.38**	3.06
Non-audit Service	3.93	3.51
Competition	3.97	3.47
Audit-firm Size	4.17	3.27

Notes: * The treatment level for each independent variable is summarized in Figure 1.
** Higher scale scores indicated a higher perceived likelihood that the client would obtain its preferred outcome to the audit conflict. (The 7-point scale used by the bankers is included in the Appendix.)

Individual Analysis

The low variance (26.3% per Table 2) explained by the experimental effects when the bankers' responses were analyzed on an overall basis is indicative of potential high between-subject response variability and suggests further investigation. Therefore, an ANOVA model was computed for each banker. Since significant first-order interactions only explained one-half of one percent of the variance when the overall analysis was performed (Table 2) and on average only accounted for 2.5 percent at the .01 level of significance (not significant for 49 out of 55 responses) when individual ANOVA models were computed, the decision was made to estimate for each banker only the proportion of variance accounted for by each significant ($p < 0.01$) main effect. All interactions were used to estimate the error term.

Table 4 contains the omega squares by main effect for each banker. As indicated, the model on average explained 54.4 percent of the variance in individual banker's judgments. The omega-square statistic summed across all significant main effects for each banker yielded an estimate of the proportion of variance which the model explained for that banker. The variance explained ranged from zero (no factors significant) for twelve individuals to 100 percent (two individuals) with the model explaining 90 percent or greater of the variance for eight individuals. Furthermore, the average of the omega-square statistic summed across all bankers (including the twelve for whom there were no significant effects) for each significant main effect was 32.1 percent for the nature of the accounting issue; 12.8 percent for the size of the audit firm; 5.8 percent for the nature of the competitive environment; and 3.7 percent for the provision of non-audit services, respectively. The finer analysis presented in Table 4 indicates that the coarser analysis inherent in Table 2 resulted in large losses of explanatory power due to sizeable individual differences. The instrument was more successful in capturing the judgments of individual bankers than indicated by the overall omega-square statistic.

Table 4. Bankers' Judgment Models From ANOVA[a]

Effect	*1*	*2*	*3*	*4*	*5*	*6*	*7*	*8*	*9*	*10*	*11*	*12*	*13*	*14*	*15*	*16*	*17*	*18*	*19*
A	—	56	26	32	66	—	23	52	39	—	—	88	—	62	—	87	—	—	51
N	—	—	9	—	—	—	—	—	14	—	42	—	56	—	—	—	—	—	—
C	—	—	—	—	—	32	—	—	25	—	—	—	33	—	—	—	—	—	—
S	—	—	52	32	—	—	43	—	14	—	—	—	—	12	37	6	57	—	—
Total	—	56	87	64	66	32	66	52	92	—	42	88	89	74	37	93	57	—	51

Effect	*20*	*21*	*22*	*23*	*24*	*25*	*26*	*27*	*28*	*29*	*30*	*31*	*32*	*33*	*34*	*35*	*36*	*37*	*38*
A	—	38	14	—	—	53	—	92	60	—	—	71	70	39	—	—	10	—	92
N	—	—	14	—	—	—	—	—	5	—	—	—	—	—	—	—	—	—	3
C	—	—	44	—	—	20	—	3	5	—	52	—	12	—	—	—	—	—	—
S	—	—	14	56	—	13	—	—	21	—	—	17	—	—	—	—	90	—	—
Total	—	38	86	56	—	86	—	95	91	—	52	88	82	39	—	—	100	—	95

Effect	*39*	*40*	*41*	*42*	*43*	*44*	*45*	*46*	*47*	*48*	*49*	*50*	*51*	*52*	*53*	*54*	*55*	*Avg.*
A	72	—	31	—	—	67	31	—	92	—	25	50	45	75	57	30	72	32.1
N	—	—	31	—	22	—	—	—	7	—	—	—	—	—	—	—	—	3.7
C	9	—	—	—	48	—	—	38	—	—	—	—	—	—	—	—	—	5.8
S	—	—	—	—	13	14	—	—	—	66	25	50	17	—	23	30	—	12.8
Total	81	—	62	—	83	81	31	38	99	66	50	100	62	75	80	60	72	54.4

Notes: A = Accounting Issue; N = Non-audit Services; C = Competition; and S = Audit-firm Size.
[a] The omega square values in the table are percentages. All interactions were used to estimate the error term. Thus interactions are not estimable.

Limitations

The findings and conclusions of this research are subject to several limitations. External validity of the study may be limited because the experimental setting may not have been sufficiently realistic and/or the factors may have been too explicitly stated. Since all the subjects were bankers, the issue remains open as to whether their perceptions can be generalized to other financial statement user groups (for instance, financial analysts). The generalizability of the results also is constrained by the specific definitions adopted. For instance, did the bankers consider a local one-office CA firm with a staff of 50 professionals to be distinctly smaller than one of the largest national CA firms in Canada? Furthermore, did the repeated measures design oversensitize the bankers to the independent variables and, thereby, enable them to predict the hypothesis and, perhaps, then respond cooperatively? Internal validity may have been threatened either by the factors included/excluded or by their operationalization.

CONCLUSIONS

Awareness that circumstances exist in which differences of opinion on matters of accounting principles or practices, or financial statement disclosure arise between client management and the external auditor appears to be growing. The results of this study, conducted prior to the October 1987 stock market slump, suggest that bankers tend to view the auditor as being vulnerable to management pressure when the technical accounting standards of the profession are either flexible or nonexistent. In addition, the results indicate other factors which may be perceived to have a detrimental impact on the ability of an audit firm to maintain its independence of management.

Bankers in this study perceive smaller audit firms as being less able to resist management pressures than larger firms. The nature of the competitive environment among audit firms, and the extent to which the audit firm also provides non-audit services to the audit client also are perceived as factors which may hamper an audit firm in its attempt to take a strong independent stance.

APPENDIX

Scenario A

In the current year's audit a dispute has arisen between Allied and its external auditors. The dispute arose over the *materiality of certain unrecorded liabilities* discovered by the auditors. The unrecorded liabilities consist primarily of expenses incurred in 1986 that were neither paid nor recorded in Allied's accounting records until 1987. Allied's controller argues that the total amount of the unrecorded liabilities is immaterial and that it is therefore unnecessary to adjust the financial statements in this regard. The auditors feel the amount is material and that the 1986 financial statements should be adjusted accordingly. *Technical accounting standards provide very little guidance* in determining the materiality of given amounts in financial statements, and thus, Allied's management believe they themselves should know as well as anyone what their financial statement readers would or would not deem to be a material amount. Other available facts include:

Case 1

- Allied's auditors will *not be providing any consulting services* to Allied in the coming twelve months.
- The immediate audit market within which Allied's auditors compete is characterized by a number of large auditing firms that are *aggressively pursuing practice development* [*expansion*] *programs.*

- Allied is audited by a *local one-office CA firm* with a staff of 50 professionals.

In your view, given the above information, how likely is it that the unrecorded liabilities wil be *ignored* for purposes of the financial statements as well as the auditor's report, which is the alternative that Allied's management desires? Record your answer by circling the most appropriate number on the following equal-interval scale.

Very low likelihood	1	2	3	4	5	6	7	Very high likelihood

ACKNOWLEDGMENTS

The author gratefully acknowledges the helpful support of the partners and staff of the Saskatoon office of Deloitte Haskins & Sells, and members of The Institute of Canadian Bankers.

NOTES

1. One indicator of this insight was provided by Banker 49 (MBA, CA) who attached the following note to his questionnaire:

> It is my perception that for large public companies, auditors tend to be more conservative and more carefully guided by GAAP than for smaller, privately held companies. Indeed, among the latter group, audits are becoming a thing of the past and these companies' auditors/accountants have become less and less independent over time with some of these accountants, actually becoming involved with business deals with their clients. An interesting study would be the effect this trend has on the ability of the banker/financial analyst to rely on their financial statements.

2. Copies of the research instrument are available upon request. Reading the Hypotheses Rationale and the Appendix, however, reveals the salient aspects of the instrument.

3. There is no apparent explanation as to why the variables order (versions 1 or 2 of the instrument) and response (early or later responders) were significant. When the 22 subjects who responded to version 1 and the thirty-three subjects who responded to version 2 of the instrument were analyzed separately as members of two separate groups, the response variable was not significant for the latter group and only marginally significant for the former group. When similar analysis was performed for the early responders ($n = 44$) and the later responders ($n = 11$), the order variable only was found to be significant for the small sample group. Given the small amount of variance explained by the order and response variables (see Table 2) and the findings of the finer group analysis, the decision was made to concentrate only on the four main independent variables in the paper.

REFERENCES

Amernic, J., and N. Aranya, "Public Accountants' Independence: Some Evidence in a Canadian Context," *The International Journal of Accounting Education and Research* [Spring 1981], pp. 11-33.

Beck, S., and P. Cherry, "How the Regulators See Us," *CA Magazine* [October 1987], pp. 40-44.

Blazouske, J.D., "Storm Clouds Are Gathering," *World Accounting Report* [January 1986], pp. 12-13.

Canadian Academic Accounting Association, *A Report to the Macdonald Commission by the Canadian Academic Accounting Association* [*CAAA*] *Task Force on the Expectations Gap* [CAAA, 1986].

Canadian Institute of Chartered Accountants, Special Committee to Examine the Role of the Auditor, "The Report of the Special Committee to Examine the Role of the Auditor," *CA Magazine* [April 1978], pp. 33-70.

Chisholm, P., "Defending the Sacred Code of the Auditing Profession," *Financial Times of Canada* [February 29, 1988], pp. 3-4.

CICA Handbook [CICA, 1988].

Corcoran, T., "Closing the 'Gap' on Chartered Accountants," *Financial Times of Canada* [June 16, 1986], pp. 1-2.

Dermer, J., M. Evans, and T. Pick, "The Compatibility of Auditing and Management Services," *Canadian Chartered Accountant* [January 1971], pp. 20-25.

Hartley, R. and T. Ross, "MAS and Audit Independence: An Image Problem," *Journal of Accountancy* [November 1972], pp. 42-51.

Johnson, A., "Glare of Spotlight Reveals Warts in Auditing System," *The Globe and Mail* [December 7, 1985], pp. B1 and B3.

Kimmitt, D., "A Calling of a Different Order," *CA Magazine* [September 1985], pp. 72-75.

Knapp, M., "Audit Conflict: An Empirical Study of the Perceived Ability of Auditors to Resist Management Pressure," *The Accounting Review* [April 1985], pp. 202-211.

Lavin, D., "Perceptions of the Independence of the Auditor," *The Accounting Review* [January 1976], pp. 41-50.

Lindsay, D., M. Rennie, G. Murphy, and H. Silvester, "Independence of External Auditors: A Canadian Perspective," *Advances in International Accounting* [Spring 1987], pp. 169-189.

Mautz, R., and H. Sharaf, *The Philosophy of Auditing* [AAA, 1961].

Sack, R., "The Anatomy of a Fraud," paper presented to the Auditing Section of the American Accounting Association at its Second Annual Luncheon, New York, [August 21, 1986].

Schulte, A., "Compatibility of Management Accounting and Auditing," *The Accounting Review* [July 1965], pp. 587-593.

Shockley, R., "Perceptions of Auditors' Independence: An Empirical Analysis," *The Accounting Review* [October 1981], pp. 785-800.

Shortell, A., "The Auditors," *Canadian Business* [November 1986], pp. 38-44.

Titard, P., "Independence and MAS—Opinions of Financial Statement Users," *Journal of Accountancy* [July 1971], pp. 47-52.

Torgerson, W., *Theory and Methods of Scaling* [Wiley, 1958].

Twigg, J., "Widen Auditors' Mandate, Hearings Told," *The Bottom Line* [December 1986 - January 1987], pp. 1-2.

Williamson, R., and E. Carmona, "PW Partner Pleads Guilty to Calgroup Charges," *The Bottom Line* [April 1988], p. 8.

ACCOUNTING FOR CHANGING PRICES IN DUTCH ANNUAL REPORTS

Dick van Offeren

ABSTRACT

This paper reports the results of an exploratory survey of 147 annual reports on the influences of the valuation method used on the reported figures of assets, equity and income. The companies of this survey were listed on the Amsterdam Stock Exchange as of December 31, 1985. First, the reports are analyzed with regard to the valuation method. The survey is continued for the companies reporting one or more items on both historical cost and current cost. The differences between the two figures are calculated for four balance sheet items and for two items of the income statement. The influence of the gearing adjustment on the reported figure of current cost group income is also calculated. Finally, the impact of the valuation method on the return on investment ratios is indicated. The most important findings are that the valuation method influences the reported figures to a large degree and that there are wide variations from company to company. These findings could adduce arguments in support of supplying both historical cost and current cost information in published financial statements. Then, users of financial statements will be able to choose the data that correspond with their needs.

Advances in International Accounting, Vol. 3, pages 87-106.

ISBN: 1-55938-078-0

Assets	*Equity + Liabilities = Capital*
Fixed assets	*Group Equity*
• *Tangible fixed assets*	• Stockholders' Equity
• Other fixed assets	• Minority interests
Current assets	Provisions and liabilities
• *Tangible current assets*	
• Other current assets	
Total assets	*Total capital*

Figure 1. Standard Format of the Consolidated Balance Sheet

Note: Italicized items are of major interest in the analysis of the data.

Net sales
Cost of sales (depreciation, depletion and amortization included)
Operating Income
Financial items
Extraordinary items
Income taxes
Gearing adjustment
Group Income
Minority interests
Net Income

Figure 2. Standard Format of the Consolidated Income Statement

Note: Italicized items are of major interest in the analysis of the data.

INTRODUCTION

As inflation declines the general public loses its interest in accounting for changing prices. However, the problem of 'inflation accounting' has not been solved. Therefore, it is interesting to investigate the effects of accounting for changing prices on published annual reports even in periods with low inflation rates.

According to Dutch law on financial reporting (Civil Code Book 2, Title 8) the valuation of assets may be based either on historical cost or on current cost. The option of Section 33 of the Fourth Directive of the European Community has been used.

The aim of this survey is to indicate the differences between historical cost accounting and current cost accounting on the reported figures of assets, equity and income. This is achieved by examining the annual reports of 147 companies

Figure 3. Consolidated Financial Statements of the ABC-Group, 1985

Consolidated Income Statement of the ABC-Group, 1985, Millions of Guilders, Historical Cost

Sales proceeds		20,094.7
Sales taxes		2,084.9
Net proceeds		18,009.8
Cost of sales		12,343.9
Gross profit		5,665.9
Selling expenses	2,857.1	
Research and development expenses	662.2	
General and administrative expenses	744.8	
Other revenues from operations	63.1	
		4,201.0
Operating income		1,464.9
Interest and other income	152.3	
Interest paid and similar expenses	337.4	
		185.1
Operating income less financing charges		1,279.8
Taxes		464.6
Earnings of consolidated companies from normal operations, after taxes		815.2
Earnings from unconsolidated companies		98.2
Group income from normal operations after taxes		913.4
Extraordinary gains	99.4	
Extraordinary losses	167.5	
Extraordinary items before taxes	68.1	
Taxes (plus)	70.6	
Extraordinary items after taxes		2.5
Group income		915.9
Minority interests		72.9
Net income		843.0

Supplementary Information on the Basis of Current Cost

Operating income on the basis of historical cost		1,464.9
Adjustments of operating income to current cost:		
Additional cost of sales	43.0	
Additional depreciation	133.0	
Total adjustments		176.0
Operating income on the basis of current cost		1,288.9
Net income on the basis of historical cost		843.0
Adjustments of operating income to current cost		176.0
Gearing adjustment (plus)		72.0
Adjustments for unconsolidated companies and minority interests (minus)		4.0
Net income on the basis of current cost		735.0

(*continued*)

Figure 3. (*continued*)

Consolidated Balance Sheet of the ABC-Group, December 31, 1985, Millions of Guilders, Historical Cost

Fixed assets		
Property, plant and equipment		3,843.0
Financial fixed assets		
Unconsolidated companies	482.3	
Other	139.5	621.8
Total fixed assets		4,464.8
Current assets		
Inventories	2,690.9	
Accounts receivables	3,114.6	
Cash and short term deposits	1,485.0	
Total current assets		7,290.5
Current liabilities		
Short term debt	438.8	
Accounts payable	2,956.2	
Total current liabilities		3,395.0
Net current assets		3,895.5
Total assets less current liabilities		8,360.3
Long-term liabilities		
Subordinated loans	184.5	
Other	1,678.1	
Total long-term liabilities		1,862.6
Provisions		2,003.0
Group net assets before minority interests		4,494.7
Minority interests		353.1
Group net assets		4,141.6

Supplementary Information on the Basis of Current Cost

Total fixed assets	5,873.8
Total current assets	7,290.5
Current liabilities	(3,395.0)
Total assets less current liabilities	9,769.3
Long-term debt	(4,458.0)
Group net assets before minority interests	5,311.3
Minority interests	(404.0)
Group net assets	4,907.3

Assets	*Historical Cost*	*Current Cost*
Fixed assets		
• *Tangible fixed assets*	3,843.0	5,252.0
• Other fixed assets	621.8	621.8
Current assets		
• *Tangible current assets*	2,690.9	2,690.9
• Other current assets	4,599.6	4,599.6
Total assets	11,755.3	13,164.3
Equity + liabilities		
Group Equity	4,494.7	5,311.3
• Stockholders' Equity		
• Minority interests		
Provisions and liabilities	7,260.6	7,853.0
Total capital	11,755.3	13,164.3

Figure 4. Restated Format of the Consolidated Balance Sheet, ABC-Group, December 31, 1985 (millions of guilders)

	Historical Cost	*Current Cost*
Net sales	18,009.8	18,009.8
Cost of sales (depreciation, depletion and amortization included)	16,544.9	16,720.9
Operating Income	1,464.9	1,288.9
Financial items, extraordinary items and income taxes (minus)	549.0	553.0
Gearing adjustment (plus)		72.0
Group Income	915.9	807.9
Minority interests		
Net income		

Figure 5. Restated Format of the Consolidated Income Statement, ABC-Group, 1985 (millions of guilders)

listed on the Amsterdam Stock Exchange as of December 31, 1985. First, the published reports were restated as described in the following section. This is followed by a description of the companies analyzed in this survey with an emphasis on those companies which provide both historical cost and current cost data in their published financial reports. The next section discusses the

Sales proceeds		20,094.7
Sales taxes		2,084.9
Net proceeds		18,009.8
Cost of sales		12,343.9
Gross profit		5,665.9
Selling expenses	2,857.1	
Research and development expenses	662.2	
General and administrative expenses	744.8	
Other revenues from operations	63.1	
Total expenses		4,201.0
Operating income (historical cost)		1,464.9
Adjustments of operating income to current cost		
Additional cost of sales	43.0	
Additional depreciation	133.0	
Total adjustments		176.0
Operating income (current cost)		1,288.9
Interest and other income	152.3	
Interest paid and similar expenses	337.4	
Total financial expenses		185.1
Operating income less financing charges		1,103.8
Taxes		464.6
Earnings of consolidated companies from normal operations, after taxes		639.2
Gearing adjustment (plus)		72.0
Earnings from unconsolidated companies		98.2
Adjustments for unconsolidated companies and minority interest (minus)		4.0
Group income from normal operations after taxes, current cost		805.4
Extraordinary gains	99.4	
Extraordinary losses	167.5	
Extraordinary items before taxes	68.1	
Taxes (plus)	70.6	
Extraordinary items after taxes		2.5
Group income		807.9
Minority interests (minus)		72.9
Net income (current cost)		735.0

Figure 6. Combination of Primary Historical Cost Consolidated Income Statement and Supplementary Information on Current Cost of the ABC-Group, 1985

results of this survey. The findings on the category "International companies" are discussed at some depth; the results of the analysis of other categories of enterprises are presented at a more general level. The conclusions are presented in the final section of this paper.

THE REPORTING MODEL

Dutch law permits four models of the balance sheet and six of the income statement. In order to process the data consistently, the published financial statements were restated. The standard formats used are shown above. Figure 1 shows the standard format of the balance sheet and Figure 2 that of the income statement.

As an illustration of the method of restatement followed in this survey, an example of the financial statements of the non-existing ABC-Group in Figure 3. Then the restatements as used in the analysis are presented in the Figures 4 and 5.

An interesting point is the combination of the primary historical cost income statement with the supplementary information on current cost accounting. This is demonstrated in Figure 6.

In order to avoid personal bias the statements were analyzed independently by two separate persons. Differences in the analysis were discussed at length. Both analysts agreed on the findings of the discussions.

DESCRIPTION OF THE LISTED COMPANIES

As of December 31, 1985 the total number of listed companies on the Amsterdam Stock Exchange was 166. Seven categories of companies are distinguished in this survey; the list of companies per category is found in Appendix 1. The categories and the number of companies belonging to each category are listed in Table 1.

The reports of 147 companies were analyzed. No analysis of the annual reports of the remaining 19 companies could be made because the companies were in liquidation, or the format of some of the reports was not comparable with the rest, or the companies did not make their reports available in time despite repeated requests.

The manufacturing sector consists of companies involved among other things in food and beverages, paper and wood, publishing, pharmaceuticals, industrial equipment, glass, chemicals, and office equipment. Of these companies, 19 belong to the top-100 manufacturing, trade, and transport companies as published by *Het Financieele Dagblad,* the leading financial newspaper in the Netherlands. In this publication the ranking is based on net sales. Only 42 of

Table 1. Categories of Companies and the Number of Companies in Each Category Listed on the Amsterdam Stock Exchange, as of December 31, 1985

Category	*Number of Companies*
Manufacturing	63
Internationals	5
Construction	7
Trade	31
Miscellaneous	7
Transportation	6
Finance	28

Table 2. Key-Items of the Five Internationals

Item	*AKZO* (*Chemicals*)	*KNHS* (*Metal*)	*PHILIPS* (*Electronics*)	*SHELL* (*Petroleum*)	*UNILEVER* (*Food*)
Net sales 1985 (millions of Dutch guilders)	18,010	7,465	60,045	252,376	66,771
Geographical sales distribution					
EC	0.51	0.72	0.53*	0.49*	0.63*
USA	0.22**	0.12	0.29**	0.26	0.17**
Rest	0.27	0.16	0.18	0.25	0.19
Number of employees as of December 31, 1985	65,000	27,383	345,600	142,000***	353,000
Rank in net sales top-100	5	11	3	1	2

Notes: * Europe.
** North America.
*** Year average.

these 100 companies are listed; the other companies are privately owned or subsidiaries of foreign companies.

The category of internationals is formed by five companies operating on a world-wide scale. In alphabetical order these companies are: (1) Akzo, (2) Koninklijke Nederlandsche Hoogovens en Staalfabrieken (KNHS) or Royal Dutch Blast-furnace and Steelworks, (3) Philips, (4) Royal Dutch/Shell Group (Shell), and (5) Unilever. As these companies are of major interest in the survey, Table 2 lists some key-items. A short description of the activities of the internationals is given in Appendix 2.

Of the 7 construction companies 3 belong to the top-100. The trade category consists of 31 companies of which 9 belong to the top-100. The miscellaneous category consists of companies that do not fit in the other categories. There are a trust company, two off-shore industries, a hotel, a dry cleaning firm, a company that operates holiday houses and parks, and a management advisory organization. One of these belongs to the top-100. The transport category consists of 6 companies including the national airline KLM (Royal Dutch Airline). Five of these belong to the top-100. The finance category groups together 28 banks, insurance, real estate, and investment companies. Among these are two major banks (ABN-Bank, Algemene Bank Nederland and AMRO, Amsterdam-Rotterdam Bank), the most important insurance company (Nationale Nederlanden), and the major investment group (Robeco).

RESULTS OF THE SURVEY

Valuation Methods Used

The information on the valuation methods used provided in the reports displays wide variations. The following table summarizes the methods and the number of companies that provide this information. It is possible to group valuation methods into four classes:

1. historical cost only;
2. current cost only;
3. mixed form and
4. both historical cost and current cost.

Companies stating assets at 'purchase price,' 'nominal value,' 'fifo,' and the like are included in the 'historical cost' class. The 'current cost' class is formed by companies stating their assets at current cost, current value, and so on. The 'mixed form' consists of companies that state one item at historical cost and the other at current cost. Companies stating one or more items at historical cost and at current cost are grouped in the 'both' class. The companies belonging to the 'both' group are most important for the results of this survey. An indication of the effects of accounting for changing prices on the reported amounts of assets, equity, and income can be obtained by comparing the figures based on historical cost and current cost.

Table 3 shows the number of companies per category grouped in one of the four classes of valuation methods, distinguished above. This table clearly illustrates that most companies (34%) are stating one or more assets and liabilities both at historical cost and current cost. The class of companies using only current cost is the smallest (2%). The mixed form and historical cost only

Table 3. Number of Companies and The Valuation Method

Category	*Historical Cost Only*	*Current Cost Only*	*Mixed Form*	*Both*
Manufacturing	14	3	19	27
Internationals	0	0	0	5
Construction	3	0	2	2
Trade	15	0	8	8
Miscellaneous	4	0	2	1
Transportation	3	0	0	3
Finance	7	0	17	4
Total	46	3	48	50
Percentage	31.3	2.0	32.7	34.0

Table 4. Items Reported on Historical Cost and Current Cost and Number of Companies Per Category

	Item					
Category	*Tangible Fixed Assets*	*Tangible Current Assets*	*Group Equity*	*Total Capital*	*Operating Income*	*Group Income*
Manufacturing	27	7	12	7	10	12
Internationals	5	5	5	5	5	5
Construction	2	0	1	0	0	1
Trade	8	1	2	1	0	2
Miscellaneous	1	0	0	0	0	0
Transportation	3	0	0	0	0	1
Finance	4	0	1	1	0	1
Total	50	13	21	14	15	22

are used by approximately 32 percent of the companies in this survey. As all five internationals belong to the 'both' class, it is fair to say that this class is, from an economic point of view, most important. This could be the result of the international debate on 'inflation accounting' in the United States (SFAS-33), the United Kingdom (SSAP-16) and by the International Accounting Standards Committee (IAS-15), and of the discussions on current cost accounting in Dutch accounting theory since Limperg developed the form known as 'replacement value accounting.'

Table 4 shows how many companies of the 'both' class state the selected items at historical cost as well as at current cost. The table shows that all companies of the 'both' class report tangible fixed assets on both valuation bases.

Table 5. Ratios of Balance Sheet Items Stated At Current Cost and At Historical Cost

	Balance Sheet Item			
Industry/ Company	*Tangible Fixed Assets*	*Tangible Current Assets*	*Group Equity*	*Total Capital*
Manufacturing	1.29	1.02	1.20	1.13
Internationals	1.35	1.09	1.50	1.21
Akzo	1.37	1.00	1.18	1.12
KNHS	1.25	1.11	1.72	1.15
Philips	1.23	1.00	1.12	1.07
Shell	1.34	1.19	1.56	1.24
Unilever	1.60	1.00	1.64	1.22

All five internationals report the selected items on the two bases. In the manufacturing category there is a large number of companies reporting one or more items on both methods. For this reason, the research focuses on manufacturing and internationals. Interesting observations in other categories are, however, also mentioned.

The Balance Sheet

As previously described, the four selected items of the balance sheet are:

1. tangible fixed assets;
2. tangible current assets;
3. group equity; and
4. total capital.

Of these the ratios of those items valued at current cost and at historical cost are calculated. As the category internationals is very diversified the findings are published for the category as a whole and for the five companies individually (see Table 5).

It is obvious that the difference in the values based on current cost and historical cost is most important in the case of tangible fixed assets. In the case of Unilever the tangible fixed assets are valued in the current cost balance sheet 60 percent higher than in the historical cost balance sheet. Due to the fast turnover the ratios calculated for tangible current assets approach 1.00. Shell and KNHS are an exception with 19 percent and 11 percent respectively higher values for these items in the current cost balance sheets compared with historical cost. This could be caused by the nature of the inventories, oil, and steel, respectively.

The differences in the reported values of the assets have their counterparts in the capital items. As previously described, group equity is formed by

Table 6. Income Statement Items Stated At Current Cost and Historical Cost

Category/ Company	*Group Income Ratio*	*Operating Income Ratio*	*Gearing Adjustment (millions of Dutch guilders)*	*Gearing As Percentage of Group Income (current cost)*
Manufacturing	0.92	0.93	—	—
Internationals	0.74	0.84	2,042	16.60
Akzo	0.88	0.88	72	8.91
KNHS	0.95	0.75	125	47.17
Philips	1.08	0.88	567	54.68
Shell	0.68	0.84	1,068	12.78
Unilever	0.83	0.83	210	11.45
Internatio-Muller	0.89	—	5	17.27

stockholders' equity (including the reserves) and minority interests. All other capital items are seen as liabilities. In the case of Philips, current cost group equity is about 12 percent higher than group equity calculated according to historical cost. For KNHS this divergence is 72 percent.

Another interesting observation is the rather wide variation in the ratios for the individual companies. However, this analysis cannot be taken further on the basis of the information provided in the published annual reports. Given that within a single valuation basis, various applications exist, it is impossible to specify unambiguously the causes of these differences. Further research needs to be done. Moreover, the way other accounting problems are solved influences the figures as well.

The Income Statement

The effects of accounting for changing prices on the income statement is best demonstrated by the figures for group income and operating income. The ratio of these items, based on current cost and historical cost, are shown in Table 6. Another interesting item is the gearing adjustment in the current cost income statement. The gearing adjustment is described as that part of realized increases of values which are deemed to be financed by liabilities. As liabilities are normally stated at fixed monetary amounts, the realized increases in values can be seen as a contribution to current cost group income. The gearing adjustment is published by all five internationals and by one trade company, Internatio-Muller. The results of the latter company are also included in the table.

Table 6 makes it clear that both income figures are materially influenced by the valuation methods used. Group income calculated on the basis of current cost is, in the case of Shell, 32% lower than income based on historical cost.

Table 7. Comparison of Current Cost Items and Historical Cost Items in the Philips 1985 Consolidated Income Statement (millions of guilders)

Item	*Current Cost*	*Historical Cost*	*Current Cost Minus Historical Cost*
Operating income	3,075	3,504	(429)
Gearing adjustment	567	0	567
Financial income and expenses	1,904	1,742	(162)
Income taxes	713	841	128
Equity in net income of unconsolidated companies	73	86	(13)
Extraordinary result after taxes	(61)	129	(190)
Result after taxes and deduction of minority interests of discontinued segments of business	0	(177)	177
Group income	1,037	959	78

Current cost operating income is also lower than historical cost operating income although these differences are not that great. In the current cost income statement the gearing adjustment plays an important role. The ratio of gearing adjustment to group income varies from 8.91 percent to 54.68 percent. Particularly noticeable is the large deviation between the calculated figures and the fact that Philips shows a current cost group income figure that is slightly higher (8%) than historical cost group income. This fact is analyzed in Table 7; six items of the current cost income statement are compared with the same items of the historical cost income statement. This table makes it clear that the gearing adjustment is the most important item that causes current cost group income to be slightly higher (78 millions of guilders) than historical cost group income.

Influence on Financial Statement Analysis

In financial statement analysis the calculation of financial ratios is a major instrument. In this section, the influence of the valuation method on the calculated return on investment ratios is demonstrated. Return on group equity is calculated as the quotient of net group income and group equity; return on total capital is the quotient of operating income and total capital employed. Both these ratios are calculated on historical cost and on current cost bases. It is clear in advance that these ratios are influenced by the valuation method in two ways. On the one hand, income figures based on current cost are normally lower than those calculated on historical cost (see Table 6) and, on the other hand, group equity and total capital are normally higher (see Table 5). Table 8 shows the effects of these two influences.

Table 8. Return On Investment Calculated On the Basis of Historical Cost and Current Cost (in percent)

	Return On			
	Group Equity		*Total Capital*	
Category/ Company	*Historical Cost*	*Current Cost*	*Historical Cost*	*Current Cost*
Manufacturing	15.33	11.95	9.70	8.03
Internationals	12.64	6.20	13.10	9.16
Akzo	20.38	15.21	12.46	9.79
KNHS	19.79	10.87	8.31	5.40
Philips	5.77	5.58	7.07	5.81
Shell	12.92	5.62	15.27	10.32
Unilever	15.64	7.89	10.18	6.96

Table 8 clearly demonstrates that there is a material difference in the calculated return on investment ratios depending on the valuation method being used. In the case of Shell, current cost return on group equity is only 43 percent of the historical cost return on group equity. Shell and Unilever report the current cost return on total capital that is 68 percent of the historical cost return on total capital.

CONCLUSION

This survey demonstrates that figures for asset, equity, and income based on current cost differ materially from those based on historical cost, even in periods with low inflation rates. This applies mainly to tangible fixed assets, group equity, and group income. The other three items surveyed—tangible current assets, total capital, and operating income—are influenced by the valuation method used to a lesser degree. Generally, the return on investment ratios are under double pressure. On the one hand, current cost income is normally lower than historical cost income and on the other hand, current cost capital is generally higher.

Another interesting observation is the rather wide variation in the ratios of items reported in current cost and historical cost statements. In current cost income statements the gearing adjustment plays an important role. The influence of this adjustment on group income varies materially from company to company.

Two results are most significant. First, the reported figures differ materially depending on the valuation method used. The other finding is that there is a wide variation from company to company. Financial reporting based on both historical cost and current cost gains an insight into the effects of changing prices. This survey makes clear that changing prices of fixed assets are more important than the changing prices of current assets in the published financial statements. As the influences are material, the outcomes of this survey could adduce arguments in support of the combination of historical cost and current cost information in published annual reports, even in periods with low inflation rates.

APPENDIX 1: LIST OF COMPANIES OF WHICH THE 1985 ANNUAL REPORTS WERE USED IN THIS SURVEY PER CATEGORY

Manufacturing

ACF Holding
Antilliaanse Verffabriek
Associatie van Uitgevers van Dagbladen en Tijdschriften, AUDET
Batenburg Beheer
Koninklijke Nederlandsche Machinefabrieken v.h. E.H. Begemann
Maatschappij van Berkel's Patent
Blydenstein-Willink
Koninklijke Drukkerij & Uitgeverij v/h C. de Boer jr
Koninklijke Distilleerderijen Erven Lucas Bols
Brink/Molyn Beheer
Buhrmann-Tetterode
Cindu-Key & Kramer
Tapijtfabriek H. Desseaux
Elsevier-NDU
Eriks
Koninklijke Nederlandse Vliegtuigfabriek Fokker
Gamma Holding
Gelatine Delft
van der Giessen-de Noord
Gist-brocades
Grasso's Koninklijke Machinefabrieken
GTI
Heineken
Hoekloos, Hoek's Machine-en Zuurstofffabriek
Holec
Constructiewerkplaatsen en Machinefabrieken Hollandia-Kloos
Hunter Douglas Groep

Industrieele Maatschappij
Koninklijke van Kempen & Begeer
Klene's Suikerwerkfabrieken
Kluwer
Koninklijke Nederlandse Papierfabrieken
Leidsche Wolspinnerij
Macintosch
Medicopharma
Meneba
Minihouse
Mulder's Fabriek van Rollend Materieel
Naarden International
Naeff
Nederlandsche Apparatenfabriek "Nedap"
Koninklijke Nederlandsche Springstoffenfabrieken
Koninklijke Nijverdal-Ten Cate
Norit
Verenigde Bedrijven Nutricia
Océ-van der Grinten
ICA holding v/h NV Industrieele Maatschappij "Palembang"
Koninklijke Delftsch Aardewerkfabriek De Proceleyne Fles, Anno 1653, Voorheen Joost Thooft en Labouchere
Rommenholler
Koninklijke D.S. van Schuppen
Schuttersveld Holding
Holdingmaatschappij De Telegraaf
Textielgroep Twenthe
Thomassen & Drijver-Verblifa
Twentsche Kabel Holding
Ubbink
Vereenigde Glasfabrieken
Verenigde Machinefabrieken Stork
Verenigde Nederlandse Uitgeversbedrijven, VNU
Verto
Wegener's Couranten Concern
Koninkllijke Wessanen
Wolters Samsom Groep

Internationals

Akzo
Koninklijke Nederlandsche Hoogovens en Staalfabrieken, KNHS
Koninklijke/Shell Groep, Shell

Philips
Unilever

Construction

Bam Holding
Koninklijke Boskalis Westminster
Verenigde Bedrijven Bredero
Hollandsche Beton Groep
Ingenieurs Bureau Bouwnijverheid-Kondor Groep
Verenigde NBM Bedrijven
Koninklijke Volker Stevin

Trade

Ahold
Automobiel Industrie "Rotterdam"
Amsterdamse Rijtuigmaatschappij
A.L. van Beek
Beers' Zonen
Koninklijke Bijenkorf Beheer
Koninklijke Borsumij Wehry
Braat Bouwstoffen
Burgman Heybroek
Handel- en Industrie-Maatschappij Ceteco
Deli-Maatschappij
Van Dorp Groep
Econosto
Emba
Eduard Goudsmit
Hagemeyer
Holdoh-Houtunie
Internatio-Muller
Koppelpoort Holding
Landré & Glinderman
MHV Amsterdam Handel Maatschappij
Otra
Koninklijke Houthandel William Pont
Productenonderneming Amsterdam Pronam
Proost en Brandt
Reesink
Riva
Rubber Cultuur Maatschappij "Amsterdam"

Schuitema
VRG Groep
Wyers Beheer

Miscellaneous

Holland American Line Trust
Holland Sea Search Holding
IHC Caland
Grand Hotel Krasnapolsky
Palthe
Sporthuis Centrum
Twijnstra Gudde

Transportation

Furness
Koninklijke Luchtvaart Maatschappij, KLM
Koninklijke Nedlloyd Groep
Phs. van Ommeren
Pakhoed Holding
Stoomvaart Maaschappij Zeeland, Koninklijke Nederlandsche Postvaert

Finance

Banks

Algemene Bank Nederland
Amsterdam-Rotterdam Bank
Crédit Lyonnais Bank Nederland
Friesch-Groningsche Hypotheek Bank
Bank Mendes Gans
Nederlandsche Middenstandsbank
Nederlandsche Scheepshypotheekbank
Westland/Utrecht Hypotheek Bank

Insurance

Aegon
Amev
Nationale-Nederlanden
Assurantieconcern Stad Rotterdam anno 1720

Real Estate Operating Companies

Bredero Vast goed
Chamotte Unie
Nagron, Nationaal Grondbezit
Ravast
Rodamco
Sarakreek Holding
Westhaven Amsterdam

Investment Companies

Calvé-Delft
Dordtsche Petroleum-Industrie Maatschappij
Heineken Holding
De Maxwell Petroleum Holding
Nederlandsche Maatschappij tot het verrichten van Mijnbouwkundige werken
Petroleum Maatschappij "Moeara Enim"
Robeco
Rorento
Administratiemaatschappij "Wester Suikerraffinaderij"

APPENDIX 2: DESCRIPTION OF THE FIRMS

General information of the activities of the internationals is given here. The descriptions are based on the annual reports of the companies.

Akzo

Akzo is a group of companies with subsidiaries in 50 countries. Akzo's main products are man-made fibers, salt, commodity and speciality chemicals, coatings, pharmaceuticals and diagnostics, consumer products, machinery, engineering plastics, membranes, and miscellaneous industrial products.

Geographically, the Group's operations are largely concentrated in the Netherlands and in the Federal Republic of Germany. Expansion of the Group's position in North America is given high priority, with high-tech products at the top of the list. Akzo's headquarters is located in Arnhem, the Netherlands.

KNHS

KNHS operates a blast-furnace and steelworks in the Netherlands. KNHS has two divisions: the steel division and the diversification and steel processing division. Its main products are steel and steel processing, aluminum, cement, and engineering and automation. KNHS has subsidiaries in 12 countries. Geographically, its operations are concentrated in the Netherlands and in the other EC countries. Its headquarters is located in IJmuiden, the Netherlands.

Philips

Philips operates in more than 60 countries. The internal organization of the Philips group is structured according to two basic patterns: the organization of activities by country and by product. Philips has separate companies for operating in the national market in a large number of countries. The product-related activities are grouped into six product sectors: lighting, consumer electronics, domestic appliances, professional products and systems, components, and miscellaneous. The product sectors are responsible for establishing world product policy in consultation with the national organizations. The headquarters of Philips is located in Eindhoven, the Netherlands.

Royal Dutch/Shell Group

Shell is a company that operates in more than 100 countries. The group is engaged in various branches of the oil and gas, chemicals, coal, metals and other related businesses. There are two parent companies: Royal Dutch Petroleum Company owns 60 percent and The "Shell" Transport and Trading Company owns 40 percent of the shares of the Group Holding Companies. Royal Dutch has its headquarters in The Hague, the Netherlands and Shell in London, United Kingdom.

Unilever

Unilever provides a wide range of products and services in some 75 countries. The larger part of its business is in consumer goods, detergents and personal products. Unilever's other activities include speciality chemicals, agribusiness operations, and animal feeds. There are two parent companies: Unilever N.V., Rotterdam, the Netherlands and Unilever PLC, London, United Kingdom. As nearly as practicable, they act as one company.

PART III

FOREIGN CURRENCY TRANSLATION

FINANCIAL AND MANAGERIAL EFFECTS OF TRANSLATING FOREIGN INVENTORIES

Kathleen Ranney Bindon

ABSTRACT

Prior to the issuance of *SFAS 8,* most companies were translating inventory at the current rate. *SFAS 8* required, in most instances, that inventory be translated at the historical rate. This paper describes the impact of translating inventory at the historical rate rather than at the current rate, referred to as the inventory translation difference (ITD). Survey data were gathered from 43 of the 150 largest U.S. multinational corporations, for up to four foreign inventories per firm. The calculated ITD had no material impact (± 10%) on the consolidated earnings of any of the 43 firms, though for some the ITD had a material effect on both foreign earnings and the reported foreign currency translation adjustment. This paper also examines whether the sample firms made changes in foreign inventory management practices as a result of *SFAS 8.* Only eight firms indicated making any changes.

Advances in International Accounting, Vol. 3, pages 109-125.

ISBN: 1-55938-078-0

INTRODUCTION

Accounting for foreign operations is an important and complex problem area, due, in part, to both the size of foreign operations and exchange rate fluctuations. The Financial Accounting Standards Board (FASB) has had difficulty resolving the foreign currency translation issue. In October 1975, the FASB issued *Statement of Financial Accounting Standards No. 8* (*SFAS 8*), "Accounting for the Translation of Foreign Currency Transactions and Foreign Currency Financial Statements." *SFAS 8* was heavily criticized, with much of the criticism centered on two of its requirements, the immediate recognition in income of all foreign exchange gains and losses and the use of only the temporal translation method, particularly the translation of inventory at the historical rate [*Business Week;* Searfass, 1976; Shank, 1976].

After an Exposure Draft, extensive public hearings and a Revised Exposure Draft, in December 1981 the FASB issued *Statement of Financial Accounting Standards No. 52* (*SFAS 52*), "Foreign Currency Translation," which replaced *SFAS 8*. The controversial nature of this topic is indicated by the Board's close vote of 4-3, with Chairman Kirk one of the dissenters.

SFAS 52 made significant changes in foreign currency translation requirements. Rather than mandating only one translation method and one treatment of exchange gains and losses, *SFAS 52* allows flexibility in the translation and reporting process. This flexibility hinges on management's choice of the functional currency for each foreign operation. Guidelines are contained in *SFAS 52* to aid management in deciding on the appropriate functional currencies. In general, the functional currency is defined by *SFAS 52* as:

> the currency of the primary economic environment in which the entity operates; normally, that is the currency of the environment in which an entity generates and expends cash flows [Par. 5].

If the local currency is designated as a foreign operation's functional currency, financial statements are translated using the current rate method, and U.S. dollar differences arising will be reported as a translation adjustment in stockholders' equity. If the functional currency is deemed to be the U.S. dollar, the *SFAS 8* temporal translation method must be used and differences arising included in net income. All gains and losses from specific transactions are reported in income under both methods.

One of the major criticisms of the temporal method was its requirement that inventory be translated at the historical rate, the rate at the time when the inventory was purchased. Under the current rate method, by contrast, all assets and liabilities are translated at the close of business rate on the last day of the fiscal year. Many opponents of *SFAS 52,* including the three dissenting

FASB members, recommended retaining the basic concepts of *SFAS 8,* but allowing locally-sourced foreign inventory to be translated at the current rate.

Criticism of translating inventory at the historical rate concentrated on two areas: (1) improper matching of sales and cost of goods sold; and (2) incorrect measurement of the risk of exposure to exchange rate fluctuations ["The New 'Reality,'" 1976, p. 34] When inventory is translated using the historical rate, it cannot be an exposed asset that balances liabilities exposed to the risk of exchange rate changes.

The magnitude of the impact of translating inventory at the historical rate rather than at the current rate, referred to hereafter as the inventory translation difference (ITD), cannot be determined from publicly-available information. Companies are not required to disclose the cost of specific foreign inventories, or the date of acqusition. This study was undertaken to determine both the magnitude and materiality of the ITD to find out whether the criticism of the historical rate required for inventory by *SFAS 8* is based on fact. In addition to quantifying the ITD, this study gathered information on the impact of foreign currency translation requirements on foreign inventory management practices (FIMP). Financial executives from a sample of U.S.-based multinational corporations were asked to provide information about dollar values of foreign inventories and about what changes, if any, were made in FIMP in response to FASB requirements.

RESEARCH PARTICIPANTS

The sample population for this study was chosen from the largest U.S.-based multinational corporations. Cook [1979] prepared a list of the 150 largest U.S. multinational corporations (MNCs), ranked in order of size of foreign revenue. Since these companies have the largest volume of foreign sales, it was anticipated that they would also have a high percentage of foreign assets, including foreign inventories. For all but six of these firms, foreign assets were at least 10 percent of total assets, indicating potentially large foreign inventories. Whereas the selection process was designed specifically to identify companies that were likely to have high levels of foreign inventories, the lack of randomness prevents any generalizations from being made to all U.S.-based MNCs.

A questionnaire was mailed to the senior financial officer of each of the 150 companies.[1] Only companies having at least one manufacturing or retailing facility abroad were eligible to participate in the study. If a company did not have at least one foreign facility, the financial officer was asked to respond that the company was ineligible and return the questionnaire uncompleted.

Responses to the initial mailing were received from 50 companies, including all who were ineligible and eight who declined to participate. Phone calls were made to 108 firms, the 100 who had not responded to the initial mailing, plus the eight who originally declined. Of these 108 firms, 47 returned the questionnaires. The others either declined to participate or did not respond.

Of the 150 companies originally identified, 21 were determined to be ineligible, and of the remaining 129 companies, 48 returned fully completed questionnaires. Thirty additional companies returned questionnaires with all questions answered except the last one requesting specific dollar information on foreign inventories. Of the remaining 51 companies, 41 declined to participate because: (1) they do not complete questionnaires as a matter of company policy (14 firms); or, (2) they did not have adequate time and/or staff to participate (27 firms). The remaining ten firms did not respond in any way.

The next section discusses the inventory translation difference while the section which follows discusses foreign inventory management practices.

THE INVENTORY TRANSLATION DIFFERENCE

The temporal translation method mandated by *SFAS 8* required the historical rate to be used for inventories instead of the current rate used by many firms to translate inventory prior to *SFAS 8*. Sixty-four percent of the firms in this sample were required to change from the current rate to the historical rate, as a result of *SFAS 8*. The rate used to translate inventory is one of the most significant factors in determining the translation gain or loss [Rodriguez, 1977].

Exchange rate changes have a two-part impact on earnings when the temporal method is used. The immediate impact occurs in the calculation of the translation gain or loss due to exposed assets and liabilities, which omits the impact of the change on inventory. The effect of currency fluctuations is recognized as the inventory is sold, which affects the gross profit margin.

Sales are translated at the weighted average rate for the period and the cost of goods sold figure matched against sales is translated at the historical rate. When the foreign currency weakens, the U.S. parent will experience a declining dollar gross profit margin. This occurs because the cost of goods sold figure is higher, in dollars, relative to the translated dollar sales revenue amount.

Using pounds sterling to illustrate this concept, assume an inventory purchase at the beginning of period 1 of £28,000,000; equal portions sold in periods 1 and 2 for £20,000,000 each: and an exchange rate in period of 1 of £1 = \$2.30 and in period 2 of £1 = \$2.00. Comparative gross profit margins are as follows:

	Period 1		Period 2	
	£	$	£	$
Sales	20,000,000	46,000,000	20,000,000	40,000,000
Cost of Goods Sold	14,000,000	32,200,000	14,000,000	32,200,000
Gross Profit	6,000,000	13,800,000	6,000,000	7,800,000
Percentage		30		19.5

If inventories represent a large percentage of total foreign assets and profit margins already are narrow, a relatively small exchange rate change can have a large impact on translated profits.

The inventory valuation method is also a significant factor in determining the importance and magnitude of the impact of inventory on gross profit. First-in, first-out (FIFO) matches the earliest inventory costs against sales revenue, while leaving the most recent costs in the ending inventory balance. Last-in, first-out (LIFO), matches the most recent inventory costs against sales revenue, while leaving the oldest costs in ending inventory. The average cost method results in costs of goods sold and ending inventory figures between those obtained using FIFO and LIFO. Table 1 illustrates the difference in gross profit and ending inventory balances, assuming different inventory valuation methods.

Table 1 is based on three purchases made during the quarter, one each month. During the same time period, the foreign currency has been appreciating relative to the dollar. A total of 9,500 units were purchased. As of the end of the quarter, 4,000 units had been sold and 5,500 remained in inventory.

Gross profit was calcluated for each of the three major inventory valuation methods, FIFO, average cost and LIFO and were, respectively, $1,500, $1,915 and $2,250. Corresponding ending inventories were $2,500, $2,915 and $3,250.

However, this study's focus is on the impact on the translation gain or loss of translating ending inventory at the current rate instead of at the historical rate, referred to as the Inventory Translation Difference (ITD), the full impact of which on cost of goods sold could not be determined due to lack of information on the size of and historical rate used to translate beginning inventory in published annual reports.

The ITD was calculated based on ending inventory data supplied by the respondents. They were requested to select and identify their four major foreign currency inventories and to supply the following information for their most recently completed fiscal year: dollar amount of ending inventory; inventory turnover; and inventory valuation method used. Also requested was the dollar amount of total foreign inventories. This information was received from 48 firms. On average, the individual inventories reported represented 68.2 percent of total foreign inventory.

Table 1. Impact of Inventory Method on Gross Profit and Ending Inventory

Month	*Units*	*FC Cost*	*Exchange Rate*	*Dollar Cost*
Purchases				
January	3,000	3,000	FC1:$1.50	2,000
February	4,000	4,000	FC1:$2.00	2,000
March	2,500	2,500	FC1:$2.50	1,000
Total purchases	9,500			
Less: Units sold	4,000			
Ending inventory	5,500			

	FIFO	*Average Cost*	*LIFO*
Dollar Gross Margins			
Sales (translated at an average rate of FC1:$2.00)	4,000	4,000	4,000
Less: Cost of goods sold[a]	(2,500)	(2,085)	(1,750)
Gross profit	1,500	1,915	2,250

Note: [a] Cost of goods sold calculations:

FIFO:	
Purchases	5,000
Less: Ending Inventory	
2,500 @ FC1:$2.50 = 1,000	
3,000 @ FC1:$2.00 = 1,500	(2,500)
Cost of goods sold	2,500
LIFO	
Purchases	5,000
Less: Ending Inventory	
3,000 @ FC1:$1.50 = 2,000	
2,500 @ FC1:$2.00 = 1,250	(3,250)
Cost of goods sold	1,750
*AVERAGE COST**:	5,000
5,500 @ .53 +	(2,915)
	2,085

$$* \quad \frac{\text{Total dollar cost}}{\text{Total units purchased}} = \frac{\$5{,}000}{9{,}500} = \$.53 \text{ per unit.}$$

The information received on individual foreign inventories provided the basis for computing the difference between the dollar amount of ending inventory in each country translated at the historical rate (as reported) and the approximate dollar amount of inventory if it had been translated using the current rate (the ITD). Firms already translating inventory at the current rate as a regular practice were excluded from this analysis.[2] Also excluded were individual foreign inventories cost using LIFO, as there was no way to determine how many LIFO layers existed and what historical rate originally was used to translate each layer. This information is necessary in order to approximate the historical rate used to translate ending inventory. After these exclusions, overall ITDs could be calculated for 43 firms, based on 157 individual ITDs.

The individual ITDs were calculated using the following procedure:

1. The approximate historical rate was applied to the reported dollar amount of ending inventory to determine the approximate amount of the inventory stated in the foreign currency.[3]
2. Ending inventory, now expressed in foreign currency units, was translated back into dollars using the current rate in effect at the close of the fiscal year reported.
3. The reported dollar inventory (translated at the historical rate) was subtracted from the calculated dollar inventory (translated at the current rate) to obtain the ITD for each individual foreign inventory reported.

The individual ITDs (up to four for each firm) were added together to obtain the overall ITD. Several factors other than the size of the inventory being translated will affect the individual ITD. These factors include: inventory turnover; inventory method; and the movement of the foreign currency relative to the dollar. Average turnover period for the 157 individual foreign inventories was 2.94 months. Unless a foreign currency had been fluctuating widely against the dollar, such as was the case with the Brazilian cruzeiro, the difference between an historical rate of less than three months ago and the current rate generally will be fairly small.

The inventory valuation method used will have a direct effect on the ITD as it determines the historical rate used to translate inventory for reporting purposes. If FIFO is used, the most recent purchases comprise ending inventory and, consequently, the historical rate would be closest to the current rate. The opposite is true for LIFO. The historical rate used to translate inventory where the average cost method is used will fall somewhere between the FIFO and LIFO historical rates. Of the 157 individual ITDs calculated, 107 (68.2%) were for FIFO inventories while the remaining 50 (31.8%) were for average cost inventories. For over two-thirds of the foreign inventories, the historical rate used to translate inventory would be close to the current rate, especially as the average inventory turnover period was just under three months.

Individual ITDS were analyzed to determine whether the foreign currency rose or fell relative to the dollar. If the currency had fallen relative to the dollar, the ITD would be be negative as the historical rate would have been less than the current rate. This would yield larger dollar amounts when translating using the current rate than when translating using the historical rate. For the time period of this study, of the 157 individual ITDs, 65 were negative. If the foreign currency had risen relative to the dollar, the individual ITD would be positive, as it was for 89 foreign inventories. For the remaining three inventories, the ITDs were zero, indicating neither a rise nor a fall of that foreign currency relative to the dollar for the time period examined.

Forty-three overall ITDs were calculated. The mean was $200,000, with a range of from -$9,001,000 to $7,286,000. Of the 43 overall (firm) ITDs, 23 were negative and 20 were positive.

Taken in isolation, the magnitude of the overall ITD is not very informative. What is of more concern is the relative size of the overall ITD. To provide relative size information, the overall ITDs were expressed as a percentage of each of three figures, consolidated earnings, foreign earnings and the reported foreign currency adjustment. Consolidated earning were chosen because often the financial press will isolate how much a MNC's reported income has been affected by the translation gain or loss. While this study does not measure the change in the entire translation gain or loss, it analyzes one significant component. Foreign earnings were chosen because often the foreign manager and/or executive in charge of foreign earnings is held at least partially responsible for the translation gain or loss. The reported foreign currency adjustment was chosen because many companies try to control and minimize this figure.

ITD expressed as a percentage of these three income statement items is contained in Appendix 1. Also included is information on the percentage of inventory reported and used to calculate the overall ITD as well as total foreign inventory as a percentage of total foreign assets. These last two figures provide information on how completely the calculated overall ITD represents total foreign inventory and how large foreign inventory is in relation to total foreign assets.

For six firms, the ITD was calculated using 100 percent of foreign inventories. The smallest ITD was 35 percent, with a mean of 68.2 percent. The size and/or sign of the overall ITDs would be expected to be different if 100 percent of foreign inventories had been used for all firms. Total foreign inventory was, on average, 28.5 percent of total foreign assets. The range was from 6 to 66 percent. While this relationship has no direct bearing on the calculation of the overall ITD, it does given an indication of the changes in net exposed position that occurred when *SFAS 8* required inventory to be translated at the historical rate.

Using ±10 percent as a significance criterion, no material changes were found for overall ITD expressed as a percentage of consolidated earnings. However, when the ITD is expressed as a percentage of foreign earnings, there were two firms for which the ITD would have caused a material change in foreign earnings. One was postiive, 14.47 percent, while the other was negative, -17.52 percent.

As would be expected, expressing the overall ITD as a percentage of the reported foreign currency adjustment generated more material changes. The relative impact of the overall ITD on the reported foreign currency adjustment is much greater as this figure, generally, is much smaller than either consolidated or foreign earnings. The range was from a low of -805 percent to a high of 442 percent. The impact was material for all but six of the firms reporting foreign currency adjustments.

Caution must be exercised when interpreting the sign of the ratio of the overall ITD to the reported foreign currency adjustment. For example, the firm with the -0.63 percent ITD/consolidated earnings percentage has a positive 98 ITD/foreign currency adjustment percentage. This indicates that the firm had a negative foreign currency adjustment and that the calculated ITD would increase the negative adjustment by 98 percent. The opposite will obtain for firms with positive ITD/consolidated earnings percentages and negative ITD/foreign currency adjustment percentages. For example, the firm with the 1.88 ITD/consolidated earnings percentage has a -71 ITD/foreign currency adjustment percentage. For this particular firm, the positive ITD would reduce the reported foreign currency adjustment by 71 percent.

The largest increase in a reported negative foreign currency adjustment was an ITD which was 263 percent of the reported adjustment. The largest increase in a positive foreign currency adjustment was 442 percent. While neither of these, nor any other, overall ITDs would have caused a material change in reported consolidated earnings, the change in almost all of the reported foreign currency adjustments, and some foreign earnings, is large and potentially could be of concern to managers and financial statement users.

The overall ITD is affected by the mix of rising and falling currencies in which the individual foreign-currency inventories are denominated. Table 2 presents a summary of the mix of currencies for the 43 firms for which overall ITDs were calculated. A total of 22 firms (51.5%) had either all rising or more rising than falling foreign currencies. For 16 firms (37.2%), either all currencies fell or more fell than rose. For the remaining five firms, foreign inventories were evenly balanced between countries with rising and falling currencies. Of even greater importance than the number of currencies rising and falling is the relative magnitude of each rate change. The individual ITDs will be affected by the direction and magnitude of the exchange rate change and by the size of the foreign inventory. The percentage exchange rate change was calculated for each currency for which a foreign inventory was reported.

A two-part computation was used to calculate the percentage exchange rate change. First, the approximate historical rate (see note 3 for an explanation of the approximate historical rate used) was subtracted from the current rate to get the direction of the change. A negative change would indicate that the foreign currency had fallen relative to the dollar, and vice versa for a positive change. Second, the exchange rate change was divided by the approximate

Table 2. Summary of Direction of Currency Fluctuations for Individual Foreign Currency Inventories

Direction of Fluctuations	*Frequency*	*Percent of Total Firms*
All rose	13	30.2
More rose than fell	9	20.9
Evenly balanced	5	11.6
More fell than rose	5	11.6
All fell	11	25.6
Total	43	99.9*

Note: * Due to rounding.

historical rate to determine the percent exchange rate for each individual ITD calculated. Table 3 summarizes the percent exchange rate changes for up to four currencies used to calculate each company's overall ITD. Some firms reported inventory information for fewer than four currencies and some of the reported inventories were LIFO inventories for which ITDs were not calculated.

For the 20 firms with positive overall ITDs, 13 had positive exchange rate changes for all currencies. Of the remaining seven firms, six had more positive than negative changes while for the last firm, inventories were evenly balanced between foreign currencies rising and falling relative to the dollar.

The distribution of rising and falling currencies was more diversified for the 23 firms with negative overall ITDs. For 11 firms, all percent exchange rate changes were negative. Of the remaining 12 firms, 5 had more negative than positive changes, 4 had an even balance, and the remaining three firms had more positive than negative exchange rate changes. All three of the latter firms reported inventories in Brazil, which was the only negative rate change they experienced. However, the cruzeiro has been falling rapidly relative to the dollar in recent years. The exchange rate fell from cruzeiro 1 = $0.615 to cruzeiro 1 = $.0153 during the period from January 1978 to December 1980. This is a decline of over 400 percent in a 36-month period, or an average monthly decline of over 11 percent. Even with a rapid inventory turnover, the difference between the historical rate and the current rate could be quite large. For these three firms, the decline in the cruzeiro was more than sufficient to negate the effects of positive exchange rate changes for their other foreign-denominated inventories.

The largest concentration of foreign inventories was in the United Kingdom. Of the total 157 foreign inventories reported, 34 (21.7%) were in the United Kingdom. For 14 firms, the United Kingdom inventory was the largest reported. It was the second, third, and fourth largest for eight, eleven, and one

Table 3. Summary of Overall Inventory Translation Difference as a Percent of Consolidated Earnings and Individual-currency Percent Exchange Rate Changes

Inventory Translation Difference (Consolidated Earnings)	*Percent Exchange Rate Change (Currency)*			
	1	*2*	*3*	*4*
4.20	1.87	0.32	2.05	A
3.55	0.52	0.56	1.27	0.22
3.30	2.49	1.66	1.89	-0.20
3.05	1.89	1.23	0.43	-0.06
2.88	1.05	1.89	0.43	1.92
2.44	0.59	1.49	0.04	-0.23
1.88	2.22	3.21	0.21	1.40
1.33	1.66	0.32	1.07	1.97
1.33	2.34	6.20	2.42	1.63
1.26	0.36	0.88	3.45	8.05
0.88	1.05	0.18	2.54	-0.01
0.84	1.77	0.72	1.31	0.42
0.75	1.39	1.89	1.86	1.12
0.58	1.17	1.23	0.22	1.55
0.54	1.55	-0.63	1.47	-0.53
0.53	0.42	1.69	0.02	-0.10
0.53	1.27	2.13	2.59	1.05
0.52	1.76	0.13	1.89	2.04
0.47	0.37	3.86	0.90	-20.66
0.06	0.72	0.01	A	A
-0.01	B	0.31	-1.06	-0.20
-0.03	0.82	-0.51	-0.51	-0.89
-0.06	-0.25	-0.14	0.12	0.00
-0.07	-0.96	A	A	A
-0.24	-5.44	-0.13	-0.40	0.00
-0.42	-10.28	1.81	0.36	2.23
-0.43	0.97	-2.44	-1.92	1.55
-0.45	B	0.76	-1.68	0.00
-0.49	-2.01	-0.24	-4.68	A
-0.53	-2.12	-0.97	-0.46	-1.07
-0.54	-1.07	1.30	A	A
-0.56	-1.66	-0.87	-3.17	-3.08
-0.63	-2.31	-0.91	-5.42	-7.19
-0.64	-1.66	-3.09	-0.01	-3.09
-0.71	0.07	-9.82	0.24	3.21
-0.83	0.73	0.82	0.63	-7.79
-1.05	0.09	-1.56	-3.32	-3.97
-1.26	-1.48	-4.66	-1.82	-0.12
-1.38	1.76	1.89	-0.06	-19.48
-1.45	-1.82	-4.77	A	A
-1.49	B	-2.63	B	-0.12
-1.78	-1.76	-1.85	-1.04	-0.02
-1.94	-0.42	0.42	-2.22	-3.69

Notes: A = no inventory reported.
B = LIFO inventory.

Table 4. Summary of the Relationships Between Change in the Exchange Rate of the Pound Versus the Dollar and the Overall Inventory Translation Difference

Change in Exchange Rate and Overall Inventory Translation Difference	*Relative Size of U.K. Inventory*				
	1	*2*	*3*	*4*	*Total*
Both positive	5	4	6	1	16
Both negative	5	2	4	0	11
Positive exchange rate change, negative overall inventory translation difference	4	2	1	0	7
Total	14	8	11	1	34

of the firms, respectively. For firms with inventories in the United Kingdom, whether the pound rose or fell relative to the dollar during the period examined had a substantial effect on the sign of the overall ITD. Table 4 summarizes the relationship between the direction of the exchange rate change and the direction of the overall ITD, by relative size of the U.K. inventory reported. For 27 of the 34 firms (79.4%), the exchange rate change for the pound and the overall ITD had the same signs. A positive rate change indicates a rise in the pound relative to the dollar, and vice versa. For seven firms, the exchange rate change in the pound and the overall ITD moved in opposite directions. For these firms, the fall in the currencies of their other foreign inventories, combined with the size of those inventories, was more than enough to offset the rise in the pound.

FOREIGN INVENTORY MANAGEMENT PRACTICES

It was anticipated that few, if any, companies would change their FIMP as a result of FASB requirements. Inventory holding patterns should minimize holding and financing costs while enabling the firm to maintain inventory levels sufficient to service customer needs. The translation process applies to externally-provided accounting figures and should not be a major determinant in operating decisions relative to inventory management. Therefore, any reported changes in FIMP are of interest.

Companies were asked to indicate whether they made changes in FIMP after the issuance of *SFAS 8* and if they anticipated making changes as a result of the new translation requirements to be contained in *SFAS 52.* Of interest, also, was if FIMP were influenced by whether inventories were denominated in currencies rising versus falling relative to the dollar. Two identical sets of

Table 5. Summary of Changes in Foreign Inventory Management Practices due to FASB Requirements

	Frequency	*Percent of Total Firms*
After the Issuance of SFAS 8		
Action Taken		
Increased inventory turnover	1	1.4
Decreased inventory size	3	4.2
Both increased turnover and decreased size	4	5.6
No change	63	88.7
Total	71	99.9[a]
Anticipated if *Exposure Draft* is Adopted		
Anticipated Action		
Increase inventory turnover	1	1.4
Decrease inventory size	2	2.8
Both increase turnover and decrease size	3	4.2
No change	65	91.5
Total	71	99.9*

Note: * Due to rounding.

questions on FIMP were included in the questionnaire. One set was to be answered only if the firm employed substantially different FIMP for inventories denominated in currencies that are rising relative to the dollar versus those currencies that are falling. The second set was to be answered only if the firm had one set of FIMP which applied to all foreign inventories. It was anticipated that few, if any, companies would have different FIMP depending on the strength of the foreign currency relative to the dollar. Only two firms indicated that they had substantially different FIMP and both of these firms also reported no changes in FIMP due to current or proposed FASB requirements.

Responses for the 71 firms providing information on FIMP which were the same for all currencies are summarized in Table 5. Possible actions listed in the questionnaire were: change inventory turnover, change inventory size; change inventory flow measurement technique; and others, which were to be described. Only eight firms (11.3%) took any action after the issuance of *SFAS 8*. The actions taken were: increased inventory turnover (one firm); decreased inventory size (three firms); and, both increased turnover and decreased size (four firms). These actions are consistent with the translation of inventory at the historical rate, as was required by *SFAS 8*. Inventory is not exposed and cannot be used to balance exposed liabilities for determining net exposure for translation purposes, as only assets and liabilities translated at the current rate are exposed. However, some of the actions undertaken may not represent good operating policies, particularly if the smaller inventory and faster turnover resulted in inability to meet customer quantity and selection needs. If these actions were taken primarily in response to changing accounting requirements, it is possible that *SFAS 8* may have had a harmful impact on the FIMP of at least some companies. If these actions were undertaken in response to having to translate inventory at the historical rate, it could be expected that firms would take opposite actions if the current rate is used to translate inventory, as is the case for most firms under *SFAS 52*. This, however, was not found to be the case for the participants in this study.

Firms reporting anticipated changes in FIMP under the new translation requirement contained in *SFAS 52* indicated that they would make the same types of changes as those reported to have been made after the issuance of *SFAS 8*. Only six firms indicated that they planned to make any changes in FIMP. These six firms indicated they planned to speed up inventory turnover (one firm), decrease inventory size (two firms) and both speed up turnover and decrease size (three firms). Since these are the same types of changes made after the issuance of *SFAS 8,* it suggests that these actions may result from operating needs and be only coincidentally related to the issuance of FASB requirements. This is consistent with the anticipation of few changes in FIMP, which should be governed by sound operating policies, as a result of FASB foreign currency translation requirements. Written comments from several respondents support this view. One respondent summed up the thrust of these comments as follows:

> Inventory management techniques have consistently stressed two objectives: achieving the minimum size necessary to support operations and increasing turnover. Accounting implications of translation are not a factor.

To determine if individual firms planned to continue the same FIMP used after the issuance of *SFAS 8* if *SFAS 52* was adopted, responses to these two questions were cross-tabulated. Table 6 presents a summary of this information. As discussed earlier, two fewer firms planned to take any action if *SFAS 52* was adopted. One of these firms increased inventory turnover and decreased inventory size after *SFAS 8,* but did not plan to continue that action. The other firm decreased inventory size but did not anticipate continuing this action if *SFAS 8* was replaced. Discontinuance of either one of these actions would be consistent with translating inventory at the current rate as turnover no longer is a factor in determining the translation rate for inventory and inventory can be used to balance exposed liabilities. However, it also is possible that these firms decided that inventory size and turnover were at appropriate levels and should not be reduced further.

Table 6. Summary of Change in Foreign Inventory Management Practices After *SFAS 8* and Anticipated if *SFAS 52* is Adopted

	Anticipated if SFAS 52 is Adopted				
After SFAS 8	*Speed Up Turnover*	*Decrease Size*	*Both*	*No Change*	*Total*
Sped up turnover	1	0	0	0	1
Decreased size	0	2	0	1	3
Both	0	0	3	1	4
No action	0	0	0	63	63
Total	1	2	3	65	71

CONCLUSION

This experiment provides information about the impact of foreign currency translation requirements for inventory on the magnitude and materiality of the inventory translation difference (ITD) for 43 U.S.-based multinational corporations. In addition, it examines the influence of foreign currency translation requirements on the foreign inventory management practices (FIMP) of 73 U.S.-based firms. Although such research is subject to certain limitations, several interesting conclusions can be drawn from the findings for these companies.

1. The ITD had no material (±10%) impact on the consolidated earnings of any of the sample firms, although for some the dollar magnitude was quite large.
2. The ITD did have some material effects on both foreign earnings and the reported foreign currency adjustment.
3. Exchange rate changes generally were small for most currencies during the time period examined, due, in part, to relatively stable currencies and to rapid inventory turnover.

Even though the number of firms with material impacts on foreign earnings was small, the dollar magnitudes were quite large. For most companies (all but six) the ITD had a material impact on the reported foreign currency adjustment. Firms complained vigorously about the impact of having to translate inventory at the historical rate required by *SFAS 8*. It is possible that their complaints, rather than being based on the impact on consolidated income, were based on the relative effects on foreign earnings and/or the reported foreign currency adjustment.

The findings with respect to FIMP were as anticipated. Only eight firms indicated changes as a result of *SFAS 8* and two fewer firms indicated they anticipated taking any action if *SFAS 52* was adopted. The changes made or anticipated were the same in both cases, to speed up turnover and/or to decrease inventory size. The FIMP changes made were consistent with sound operating policies, indicating that these changes most likely were made coincidentally with, and not due to, accounting requirements.

APPENDIX

Summary of Firms Ranked by Inventory Translation Differences (ITD) as a Percent of Consolidated Earnings Including Additional Demographic Information (In Percent)

ITD				
Consolidated Earnings	*Foreign Earnings*	*Foreign Currency Adjustment*	*Total Foreign Inventory*	*Total Foreign Assets*
4.20	14.47	A	100	38
3.55	5.30	-14	47	18
3.30	5.44	-31	62	33
3.05	7.45	32	88	37
2.88	8.48	-41	77	29
2.44	6.79	78	100	40
1.88	7.00	-71	69	66
1.33	5.78	442	100	27
1.33	5.34	291	79	9
1.26	4.07	376	58	35
0.88	5.84	A	98	38
0.84	2.64	-10	76	19
0.75	2.49	-32	48	26
0.58	2.77	25	83	44
0.54	1.19	-18	39	26
0.53	1.43	-53	100	18
0.53	3.54	-805	84	30
0.52	1.61	A	41	36
0.47	2.13	-30	48	12
0.06	2.70	-18	B	B
-0.01	-0.02	-263	100	10
-0.03	-0.25	1	78	29
-0.06	-0.27	-4	58	25
-0.07	-0.14	-12	B	B
-0.24	-1.57	23	39	23
-0.42	-2.21	4	52	16
-0.43	-1.24	9	61	54
-0.45	-3.22	33	74	32
-0.49	-1.75	-5	B	B
-0.53	-1.90	45	B	B
-0.54	-3.86	-120	100	22
-0.56	-1.74	-494	35	25
-0.63	-1.75	95	79	6
-0.64	-1.39	-64	42	29
-0.71	-3.21	77	79	20
-0.83	-2.44	10	66	37
-1.05	-3.20	1	69	38
-1.26	-5.23	48	68	33
-1.38	-3.06	27	42	32
-1.45	-17.52	38	71	12
-1.49	-6.47	-32	69	44
-1.78	-4.05	55	41	28
-1.94	-5.87	-243	52	65

Notes: A = no foreign currency adjustment reported.
B = total foreign inventory information not supplied.

ACKNOWLEDGMENTS

The author gratefully acknowledges the support of the Arthur Andersen & Co., Deloitte Haskins and Sells, and Richard D. Irwin Foundations.

NOTES

1. This study was conducted prior to the issuance of *SFAS 52,* but during the time period the Exposure Draft, "Foreign Currency Translation," was being deliberated. It is believed that the responses relative to FIMP would not have been significantly different after *SFAS 52* was formally adopted.
2. Seven firms continued to translate inventory at the current rate after *SFAS 8* was issued. The three firms explaining their reason for doing so indicated that foreign inventory was not material.
3. The approximate historical rate was determined differently depending upon whether the FIFO or average cost inventory valuation method was used. For FIFO inventories, the calculation was based upon the inventory turnover, expressed in months. A weighted average monthly historical rate was then determined, using rate quotations from the *Wall Street Journal.* For the average cost method, turnover again was used to determine how frequently inventory is replaced, in numbers of months. A weighted average historical rate, based upon the number-of-months inventory on hand at the end of the fiscal year, was determined. These procedures were developed after telephone conversations with six respondents, three each using FIFO and average cost.

REFERENCES

Cook, J., "A Game Any Number Can Play," *Forbes* [June 25, 1979], pp. 56-62.

Financial Accounting Standards Board, *Statement of Financial Accounting Standards No. 8,* "Accounting for the Translation of Foreign Currency Transactions and Foreign Currency Financial Statements" [FASB, 1975].

Rodriguez, R.M., "FASB No. 8: What Has It Done For Us?," *Financial Analysts Journal* [March 1977], pp. 40-47.

Searfass, W.D., "Possible Undesirable Effects of FASB No. 8," *The CPA Journal* [May 1976], pp. 59-60.

Shank, J.K., "FASB Statement No. 8 Resolved Foreign Currency Accounting—Or Did It?," *Financial Analysts Journal* [July/August 1976], pp. 55-61.

"Shifting Rates Throw Earnings Out of Kilter," *Business Week* [April 12, 1975], pp. 28-29.

"The New 'Reality'." *Forbes* [April 15, 1976], p. 34.

THE SPECIAL DRAWING RIGHT AS A REPORTING CURRENCY

M. Ali Fekrat

ABSTRACT

Current accounting standards governing the translation of financial statements from one currency into another are unsuitable for multinational enterprises (MNEs), and a multicurrency unit of account such as the Special Drawing Right (SDR) would portray the currency environment of MNEs more realistically than any single national currency. By capturing the essence of the MNEs' economic environment, financial statements using a multicurrency unit of account would provide information not contained in the single-currency statements. This paper starts with the argument that mature MNEs operate in a global multicurrency environment, and hence no single national currency could legitimately serve as their reporting currency. It shows the computation of the SDR and discusses the role of both SDRs and European Currency Units (ECUs) in international finance, leading to a new reporting hypothesis, its illustration and analysis.

Advances in International Accounting, Vol. 3, pages 127-137.

ISBN: 1-55938-078-0

BACKGROUND

Extensive currency realignments and volatility in exchange markets since the 1970s have forced attention on finding appropriate solutions to the problem of converting a set of multicurrency financial statments into a common currency for reporting purposes. In 1975, the U.S. Financial Accounting Standards Board (FASB) issued *Statement No. 8,* "Accounting for the Translation of Foreign Currency Transactions and Foreign Currency Financial Statements" (*SFAS 8*), which soon gave rise to one of the most heated controversies in the history of accounting standard-setting [Seidler, 1978]. The main conceptual flaw with this Statement, and the reason for controversy, was its implicit assumption that MNEs essentially operated in a single currency environment, namely the currency of the country in which the parent company was located [Connor, 1978]. This meant that the financial statements of subsidiaries had to be translated into the currency used by the parent company without changing the measurement basis of the original transactions. Local currency financial statements had to be translated using exchange rates between the local currency and the currency of the parent company, the historical rate for almost all nonmonetary accounts, and the current rate for all monetary accounts.

This Statement was superseded in 1981 by *Statement No. 52,* "Foreign Currency Translation" (*SFAS 52*), which, in effect, abandoned the single-currency assumption of *SFAS 8.* Instead, it explicitly recognized the multicurrency environment in international operations, and therefore, required (1) identifying the "functional" currency of an entity's economic environment (2) measuring all elements of the financial statements in the functional currency, (3) using the current exchange rate for translation from the functional currency into the reporting currency, if different, and (4) distinguishing the economic impact of changes in exchange rates on a net investment from the impact of such changes on individual assets and liabilities that are receivable or payable in currencies other than the functional currency.

The substantive contribution of *SFAS 52* was its explicit recognition that an entity's functional and reporting currencies may be different. An entity's functional currency is the currency of the primary economic environment in which it operates and in which it is expected to generate net cash flows. An entity's reporting currency is the currency in which it reports its financial statements. For a corporation without foreign subsidiaries, the functional currency and the reporting currency are identical. However, a subsidiary located in a country other than that of the parent, doing the bulk of its business with other countries and in other markets, may have a functional currency other than the currency of the country in which it is located, while its reporting currency may be the currency of the country in which its parent company is located. For a foreign subsidiary with relatively self-contained operations, the functional currency is typically the local currency of its country of incorporation. On the other hand, if foreign operations are a direct and integral component or extension of a parent company's operations, the reporting currency, that is, the currency in which the parent prepares its financial statements, is also the functional currency of those operations [Kubin, 1984].

This distinction between integrated and self-contained foreign entities is critical, because the economic effect of exchange rate changes on their cash flows is quite different. Whereas the economic effect of such changes on fully integrated operations concerns individual foreign currency assets and liabilities, which have a direct bearing on the parent's cash flows, the economic effect of an exchange rate change on self-contained foreign operations concerns the parent's net investment in those operations, and translation adjustments arising from consolidating the operations of such a foreign concern do not directly affect cash flows.

The application of *SFAS 52* implies the ability to identify the functional currency. The Board has suggested a list of economic factors to be considered both individually and collectively in determining the functional currency of a foreign entity. A foreign entity's currency will be the functional currency if (1) its cash flows are primarily in foreign currency (do not directly impact the parent's cash flows), (b) its sales prices are not responsive to short-term exchange rate changes (determined by local competition), (c) it has an active local market, (d) its expenses are primarily incurred locally, (e) its financing is denominated in foreign currency (funds for debt service generated locally), and (f) its intercompany transactions are low (no extensive interrelationships between parent and foreign entity).

While *SFAS 52* provides detailed guidance on how to determine the functional currency, it provides no such guidance with respect to the reporting currency. It implicitly assumes that the reporting currency is always the currency of the country of incorporation of the parent company. As we shall see, this assumption is unwarranted for a multinational enterprise and leads to distorted reporting of performance results.

SFAS 52's INCOMPATIBILITY WITH MULTINATIONALS

The translation method recommendation in *SFAS 52* is essentially incompatible with the basic tei ets, orientation and operation of mature multinational enterprises. This is mainly because the Statement implicitly views such enterprises as a collection of unrelated units without considering the interwoven relationships that link the different units into a unified whole. According to Perlmutter [1969], multinationals pass through the following three stages as they grow to maturity.

1. *Ethnocentric* enterprises are strongly oriented toward domestic interests. This is the first stage of the life of an MNE. At this stage, management is still not aware of the problems that arise from differences in the economic environment an MNE faces. Among other things, the ethnocentric approach implies—if we use American companies as an example—that American principles of doing business are enforced everywhere, no matter whether they fit or not.

2. *Polycentric* enterprises are strongly oriented toward local interests. This type exists during the second stage of an MNE's life, when top management realizes, for example, that American business principles are not very useful in situations that are entirely different from the American model. The result is a major effort to decentralize and manage the group as though it were "more akin to a confederation" [p. 12], giving each subsidiary a large degree of freedom.

3. *Geocentric* enterprises have strongly adopted a global viewpoint, thus abstracting from local or domestic "national" interests. In this third and highest stage of an MNE's truly becoming "multinational," the group is regarded as "a whole whose focus is on worldwide objectives as well as local objectives, each part making its unique contribution with its unique competence" [p. 12]. This stage of MNE operations, now considerably accelerated by rapid technological change and globalization of the marketplace, is regarded as the most efficient and streamlined form of an MNE. It is also the most difficult to achieve mainly because it requires a shift in top management's outlook and approach.

What this implies for our analysis may be stated as follows: exactly what currency or currency mixes best reflect the totality of the economic environment of an MNE depends on the MNE's stage of development. For ethnocentric MNEs, the parent company's currency appears to be the focus of attention and that currency is likely to be both the functional and the reporting currency (as assumed by *SFAS 8*). Since the MNE is still at the early stage of its development and multinational operations are still relatively small as a component of overall operations, the parent-currency focus seems both appropriate and practical. However, for polycentric MNEs, local interests become important and local currencies emerge as one focus of foreign operations. But given that the MNE has not yet achieved the global orientation and outlook, the parent company focus continues to dominate. There are, therefore, local functional currencies and a reporting currency which reflects the parent company focus. For geocentric MNEs, however, the situation is substantially different. These multinational enterprises operate in the global marketplace in a truly multicurrency environment in that their receipts and payments are made in any one of several key convertible currencies. Collectively these currencies serve as both functional and reporting currencies. Under these conditions, no single currency may realistically be singled out as either the MNE's functional or reporting currency and none would portray fairly the substance of its operating business environment. The fact that multiple functional currencies are used by a multinational enterprise was not recognized by the FASB in *SFAS 8,* but was later conceded in *SFAS 52,* however not multiple reporting currencies.

The multicurrency environment of a geocentric MNE is illustrated by many of today's multinational companies in the world. The U.S.-based companies earned 24 to 73 percent of their gross revenues from nondomestic sources. The non-U.S.-based companies earned 38 to 60 percent of their gross earnings from nondomestic sources [Mueller, Gernon, and Meek, 1987]. A case that highlights the details of actual currency flows in a multinational enterprise is that of the Bulova Watch Company [Anthony, Dearden, and Bedford, 1984]. During the 1970s, this company was composed of 32 operating subunits, each with its own profit responsibility. Of the total number of profit centers, 22 were located outside the United States. Manufacturing took place in 21 plants, 12 located in the United States and 9 overseas. Products moved among plants and responsibility centers frequently, as intercompany sales were essential for attaining competitive profitability goals. Of all the watches sold by Bulova in the United States, about 85 percent contained movements imported from other countries. In some instances, from the time components were manufactured at a foreign site to the time finished watches were ready for sale in the United States, as many as five intercompany transactions took place. Aside from the purely managerial control issues that such multinational operations present, deciding exactly which currency should serve as the reporting currency for the enterprise as a whole when company products move continually across currency borders is hardly self-evident.

SDR: A MULTICURRENCY CURRENCY

Special drawing rights (SDRs) were originally created by the International Monetary Fund (IMF) in 1969 as a means of augmenting its resource base to cope with the growing liquidity requirements of its member countries. Since then the SDR has gained widespread acceptability not only as a key official reserve asset among central banks, but also as an important component of private international finance.

Official SDRs are entries on the books of the International Monetary Fund and of certain other official organizations. The IMF entries are used to record all Fund transactions and as a means of settling balance-of-payments deficits/surpluses among member states. The SDR value was originally tied to the gold content of the U.S. dollar, but was later changed to a basket of sixteen currencies chosen on the basis of their importance in international trade and finance. The basket was subsequently simplified to include only five currencies—the U.S. dollar, the German mark, the French franc, the Japanese yen, and the British pound. The amount of each currency in the basket is fixed, but the weight fluctuates with changes in exchange rates. The calculation of the U.S. dollar value of the SDR for two randomly selected dates is shown below:

	(1)	(2)		(3)	
	Currency	*Spot Rates*		*Dollar Value*	
Currency	*Units*	*1/83*	*4/87*	*1/83*	*4/87*
U.S. Dollar	.540	1.000	1.000	.5400	.5400
German Mark	.460	2.430	1.787	.1893	.2574
Japanese Yen	34.000	236.200	139.750	.1439	.2433
French Franc	.470	6.886	5.958	.1075	.1242
Pound Sterling	.071	.650	.602	.1092	.1179
U.S. dollar value of SDR				1.0899	1.2828

Explanation of columns:

(1) The currency components of the basket.

(2) The exchange rates in terms of currency units per U.S. dollar as quoted in *The Wall Street Journal* on the last day of the months indicated above.

(3) The U.S. dollar equivalent of the currency amounts in column (1) at the exchange rates in column (2), that is, column (1) divided by column (2).

Private SDRs function as a medium of exchange, a store of value, and a unit of account—the traditional functions of money. Essentially, SDR-based transactions use the official basket to fix obligations among private parties, not against the International Monetary Fund. The prime attribute of such transactions is less exchange rate variability than any one of the basket currencies [Dheeriya, 1985], thereby providing a built-in protection against exchange rate fluctuations. As a weighted average of the exchange rates of the component currencies, the SDR's value generally moves by less than that of its components.

An alternative composite currency, the use of which is rapidly growing in private financial markets, is the European Currency Unit (ECU). The ECU consists of a fixed quantity of each of 10 European currencies: .719 German marks; 1.31 French francs; .256 Dutch guilders; 3.71 Belgian francs; .14 Luxembourg francs; .219 Danish kroner; 140 Italian liras; .00871 Irish pounds; .0878 British pounds; and 1.15 Greek drachmas. Since its introduction in March 1979, the ECU has been used by the governments of the eight European countries particularly in the European Monetary System (EMS) for debt settlements among central banks. It has also played a rapidly growing role in private finance, including interbank markets, short-term deposit markets, the Eurobond market, and most recently, the futures and options markets in the United States and other countries with leading stock and commodity exchanges.

The private commercial use of the ECU has also been expanding, as indicated by the increasing number of trade contracts, export credits, and other transactions denominated in ECUs. Some companies have chosen to invoice transactions with foreign affiliates in ECUs. Even ECU travelers checks have recently become available [Glick, 1987]. Two factors account for this growing use of the ECU. First, because the composition of the ECU excludes the U.S. dollar, the value of the ECU in terms of any of its component currencies is generally unaffected by changes in the value of the dollar. Consequently, one of the ECU's appeals stems from its use as a hedge against the dollar. Second, the official EMS commitment to stabilize the ECU within a band called the "parity grid" instills confidence in the private sector and helps boost its market.

In many respects, the ECU has moved toward becoming the common currency in Europe. A new international clearinghouse for private ECUs is now being organized by commerical banks in conjunction with the Bank of International Settlements (BIS). Thus the ECU's role as a genuine international currency makes it a logical candidate for use as a functional currency by enterprises whose receipts and payments are actually denominated in ECUs.

But what about its role as a reporting currency for geocentric multinational enterprises? The answer to this question should probably be in the negative, mainly because the ECU excludes the most important key international currencies, that is, the U.S. dollar, the Japanese yen, and the Swiss franc. The ECU market, though growing, is still small and immature compared with the huge Eurodollar market. The bulk of international bank lending and private and institutional investing is still in U.S. dollars, followed by German marks, Swiss francs, and Japanese yen. Consequently, just like national currencies, a composite currency that excludes the key international currencies would not be suitable as a reporting currency by multinationals.

INFORMATION CONTENT OF SDR STATEMENTS

The main point of this paper may be stated in the form of a hypothesis as follows:

> *The use of the SDR as a reporting currency results in new and more realistic information than that contained in single-currency financial statements.*

This hypothesis will be examined with the aid of a generalizable illustration and deductive analysis.

Assume the following beginning and ending balance sheets for a U.S. multinational company and its Japanese subsidiary (Sub):

Beginning Balance Sheets

	U.S. Company	*Japanese Sub*
Assets	$1,300	Y22,730
Investments in Sub	100	
Total	$1,400	Y22,730
Liabilities	$600	Y0
Equity	800	22,730
Total	$1,400	Y22,730

Ending Balance Sheets

	U.S. Company	*Japanese Sub*
Assets	$1,300	Y62,730
Investment in Sub	100	
Total	$1,400	Y62,730
Liabilities	$0	Y0
Equity	$1,400	62,730
Total	$1,400	Y62,730

Assume further that the increase in the equities of the U.S. Company and its Japanese Sub resulted from the following transactions during the period:

Revenues	$1,000	Y50,000
Expenses	400	10,000
Net Income	$ 600	Y40,000

Exchange rates at the beginning and at the end of the period are assumed to be as follows:

Beginning:	Y227.30 = $1.00	SDR .87020 = $1.00	SDR 1 = Y261.26
Ending:	Y138.90 = $1.00	SDR .76253 = $1.00	SDR 1 = Y182.16

The translated statements of the subsidiary in dollars are as follows:

Beginning Balance Sheet

Assets (Y22,730/227.30)	$100.00
Equity (Y22,730/227.30)	$100.00

Income Statement

Revenues {Y50,000/[(227.30 + 138.90)/2]}	$273.07
Expenses {Y10,000/[(227.30 + 138.90)/2]}	54.61
Net Income	$218.46

Ending Balance Sheet

Assets (Y62,730/138.90)	$451.62
Equities (Y62,730/138.90)	$451.62

Translation Gain

Increase in Equities ($451.62-$100.00)	$351.62
Net Income	218.46
Translation Gain	$133.16

Under *SFAS 52,* the U.S. company will include profits of $218.45 in its consolidated income statement and an increase of $133.16 as a valuation adjustment in its equity on the balance sheet. The consolidated net income of the enterprise will be $818.46 while the increase in consolidated equity will be $951.62. The difference of $133.16 represents the financial effect of the fall in the value of the dollar in relation to the yen.

Now let us see how the results change if we use the SDR as the reporting currrency. Here both sets of financial statements must be translated into SDRs before consolidated statements for the whole enterprise can be prepared. Following the same computational procedures used above, the SDR financial statement of the U.S. Company and its Japanese Sub are shown below.

Beginning Balance Sheets

	U.S. Company		*Japanese Sub*	
Assets	SDR	1,131.26	SDR	87.02
Investment in Sub		87.02		
Total	SDR	1,218.28	SDR	87.02
Liabilities	SDR	522.12	SDR	0
Equity		696.16		87.02
Total	SDR	1,218.28	SDR	87.02

Ending Balance Sheets

Assets	SDR	991.29	SDR	344.37
Investment in Sub		76.25		
Total	SDR	1,067.54	SDR	344.37
Liabilities	SDR	0		0
Equity		1,067.54		344.37
Total	SDR	1,067.54	SDR	344.37

	Income Statements			
Revenues	SDR	816.36	SDR	225.52
Expenses		326.55		45.10
Net Income	SDR	489.81	SDR	180.42
	Translation Gains (Losses)			
Increase in Equities	SDR	371.38	SDR	257.35
Net Income		489.81		180.42
Translation Gain (Loss)		(118.43)		76.93

The consolidated statements at the end of the period would show a combined net income of SDR 670.23 offset by a net translation loss of SDR 41.50, resulting in an increase in the equity of the enterprise as a whole of SDR 628.73.

Why does the translation effect change so significantly when the reporting currency is changed from a single currency to a multicurrency unit? The ingredients of an answer to this question lie in the distinctions already made in the first part of the paper. Recall that the geocentric enterprise has a strong global marketplace orientation. In the case of such a multinational enterprise, with relatively high dollar asset holdings, it would seem fallacious to report a translation gain when in fact the value of its dollar assets has suffered a decline. In the words of the Financial Accounting Standards Board's Concept Statement No. 2, this would hardly be "representationally faithful." The SDR statements, on the other hand, report a net translation loss, which seems to be in keeping with what has actually transpired. This outcome confirms the conclusion reached elsewhere [Jacobi, 1984] that a given set of multinational operating results will be reported favorably or unfavorably depending on the reporting currency into which the results are translated. It seems possible to generalize that single currency statements distort the operating results of multinational enterprises. Given that SDR statements automatically take into account the changes in the values of a group of currencies in relation to each other and not just in relation to a single currency, they would show the net effect of currency changes (i.e., unfavorable movements in some offset by favorable movements in others) on a multinational enterprise. In this sense, SDR statements would have greater representational faithfulness than single currency statements.

REFERENCES

Anthony, R.N., J. Dearden, and N.M. Bedford, *Management Control Systems* [Irwin, 1984], pp. 664-674.

Connor, J.E., Jr., "Accounting for Foreign Currency Translation," in *Accounting for Multinational Enterprises,* edited by D.D. AlHashim and J.W. Robertson [Bobbs-Merrill Educational Publishing, 1978], pp. 130-139.

Dheeriya, P.L., "A Case for Special Drawing Rights as a Unit of Account," *The International Journal of Accounting Education and Research* [Fall 1985], pp. 71-87.

Financial Accounting Standards Board, *Statement of Financial Accounting Standards No. 8,* "Accounting for the Translation of Foreign Currency Transactions and Foreign Currency Financial Statements" [FASB, 1975].

________, *Statement of Financial Accounting Concepts No. 2,* "Qualitative Characteristics of Accounting Information" [FASB, 1980].

________, *Statement of Financial Accounting Standards No. 52,* "Foreign Currency Translation" [FASB, 1981].

Glick, R., "ECU, Who?," *FRBSF Weekly Letter* [January 1987].

Jacobi, M.H., "The Unit of Account in Consolidated Financial Statements of Multinational Enterprises," in *International Accounting,* edited by H.P. Holzer [Harper & Row, 1984], pp. 105-119.

Kubin, K.W., "Financial Accounting and Reporting for International Business Operations," in *International Accounting,* edited by H.P. Holzer. [Harper & Row, 1984], pp. 47-85.

Mueller, G.G., H.Gernon, and G. Meek, *Accounting: An International Perspective* [Irwin, 1987], p. 2.

Perlmutter, H.V., "The Tortuous Evolution of the Multinational Corporation," *Columbia Journal of World Business* [January-February 1969], pp. 9-18.

Seidler, L.J., "Accounting for Foreign Currency Translation," in *Accounting for Multinational Enterprises,* edited by D.D AlHashim and J.W. Robertson [Bobbs-Merrill Educational Publishing, 1978], pp. 107-129.

IMPACT OF SFAS 52 ON THE ACCURACY OF ANALYSTS' EARNINGS FORECASTS

Bikki Jaggi and Gurprit Chhatwal

ABSTRACT

This study examines the impact of the Financial Accounting Standards Board's *Statement of Financial Accounting Standards No. 52,* "Foreign Currency Trnaslation," on the accuracy and variability of security analysts' forecasts. The total sample consisted of 212 analysts' forecasts for firms affected by the standard; 106 firms which adopted the standard in 1981 formed the test group, and 106 firms which did not adopt the standard during this year belonged to the control group. Forecasts for test and control groups for the pre-adoption period were compared with forecasts for the post-adoption period and comparative analyses were also conducted on subsets matched by firm size and earnings variability. The results of the comparative analyses indicate that there was no significant difference in accuracy or variability of analysts' forecasts between pre- and post-adoption periods. These results, therefore, imply that the adoption of *SFAS 52* did not result in a significant improvement in the accuracy or variability of analysts' forecasts.

Advances in International Accounting, Vol. 3, pages 139-154.

ISBN: 1-55938-078-0

INTRODUCTION

Earnings forecasts which form the basis for cash flow predictions play an important role in investors' decisions [FASB *Statement of Financial Accounting Concepts No. 1*]. The importance of these forecasts has led many researchers to examine their accuracy. Some compared the accuracy of management forecasts with that of analysts' forecasts [Basi, Carey, and Twark, 1976: Ruland, 1978; Jaggi, 1980]; others examined the accuracy of management and security analysts' forecasts in relation to the accuracy of model forecasts [Copeland and Marioni, 1972; Brown and Rozeff, 1978-1979].

The accuracy of forecasts developed by security analysts and investors greatly depends upon the quality of available historical earnings data which are developed on the basis of Financial Accounting Standards (FAS). In 1981, *SFAS 52* replaced the prior standard, *SFAS 8,* with the objective of better reflecting the economic performance of subsidiaries in consolidated financial statements and improving the quality of reported earnings. This study examines whether financial information generated on the basis of *SFAS 52* improved the accuracy and variability of earnings forecasts developed by security analysts.

BACKGROUND AND RATIONALE FOR CURRENT STUDY

Background

Several foreign currency translation methods have been suggested in the literature in order to incorporate financial information of subsidiaries into consolidated financial statements. The selection of these methods is, however, guided by the accounting standards which have been developed from time to time, such as Accounting Principles Board (APB) Opinions Nos. 6, and 22, *SFAS 8,* and *SFAS 52.*

Until recently, *SFAS 8* provided the detailed guidelines for translation of foreign currency into U.S. dollars. However, in view of differences in the economic environments of the countries in which subsidiaries operate, translation methods laid down in this standard were criticized by academics and practitioners. A survey of the financial community indicated that *SFAS 8* made income figures highly variable with changes in foreign exchange rates [Massaro, 1978]. Several researchers who examined the effect of *SFAS 8* on the exchange risk management activities of multinational corporations also found that variability of earnings because of *SFAS 8* seemed to be a major concern of the management of several corporations [Evans, Folks, and Jilling, 1978; Shank, Dillard, and Murdock, 1979; Morsicato, 1980] (also see *SFAS 52* itself for comments).

Brown [1983] investigated whether adoption of *SFAS 8* improved the accuracy of earnings forecasts developed by security analysts. He compared the accuracy of Value Line Earnings Forecasts developed after and before the adoption of *SFAS 8*. He also compared the accuracy of adopting firms with that of non-adopting firms. His findings indicated that the accuracy of forecasts of adopting firms showed some improvement for the post-adoption period compared with that of the pre-adoption period. He also detected a similar improvement for firms which did not adopt *SFAS 8*. His results, however, did not show a statistically significant difference in the improvement of accuracy for the post-adoption period either for adopting or non-adopting firms. On the basis of these results, he concluded "that even though the results were in the expected direction (percentage improvement < 50 percent; negative Wilcoxon), *SFAS 8* did not exert a significant effect on the impaired predictive ability" [Brown, 1983, p. 439]. No study has so far been conducted to evaluate the impact of *SFAS 52* on the accuracy of earnings forecasts developed by security analysts.

Statement of Financial Accounting Standards No. 52

The perceived weaknesses of *SFAS 8* led the Financial Accounting Standards Board (FASB) to re-examine the issue of foreign currency translation. As a result, a new standard (*SFAS 52*) superseded all existing standards on the subject and provided comprehensive guidelines to deal with different aspects of foreign currency translation. The major objective of *SFAS 52* was to lay down the rules for foreign currency results generally compatible with the expected economic effects of a change in the rate of exchange on an enterprise's cash flows and equity [*SFAS 52,* paragraph 4]. To accomplish this objective, the concept of a functional currency has been introduced.

"Functional currency" is defined as the currency of the primary economic environment in which the foreign entity operates. Normally, the functional currency would be the currency in which the entity generates and expends cash. However, it is not necessary that under all circumstances the functional currency be the foreign currency. If the entity is relatively self-contained and integrated within a particular country or economy, then the currency of the country in which it operates will be the functional currency, otherwise the currency of the country in which the parent company is located will become the functional currency. If the economic circumstances warrant the use of foreign currency as the functional currency, the current rate method is used for translating foreign currency into the reporting currency.

In addition to the introduction of the functional currency concept, *SFAS 52* provided for direct adjustments for a number of items to owners' equity on the balance sheet instead of the income statement. The most important adjustment related to the foreign currency translation, which was to be removed from the income statement when the functional currency was the foreign currency.

Rationale and Hypothesis for the Study

The new standard (*SFAS 52*), which introduced the concept of functional currency and changed the method for adjustments resulting from foreign currency translation, was expected to better reflect the economic results of subsidiaries in foreign countries. This expectation is based on the premise that the changes in the reporting methods would reduce the earnings volatility.

The important research question arises, did the changes introduced by *SFAS 52* improve the quality of reported earnings (and other financial information) so that it provided better and more accurate earnings forecasts? This study empirically tests whether the accuracy of earnings forecasts improved after adoption of *SFAS 52.* Because it is possible that the adoption of *SFAS 52* may have created ambiguities and uncertainties for forecasters during the early post-adoption period, which could temporarily have an adverse affect on the accuracy of forecasts, this study will isolate this temporary uncertainty by conducting an analysis with a time lag of one year from the time of adoption of *SFAS 52.*

The following general hypothesis was developed for the study:

H_0: There is no difference in the accuracy of security analysts' earnings forecasts developed after the adoption of *SFAS 52* compared to those developed before that standard.

If the hypothesis is rejected, the results will indicate there is a difference in the accuracy of earnings forecasts for the post- and pre-adoption periods, and the sign of the difference will enable us to determine whether the accuracy of forecasts developed after the adoption of *SFAS 52* improved or not.

RESEARCH METHODOLOGY

Sample Selection and Data Collection

We used a sample of firms which have substantial international operations and were affected by *SFAS 52.* A list of firms that adopted *SFAS 52* in 1981, 1982, and 1983 was obtained from the American Institute of Certified Public Accountants (AICPA). The number of adopting firms in these years was 151, 133, and 60 respectively. These numbers indicate that most affected firms adopted the standard within the first two years of its promulgation although they were not required to adopt it until the fiscal year commencing on or after

Table 1. Characteristics of Sample Firms

	Test Group	*Control Group*
Size Characteristics for 1981		
Average Sales ($ millions)	$2,871	$4,404
Average Assets ($ millions)	2,166	3,442
Variability in Earnings Per Share		
Standard Deviation	1.79	2.02

December 15, 1982. However, an earlier compliance, though not required, was encouraged and a majority of firms opted for an earlier compliance.

To eliminate the impact of factors other than the adoption of *SFAS 52,* a research design was developed to compare the forecast accuracy of adopting firms with those of non-adopting firms. The following procedures were followed to classify all firms affected by *SFAS 52* into adopting and non-adopting firms.

First, firms which adopted *SFAS 52* in 1981 formed the preliminary group of adopting firms (test group) and firms which adopted the standard in later years, (1982 and 1983), were classified as a non-adopting group. Second, in order to isolate the industry effect, the control group firms were matched with the test group firms on the basis of two-digit SIC code. If the test group firms could be matched with a control group firm, both firms were retained in their respective group of the sample; nonmatched firms were excluded. As a result of this procedure, 120 firms were included in the test group and the same number of firms in the control group.

Third, the sample obtained through the first two steps was further evaluated to examine whether the earnings values of the firms were significantly small. Relative forecast accuracy determined on the basis of very small earnings values is likely to produce biased results. Therefore, in order to control for the effect of small values on the percentage accuracy of forecasts, firms with earnings of less than fifteen cents per share were dropped from the study, along with their corresponding match. As a result of this procedure, 14 firms were dropped both from the test and control group. The final sample consisted of 106 test and 106 control firms.

The above procedures enabled us to meet the following criteria. First, only firms with substantial foreign operations were included in the study. Second, the industry impact was controlled through the use of test and control groups matched by industry codes. Third, the effect of a small denominator on the calculation of relative forecast error was minimized.

The test and control group firms were compared with regard to their sales, assets and earnings variability. The statistics contained in Table 1 show that the average size of the test group firms is smaller than that of the control firms.

The earnings variability, determined as the standard deviation of Earnings Per Share over the preceding four years, is also smaller for the test group firms (1.79 vs. 2.02). In order to eliminate the impact of differences of size and earnings variability of the two groups, subsets of the sample matched on firm size and earnings variability were generated and additional tests were conducted on these subsets.

Security Analysts' Forecasts and Prediction Period

The earnings forecasts developed by the *Value Line Investment Survey* (*VLIS*) were used in this study. These forecasts were selected because they have been found to be accurate [Roseff and Brown, 1979] and have been widely used by researchers and investors.

The VLIS earnings forecasts developed in the quarter immediately following the end of the fiscal year in which the adoption took place were selected for the study. This was done to ensure that the actual earnings on which predictions were based, were generated in accordance with *SFAS 52*. The same period was also used for the control group to ensure the comparability of forecasts for the two groups. In order to ensure temporal comparability, earnings forecasts before adoption of *SFAS 52* were selected from the quarter immediately following the end of the preceding year.

The study is based on annual earnings forecasts rather than on quarterly earnings forecasts because only annual earnings are affected by this standard.

Test Procedures

The accuracy of earnings forecasts has been evaluated on the basis of the Relative Prediction Error (RPE) and Absolute Relative Prediction Error (ARPE):

$$\text{RPE} = \frac{A_{i,t} - P_{i,t} \mid A_{i,t-1}}{A_{i,t}} \tag{1}$$

$$\text{ARPE} = \mid \text{RPE} \mid \tag{2}$$

where,

$A_{i,t}$ = Actual annual earnings per share for firm i in year t;

$P_{i,t} \mid A_{i,t-1}$ = Predicted earnings per share for firm i in year t after the availability of actual earnings per share for the year t-1.

$\mid \; \mid$ = Absolute value operators

The actual earnings figure is used as a denominator to achieve the relative error measure because this is theoretically more supportable [for example, see Theil, 1966], and is widely used in the accounting research studies [for example, see Silhan, 1982; Brown, 1983]. In order to ensure the reliability of the denominator, the sample was examined to see if for any firm the actual earnings figures were negative. No such observation was detected in the sample. It is recognized that the size of actual earnings is likely to influence the results of the study, but this situation will also be faced when the predicted figure is used as a denominator.

To reduce the impact of other factors on the accuracy of forecasts, a comparative analysis of the test and control group was conducted. For this purpose, a difference measure in the prediction error (*d* PE) for two periods is calculated:

$$d\,\text{PE} = \text{ARPE}_t - \text{ARPE}_{t-1} \tag{3}$$

where,

t = period immediately following the adoption of *SFAS 52*
$t-1$ = period before adoption of *SFAS 52*

A positive value of *d* PE signifies that the prediction error for the post-adoption period is comparatively higher, while a negative value of *d* PE indicates an improvement in the accuracy of forecast after adoption of *SFAS 52*. The Matched Pair Wilcoxon test is conducted to determine whether a significant improvement in the earnings forecasts could be detected for adopting firms compared to non-adopting firms.

The relative accuracy of earnings' forecasts for adopting firms vis-à-vis non-adopting firms is further evaluated on the basis of the following D1 statistic:

$$\text{D1} = \frac{\text{ARPE}_{ns,tj}}{\text{ARPE}_{ns,t-1j}} - \frac{\text{ARPE}_{s,ti}}{\text{ARPE}_{s,t-1i}} \tag{4}$$

where s_i and ns_j define the adopting and non-adopting firms respectively.

The measure of D1 compares the relative accuracy of test group firms with the control group firms whereby the relative accuracy represents the relationship between the post- and pre-adoption periods. If the difference between the accuracy of forecasts of the two groups is positive, that is, D1 value is positive, it will indicate that adopting firms exhibited comparatively lower error rate during the post-adoption period and this will imply that there was an improvement in earnings forecasts for these firms during the post-adoption period. If the D1 value is negative, it would mean that the relative prediction error of adopting firms was higher for the post-adoption period indicating that the accuracy of forecasts of adopting firms deteriorated after adopting *SFAS 52*.

The comparative accuracy of analysts' forecasts for adopting and non-adopting firms will also be evaluated on the basis of a statistic introduced by Brown [1983] which is termed as D2 statistic:

$$D2 = \frac{ARPE_{s,t-1i}}{ARPE_{ns,t-1,}} - \frac{ARPE_{s,ti}}{ARPE_{ns,tj}} \qquad (5)$$

The measure D2 is based on the difference between the relative prediction errors of adopting and non-adopting firms for the pre- and post-adoption periods. A positive value of D2 indicates that the relative error in the post-adoption period was smaller, indicating an improvement in the accuracy of earnings predictions for the post-adoption period.

TEST RESULTS AND DISCUSSION

Forecast Accuracy Results for Test and Control Groups

The error measures of RPE and ARPE were calculated for all test and control group firms using Equations (1) and (2) for pre- and post-adoption periods. The Matched Pair Wilcoxon tests were conducted on ARPE of the adopting as well as non-adopting firms to determine whether forecast errors for the period after adoption of *FAS 52* differed significantly from those for the period before adoption of this standard. The ARPE measure was used because both under and over estimates were considered to be prediction errors, and the Matched Pair Wilcoxon test was used because the error measures were not found to be normally distributed (Kolmogorov *D*-statistic). Table 2 contains the results.

The test results contained in Column 1 of Table 2 indicate that forecast errors for the post-adoption period—1982—were significantly different from those of the pre-adoption period—1980—and the forecast errors were higher for the post-adoption period compared to the pre-adoption period. The higher forecast errors both for adopting and non-adopting firms suggested that the accuracy of forecasts was influenced by factors other than adoption of *SFAS 52*. Therefore, the results of this test did not enable us to properly evaluate the impact of *SFAS 52* on the accuracy of earnings forecasts.

Table 2. Test Results of Differences in Relative Prediction Errors—Pre- versus Post-Adoption Periods

	Z-Values: Wilcoxon Test	
	1980 vs. 1982 ($n = 106$)	*1980 vs. 1983* ($n = 37$)
Adopting Firms (Test Group)	-4.58*	-0.28
Non-Adopting Firms (Control Group)	-1.99**	-1.48

Notes: * Significant at the 0.01 level.
** Significant at the 0.05 level.

Comparative Forecast Accuracy Results

Three additional tests were conducted to evaluate the comparative accuracy of adopting and non-adopting firms to determine whether the adoption of *SFAS 52* improved the accuracy of security analysts' forecasts. The first test of comparative analysis was based on the *d* PE measure of adopting and non-adopting firms. This measure was calculated by using Equation (3). As mentioned earlier, the *d* PE measure reflected the difference between the forecast errors for post- and pre-adoption periods. The positive sign of the error measure indicated that the prediction error for the post-adoption period was comparatively higher, while a negative sign of the measure reflected an improvement in the accuracy of forecasts after adoption of *SFAS 52.*

In order to examine whether there was an association between *d* PE and adoption of *SFAS 52,* we conducted the Chi-Square and Matched Pair Wilcoxon tests on the test and control groups. The results on the Chi-Square test are presented in Table 3.

The results in Panel A of Table 3 show that there were no significant differences between negative and positive *d* PEs of the two groups (Chi-Square = .09 for 1980 vs. 1982 forecasts). This meant that the RPEs for pre- and post-adoption periods for adopting firms were different compared to those of non-adopting firms.

The results on the Matched Pair Wilcoxon Test contained in Table 4 Column 1 also indicated that there was no statistically significant difference in the *d* PE measure for the two groups ($Z = -.026$). These results thus confirm the Chi-Square results that RPEs for pre-and post-adoption periods for adopting firms did not differ significantly from those of non-adoption firms.

The second and third tests on comparative accuracy of the two groups were based on D1 and D2 measures, calculated by using Equations (4) and (5) respectively. The Matched Pair Wilcoxon test on D1 measure was conducted upon the assumption that the distribution of forecast error ratios between the

Table 3. Association Between Positive and Negative *d* PE Values for Adopting and Non-Adopting firms

	Adopting Firms	*Non-Adopting Firms*	*Total*
Panel A: Comparison of 1980 and 1982 Forecasts			
Positive	75	61	136
Negative	31	45	76
Column Total	106	106	212
Chi-Square = 0.09			
Panel B: Comparison of 1980 and 1983 Forecasts			
Positive	14	23	37
Negative	23	14	37
Column Totals	37	37	74
Chi-Square = 0.24			

Table 4. Test Results of Differences in Relative Prediction Errors—Adopting versus Non-Adopting Firms

	Wilcoxon Z-Values	
	1980 and 1982 (n = 106)	*1980 and 1983 (n = 37)*
d PE	-.026	-.87
D1	-1.86	-1.22
D2	-1.55	0.92

pre- and post-adoption periods of non-adopting firms (control group) was no different than that of adopting firms (test group). The Wilcoxon test on D2 measure was conducted upon the assumption that the distribution of forecast error ratios between adopting and non-adopting firms for the post-adoption period was no different than that for the pre-adoption period. The results of Wilcoxon tests on D1 and D2 measures are contained in Table 4.

The test results relating to D1, contained in column 1 of Table 4, indicate that there was no statistically significant difference between the forecast error ratios of adopting and non-adopting firms ($Z = -1.86$). The test results on D2 are similar to those of D1 results (Table 4, Column 1) and they indicate that the forecast error ratios for the pre-adoption period were no different from those of the post-adoption period ($Z = -1.55$).

The results of all three tests on comparative analyses consistently show that there was no significant difference between the forecast errors of adopting and non-adopting firms for the post-adoption period compared to the pre-adoption period.

Additional Tests on Firms Matched on Size

It is, however, possible that the accuracy of forecasts for large and small firms may differ because analysts are able to obtain additional information from management of small firms which may enable them to make more accurate forecasts for such firms. Therefore, the comparative analysis of adopting and non-adopting firms may not be valid if their sizes are significantly different. In order to isolate the impact of firm size on the comparative analysis of adopting and non-adopting firms, tests were repeated on a subset of the sample matched on the basis of asset size in addition to the SIC code. The asset size of adopting firms and of the matched non-adopting firms was compared and the firms were included in the subset if the assets of the non-adopting firm were within 30% of the total assets of its matching adopting firms; otherwise both adopting and non-adopting firms were excluded from the subset. As a result of this procedure, only 33 firms could be matched. Thus, the subset consisted of 33 adopting and 33 non-adopting firms.

The results of the comparative analysis were similar to those reported for the total sample. There was no statistically significant difference in the forecast errors of adopting and non-adopting firms for the pre- and post-adoption periods. The results with regard to the difference in the ARPE of the pre- and post-adoption periods for both groups, however, differed from those reported for the total sample. They indicated that there was no difference in the forecast errors for the two periods for either of the groups.

Additional Tests on Firms Matched on Earnings Variability

Variability in historical earnings can be crucial for prediction of future earnings. A high variability is likely to generate more uncertainty which can make the prediction process more difficult. To minimize the effect of earnings variability on the comparison of adopting and non-adopting firms, firms were matched on the basis of earnings variability in addition to the SIC code. Earnings variability of all firms was computed on the basis of variance over the five years' period preceding the year of adoption (1977-1981). If the earnings variability was statistically different for the matched pair of adopting and non-adopting firms, both firms were dropped from the sample (*F*-value, 90% level of significance). As a result of this procedure, 56 adopting and 56 non-adopting firms formed the subset.

All tests were repeated on this subset. The results indicated that the forecast errors for the 1982 forecasts of adopting firms were higher compared to those of the 1980 forecasts, and that there was no difference in the forecast errors of the two periods for non-adopting firms. The results of the comparative analysis, however, were similar to those of the total sample and no statistically significant difference was found in the forecast errors of adopting and non-adopting firms for the pre- and post-adoption periods.

Results on Variation of Forecast Accuracy

In addition to the accuracy of forecasts, we also evaluated the variances of the forecast errors for adopting and non-adopting firms. It could be argued that comparatively smaller variation in forecast errors of adopting firms after adoption of *SFAS 52* will indicate that security analysts were able to develop better forecasts during the post-adoption period. A smaller variation represents a narrower range of forecast error which provides higher reliability to forecasts. A wider fluctuation in the forecast errors, on the other hand, does not provide the desired reliability because it would involve a higher uncertainity for their realization. This uncertainty aspect of forecasts has been especially underlined by the FASB's *Statement of Financial Accounting Concepts No. 1.*

The variances of Relative Prediction Errors (RPE) were calculated for test and control groups for the pre- and post-adoption periods. The variation of forecast errors for the test group during the post-adoption period was compared to that of the pre-adoption period using the *F*-test. Similarly, an *F*-test was also conducted on the variances of the control group forecasts. The results are contained in Table 5.

The results contained in Panel A indicate a statistically significant difference in the variances of forecast errors for the post- and pre-adoption periods, and this significant difference is evident both for adopting and non-adopting firms (*F*-values 12.43 and 7.78 respectively). For both groups, the variances are higher in the post-adoption period. The higher variances could have been caused by factors other than adoption of *SFAS 52.*

Test Results for the Period with a Lag

Further tests were conducted to examine whether a presence of the learning process could be detected. Analysts would be able to develop better forecasts after they have more experience with the new standard. The impact of the learning lag was examined by comparing the forecast errors of 1980 forecasts with those of 1983 forecasts. An analysis of the impact of a lag beyond one year could not be performed because there were no control group firms after 1983. As mentioned earlier, all firms affected by the standard adopted the standard by 1983.

Table 5. Test Results of Differences in Variances of Relative Prediction Errors—Pre- versus Post-Adoption Period

	Adopting Firms		*Non-Adopting Firms*	
	Variance of RPE	*F-Value*	*Variance of RPE*	*F-Value*
Panel A: Comparison of 1980 and 1982 Forecasts ($N = 106$)				
1980	0.65		6.53	
		12.43*		7.78*
1982	8.08		50.79	
Panel B: Comparison of 1980 and 1983 Forecasts ($N = 37$)				
1980	0.63		14.64	
		1.62		1.06
1983	1.02		15.48	

Note: * Significant at the 0.01 level.

Several firms which were included in the control group as non-adopting firms adopted *SFAS 52* in 1982. In order to be consistent with the methodology used in comparing the accuracy of 1982 forecasts with 1980 forecasts, all firms which became adopting firms in 1982, were dropped from the control group, and the respective matched firms were dropped from the test group. Consequently, the sample for this analysis consisted of 37 firms each in the test and control groups.

All tests were repeated on this reduced sample. The results of these analyses are contained in column 2 of Tables 2 and 4, and panel B of Tables 3 and 5. The results in Table 2 indicate that there was no statistically significant difference in the accuracy of 1983 forecasts compared to 1980 forecasts. This was true for the test group (Z=-0.28) as well as the control group (Z=-1.48). These results differ from the results relating to the 1982 period which indicated a difference in the forecast errors for pre- and post-adoption periods.

The results on the comparative accuracy of the two groups contained in Tables 3 and 4 are similar to those relating to the 1982 results. These results indicate that the difference between the forecast errors of adopting and non-adopting firms for the post- and pre-adoption period was not statistically significant.

The results on the forecast variances contained in Table 5 indicate that the variances of adopting firms as well as non-adopting firms were higher for 1983 forecast errors compared to 1980 forecast errors (adopting: 1.02 vs. 0.63; non-adopting: 15.48 vs. 14.64). However, the differences were not significant.

Discussion of the Results

The results presented above show that the accuracy of security analysts' 1982 forecasts for adopting as well as non-adopting firms was lower compared to that of the 1980 forecasts. Similar results were also found for the subset of the sample matched on the basis of firm size. However, the results for the subset matched on the basis of earnings variability were slightly different. The accuracy of 1982 earnings forecasts was lower only for adopting firms. Similar to the results of the accuracy of forecast errors, the results on the variances of forecast errors for the total sample indicated that the variances for 1982 forecast errors were higher compared to the 1980 forecast errors both for adopting and non-adopting firms.

The deterioration in the accuracy and variances of forecast errors during the post-adoption period both for adopting and non-adopting firms was probably due to the impact of external factors, such as changes in economic environments. But the results relating to the subset matched on the basis of variability in earnings, indicating the deterioration in the accuracy of forecasts for adopting firms only, could have been due to adoption of *SFAS 52*. This impact was, however, temporary. The 1983 results indicated that the accuracy of earnings forecasts of the total sample as well as subsets of the sample, was no different than that of 1980. Therefore, even if the 1982 deterioration in the accuracy of earnings forecasts was caused by the uncertainty resulting from the adoption of the standard, it was eliminated in 1983.

A clear indication of the impact of *SFAS 52* on the earnings forecasts, however, would come from the results of comparative analyses of adopting and non-adopting firms for the pre-and post-adoption periods. The results contained in tables 3 and 4 indicate that there was no significant change in the accuracy of forecasts of adopting and non-adopting firms during the post-adoption period compared to pre-adoption period. The results of comparative analyses on all three measures, namely, d PE, D1, and D2 consistently show that the change in accuracy from 1980 to 1982 for adopting firms was no different than the change in accuracy for non-adopting firms. The results of comparative analyses on 1983 forecasts also support these findings. Furthermore, the results on the subsets matched on firm size and earnings variability confirm the findings of the comparative analyses.

In view of these findings, we cannot reject the null hypothesis that there is no difference in the accuracy of security analysts' forecasts for the post-adoption period compared to the pre-adoption period. These results, therefore, suggest that the adoption of *SFAS 52* has not significantly improved the quality of earnings in such a way that enabled security analysts to develop more accurate earnings forecasts.

SUMMARY AND CONCLUSION

This paper has presented the findings of a study that examined the impact of *SFAS 52,* "Foreign Currency Translation," on the accuracy of security analysts' forecasts. The test group consisted of 106 analyst forecasts for firms that adopted *SFAS 52* in 1981. The matched group consisted of 106 forecasts for firms that did not adopt the standard in 1981 but were affected by the standard and subsequently adopted it.

The impact of the standard was first examined by comparing the accuracy of forecasts for the post-adoption period with the pre-adoption period, and the statistical significance of the results was tested by using the non-parametric Matched Pair Wilcoxon test. The test results indicated that the accuracy of forecasts of adopting as well as of non-adopting firms was lower for the post-adoption period than for the pre-adoption period. The results of the comparative analysis, however, did not indicate any difference in the change of accuracy from pre-adoption period to post-adoption period between adopting and non-adopting firms. The tests on variances in forecast errors, on subsets of the sample matched on firm size and earnings variability, and on a sample for an extended period, provided similar results. The results of this study, therefore, indicate that there was no significant impact of *SFAS 52* on the accuracy or variability of security analysts' earnings forecasts.

The above results, however, need to be interpreted with caution because of the limitation of the study. The study could not isolate the impact of the percentage of foreign operations in total earnings because this information could not be obtained from any source.

ACKNOWLEDGMENTS

The authors gratefully acknowledge helpful comments and suggestions from the editor and reviewer. We also thank Larry Brown, Yaw Mensah, and William Salowe for their helpful comments on earlier drafts of this paper.

REFERENCES

American Institute of Certified Public Accountants, *Accounting Trends and Techniques,* Vols. 35-38 [AICPA, 1981-1984].

Basi, B.A., K.J. Carey, and R.D. Twark, "A Comparison of the Accuracy of Corporate and Security Analysts' Forecasts of Earnings," *The Accounting Review* [April 1976], pp. 244-254.

Brown, L.D., "Accounting Changes and the Accuracy of Analysts' Earnings Forecasts," *Journal of Accounting Research* [Autumn 1983], pp. 432-443.

Brown, L.D. and M.S. Rozeff, "The Superiority of Analyst Forecasts as Measures of Expectations: Evidence from Earnings," *Journal of Finance* [March 1978], pp. 1-16.

________. "Adapting Expectations, Time Series Models and Analyst Forecast Revision," *Journal of Accounting Research* [Autumn 1979], pp. 341-351.

Collins, W.A., and W.S. Hopwood, "A Multivariate Analysis of Annual Earnings Forecasts Generated from Quarterly Forecasts of Financial Analysts and Univariate Time-Series Models," *Journal of Accounting Research* [Autumn 1980], pp. 490-506.

Conover, W.J., *Practical Nonparametric Statistics* [Wiley, 1980].

Copeland, R.M., and R. Marioni, "Executives' Forecasts of Earnings Per Share Versus Forecasts of Naive Models," *Journal of Business* [October 1972], pp. 497-512.

Evans, T.G., W.R. Folks, Jr., and M. Jilling, *The Impact of Statement of Financial Accounting Standards No. 8 on the Foreign Exchange Risk Management Practices of American Multinationals: An Economic Impact Study* [FASB, 1978].

Financial Accounting Standards Board, *Statement of Financial Accounting Standard No. 8,* "Accounting for the Translation of Foreign Currency Transactions and Foreign Currency Standards" [FASB, October 1975].

________, *Statement of Financial Accounting Concepts No. 1,* "Objectives of Financial Reporting of Business Enterprises" [FASB, 1978].

________, *Statement of Financial Accounting Standards No. 52* "Foreign Currency Translation" [FASB, December 1981].

Jaggi, B., "Further Evidence on the Accuracy of Management's Forecasts vis-à-vis Analysts' Forecasts," *The Accounting Review* [January 1980], pp. 96-101.

Mansfield, E., *Statistics for Business and Economics* [Norton, 1980].

Massaro, V.G., "Corporate Experience with FASB Statement No. 8," *Conference Board Information Bulletin, No. 40* [June 1978].

Morsicato, H.G., *Currency Translation and Performance Evaluation in Multinationals* [UMI Research Press, 1980].

Richmond, S.B., *Statistical Analysis* [Ronald Press, 1964].

Ruland, W., "The Accuracy of Forecasts by Management and by Financial Analysts," *The Accounting Review* [April 1978], pp. 439-447.

Shank, J.K., J.F. Dillard, and R.J. Murdock, *Assessing the Impact of FASB 8: A Research Study* [Financial Executives Research Foundation, 1979].

Silhan, P.A., "Simulated Mergers of Existent Autonomous Firms: A New Approach to Segmentation Research," *Journal of Accounting Research* [Spring 1982], pp. 256-262.

Theil, H., *Applied Economic Forecasting* [North Holland, 1966].

FASB STATEMENT 52, AN ACCOUNTING POLICY INTERVENTION:

U.S.-BASED MULTINATIONAL CORPORATE PREENACTMENT LOBBYING BEHAVIOR

Robert J. Kirsch, Thomas G. Evans, and Timothy S. Doupnik

ABSTRACT

This study examines the accounting policy intervention process from the perspective of U.S.-based multinational corporate lobbying prior to FASB *Statement of Financial Accounting Standards No. 52,* "Foreign Currency Translation" (*SFAS 52*). The formulation of an appropriate foreign exchange risk management strategy depends on how corporate management defines and measures its exposure to changes in foreign currency values. If management's objective is primarily economic, protection against economic exposure is a first priority. If management's objective is primarily accounting, it will give priority to protection against transaction and translation exposure. Consequently, firms

Advances in International Accounting, Vol. 3, pages 155-171.

ISBN: 1-55938-078-0

whose primary objectives are accounting should behave differently from those with primarily economic objectives in lobbying for/against specific accounting standards. These differences should be both observable and quantifiable. This study employs data from the 1984 FASB-sponsored Evans and Doupnik survey of corporate foreign exchange risk management, COMPUSTAT tapes, correspondence with FASB, and corporate financial statements and proxies. Multiple discriminant analysis, analysis of variance on ranks, and contingency tables are employed to investigate research hypotheses concerning firms' lobbying behavior. The results suggest there is a relationship between a firm's basic objective and its propensity to lobby FASB; smaller multinational firms and firms *without* a management compensation scheme were more likely to lobby over *SFAS 52*.

INTRODUCTION

Accounting policy intervention constitutes the government or quasi-government imposition of a financial accounting standard on domestic and foreign corporations operating and reporting in the United States. We examined the accounting policy intervention process from the perspective of preestablishment multinational corporate (MNC) lobbying effort. We focused specifically upon U.S.-based corporate lobbying effort prior to establishment of *Statement of Financial Accounting Standards No 52,* "Foreign Currency Translation" (*SFAS 52*). The research question of interest is whether firms with accounting objectives were more likely to lobby the FASB over *SFAS 52* than firms with economic objectives, since *SFAS 52* as proposed and ultimately adopted could have a major impact on firms' accounting net income by removing translation gains and losses from the income statement and reconstituting them as a separate balance sheet owners' equity component. *SFAS 52* changes the calculation of net income without causing any substantive change in future cash flows; consequently firms with accounting objectives should be more interested in it.

A limited number of studies have explored lobbying efforts of management to influence accounting standards. Watts and Zimmerman [1978] explored those factors influencing management's attitudes towards accounting standards which are likely to affect corporate lobbying on accounting standards. Certain factors are expected to affect a firm's cash flows and in turn are affected by accounting standards. They focused on taxes, regulation, management compensation plans, bookkeeping costs, and political costs. They examined corporate submissions to the FASB's discussion memorandum on general price level adjustments. They found that large firms which would experience reduced earnings due to the changed accounting standard favored the change. All other firms opposed the change if the additional bookkeeping costs justified the cost of lobbying.

In a follow-up study, Dhaliwal [1981] examined a representative sample of the 120 position papers submitted in response to the FASB discussion memorandum on the issue of accounting for interest costs. He found that because of the protective covenants that usually exist in loan agreements, firms with higher leverage oppose an accounting standard which would decrease their reported income or equity, or increase the volatility of reported earnings.

Our study examined corporate submissions on the exposure draft and the revised exposure draft dealing with foreign currency translation that became *SFAS 52* and the data obtained by Evans and Doupnik [1986] in their FASB-sponsored survey of corporate foreign exchange risk management practices and policies. It employed univariate and multivariate techniques to test a series of research hypotheses on corporate lobbying of FASB over the proposed foreign currency translation standard. The aim of the study was to examine for a systematic relationship between the character of a firm's basic objective and its lobbying effort in order to contribute to a better understanding of the accounting policy intervention process. The independent variables were the firm's basic objective, the debt-to-equity ratio, the ratios sales from foreign operations to total sales, net income from foreign operations to total net income, and net assets in foreign operations to total net assets, and the presence (absence) of a management compensation scheme. The results suggest that there is a relationship between a firm's basic objective and its propensity to lobby FASB, that smaller multinational firms and firms *without* a management compensation scheme were more likely to do so over *SFAS 52*.

This paper examines the accounting standard setting process in a systems context. Systems theory provided a framework in which to examine the accounting intervention process from an extrafirm perspective. Since systems theory does not provide insight into the internal decision-making processes within the firm, agency theory is reviewed for its theoretical contribution to understanding intrafirm behavior.

Six lobbying effort hypotheses were developed and empirically tested to probe for a systematic relationship between the character of a firm's basic objective and its propensity to lobby FASB over *SFAS 52*.

THE STANDARD SETTING PROCESS

The accounting policy intervention process may be considered in the systems context. Accounting standards, whether set by the U.S. Congress, the Securities and Exchange Commission (SEC), or the Financial Accounting Standards Board (FASB), constitute policy interventions (inputs) into the MNC. The firm may anticipate such standards and attempt to influence them (lobbying), it may react to them once established, or it may do both.

The manner in which MNCs react to a proposed accounting standard, as well as to a standard already promulgated, may generate feedback externally which ultimately may influence the standard setting authority to revise the standard. Since its esablishment in 1973, the Financial Accounting Standards Board has been the primary financial accounting standard setting body for U.S.-based firms.

Because the FASB operates in the sunshine, as an element of standard setting due process firms are encouraged to communicate with (lobby) the Board with respect to both proposed standards and standards already established. Such communication is taken into account by the FASB in the drafting and imposition of a new standard, as well as in the revision and/or replacement of an existing standard.

The way in which a firm responds to a new standard may depend upon the objectives of corporate management. Management objectives may be regarded as either accounting-based—concerned with maximizing accounting net income—or economic-based—concerned with maximizing the present value of expected future net cash flows. While it is recognized that some mix of objectives, accounting and economic, is most likely to be found in practice, it seems reasonable that firms' objectives may be characterized according to their primary orientation—primarily accounting versus primarily economic.

An accounting standard, proposed or established, may be perceived by a firms' management as having corporate behavioral consequences, either desirable or undesirable, which may have significant economic impact on the firm. Consequently, the firm may seek to influence the outcome of the accounting standard setting process in order to achieve the desired post-enactment corporate behavioral consequences. It is important to have a clear understanding of this relationship if the accounting policy intervention process is to function most effectively.

The formulation of an appropriate foreign exchange risk management (FERM) strategy depends on how corporate management defines and measures its exposure to changes in currency values. As Robock and Simmonds [1983, p. 540] noted: "(1) if management's goal is to maximize long-run stockholder wealth, i.e., management's objective is primarily economic, protection against economic exposure is a first priority; and (2) if management feels its performance is judged on short-term results, i.e., management's objective is primarily accounting, it will give priority to protection against transaction and translation exposure." Accounting (translation) exposure results because any foreign item that is translated into dollars for financial reporting purposes at the current rate may result in a foreign exchange gain or loss. If the exposed assets exceed the exposed liabilities, asset exposure occurs. If the exposed liabilities exceed the exposed assets, liability exposure occurs. Accounting risk refers to the possibility of exchange gains and losses resulting from balance sheet exposures.

Reacting to economic exposure—the impact of exchange rate fluctuations on the long-term value of expected after-tax net cash flows—can require strategic changes that encompass nearly all decision areas, including diversification of financing, changed production setting, and sourcing. Techniques to minimize accounting exposure center around hedging. Hedging means entering into a contract to buy (sell) foreign currency at a future fixed rate; it provides defense against the risk of loss from a change in foreign exchange rates.

The various forms of exchange risk have different implications for the MNC. Accounting risk of foreign assets and liabilities presents operational problems which can be covered (hedged) at an implicit or explicit cost to the firm. Economic risk of net assets cannot be covered, although it may be reduced through a variety of diversification techniques [Siegel, 1983, pp. 16-17].

Thus, firms whose primary objectives are accounting should behave differently from those with primarily economic objectives in lobbying for/against *SFAS 52*. These differences should be both observable and quantifiable.

IMPLICATIONS FOR MANAGEMENT BEHAVIOR

The systems framework does not provide insight into the internal decision making processes which convert those inputs into outputs. Agency theory suggests a way to gain such insight.

In agency theory, the firm is regarded as a "set of contracts" between principal(s) and agent(s) [Fama, 1980]. The principals engage the agent(s) to perform some service on their behalf which requires the delegation of some decision making authority to the agent(s) [Jensen and Meckling, 1976]. Members of the firm are assumed to be motivated solely by self-interest.

Owners and creditors experience more confidence in corporate management which is able to report stable earnings rather than earnings which fluctuate considerably. By making decisions that lead to a smoother pattern of earnings, management may increase the perceived value of its services. This may translate into increased job security, salary increases, enhanced management compensation packages, and the like. Thus, management may increase its own welfare by engaging in income smoothing behavior [Lambert, 1984].

Thus, in the principal/agent relationship, the agents serve the principals through self-interested activity. Agency theory concentrates on the principal/agent relationship while largely ignoring environmental factors, such as governmental and/or quasigovernmental regulation, which may influence agent behavior. Systems theory allows the incorporation of awareness of environmental impact upon the principal/agent relationship.

LOBBYING EFFORT HYPOTHESES

The independent variables under consideration were the firm's basic objective, the debt-to-equity ratio, the ratios sales from foreign operations to total sales, net income from foreign operations to total net income, and net assets in foreign operations to total net assets, and the presence (absence) of a management compensation scheme. These variables were incorporated into a discriminant model which was employed to test the lobbying effort hypotheses.

The following research hypotheses were evaluated:

H_1. Proportionately more firms with accounting based-objectives lobbied the FASB in support of proposed accounting standard *SFAS 52* than firms with economic-based objectives.

H_2. Firms supporting the adoption of *SFAS 52,* which permits the inclusion of translation gains and losses in equity, had higher debt/equity ratios.

H_3. Firms supporting the adoption of *SFAS 52* had a higher percentage of sales from foreign operations.

H_4. Firms supporting the adoption of *SFAS 52* had a higher percentage of net income from foreign operations.

H_5. Firms supporting the adoption of *SFAS 52* had a higher percentage of net assets in foreign operations.

H_6. Proportionately more firms supporting *SFAS 52* had management compensation plans tied to accounting data.

The firm's basic objective was included because accounting-based firms seemed more likely to lobby in favor of *SFAS 52* due to its income smoothing implications than economic-based firms. Furthermore, if the basic objective of corporate management is grounded on accounting measures, such as net income, and the FASB proposes to change the method of calculating that measure, there should be observable proportionately more lobbying effort by those MNCs (1) which would be required to change accounting methods, and (2) which pursue accounting-based objectives. On the other hand, the behavior of management, whose basic objective is defined in terms of economic results, should be less affected by a required change in accounting methods.

Debt/equity was selected because creditors focus on this ratio and loan covenants often specify that a firm must maintain a certain debt/equity level. By requiring inclusion of translation losses in equity, *FASB 52* could adversely affect this ratio and cause violation of loan covenants. Thus, firms with high debt/equity ratios would be likely to oppose *SFAS 52* if they perceived that it would result in a higher debt/equity ratio.

The ratios sales from foreign operations to total sales and net income from foreign operations to total net income were chosen as related indices of the ultimate contribution of foreign operations to consolidated net income, which capture the impact of transactions upon consolidated net income. The ratio net assets in foreign operations to total net assets was chosen as an index of translation impact upon the consolidated balance sheet. Thus, these ratios seem to be appropriate indices of corporate concern for and/or interest in financial accounting standards which affect the measurement and reporting of foreign currency transactions and translation.

The presence of a management compensation scheme seemed a good predictor of pro *SFAS 52* lobbying effort. Given its potential to reduce income volatility and facilitate income smoothing, *SFAS 52* was likely to be positively regarded by top corporate officers. *SFAS 52's* smoothing potential, its promise of enhancing management's perception by monitoring principals, and its potential for improving management's incentive compensation seemed to suggest that managers of firms with executive compensation packages would be inclined, in their own self interest, to lobby FASB in favor of the standard.

Therefore, it should be possible to discriminate between MNCs which pursue primarily an accounting objective and those which pursue an economic one in terms of their pre-enactment lobbying; and between those with management compensation plans and those without: and between those with larger debt/equity ratios and foreign operations and those with smaller ones.

One limitation in testing the above hypotheses was that much of the data employed in the analysis was gathered in 1984, but the lobbying efforts occurred in 1980-1981. This necessitated that a simplifying assumption be made: firms involved in lobbying the FASB have undergone no major changes in (1) basic objective (accounting or economic), (2) percentages of sales and net income from foreign operations, or (3) percentages of net assets in foreign operations since late 1980.

SOURCES OF DATA ON FIRMS

Most of the data analyzed in this study are a subset of the responses obtained by Evans and Doupnik [1986] in their FASB-sponsored questionnaire survey of foreign exchange risk management practices. The survey, conducted from September to December 1984, yielded usable responses from 167 U.S.-based multinational corporations. The MNCs surveyed were predominantly *Fortune 500* firms (145 companies or 86.8%).

The Evans and Doupnik data were supplemented with relevant data from the 1980 COMPUSTAT tape, corporate financial statements and proxies, and corporate correspondence with the FASB. Data to calculate the debt-to-equity ratio was obtained from the COMPUSTAT tape. The corporate financial statements and proxies were examined to determined the presence (absence) of a management compensation scheme, and to supplement the COMPUSTAT tape when specific MNCs were not included on the tape. Corporate correspondence with the FASB was examined to learn the lobbying position of each MNC in the sample.

From the full set of 167 MNCs in the E&D data base, a subset was chosen based upon completeness of data, comparability of firms, and unambiguous responses. To ensure greater comparability, the MNCs included in the sample were *Fortune 500* firms. Any firms whose foreign operations changed dramatically since adoption of *SFAS 52* were eliminated.

In addition, the sample was restricted to those MNCs which commented on the August 28, 1980, FASB Exposure Draft, the June 30, 1981, FASB Revised Exposure Draft, or both, and also responded to the Evans and Doupnik's survey. The sample was further limited to those MNCs whose FERM objective, accounting or economic, could be inferred unambiguously from their completed E&D questionnaire. As some corporate responses to questions regarding objectives left the firm's primary goal open to conjecture, such respondents were dropped from the sample.

Inferred Objective

Evans and Doupnik's question I-1 (see Figure 1) listed seven possible objectives of foreign exchange risk management.[1] Respondents were asked to evaluate the importance of each objective to their their firm on a 5-point Likert scale from "1=very important" to "5 =unimportant." Three of the objectives—b, f, and g—are clearly concerned with managing accounting risk, while objective d deals with economic risk. The remaining three objectives are ambiguous in terms of the accounting/economic risk dichotomy.

Evans and Doupnik's question III.8.e. asked the respondents to indicate which exposure measure(s) their firms developed for managerial use: economic, accounting, operations, or other.

If the following conditions were met, a respondent's basic FERM objective was inferred to be the management of *accounting* risk: (1) at least one of the three accounting objectives was rated "1" or "2"; and (2) either the economic risk objective was assigned a lower priority; or an accounting risk measure was calculated.

Management of *economic* risk was inferred as the firm's basic FERM objective if the economic goal was rated either "1" or "2," and either two of the three accounting objectives received lower priority, or the firm calculated an economic measure of exposure.

I. 1. Please provide your evaluation of the current importance to your firm of the following possible objectives of exchange risk management by circling the appropriate number on a scale of 1 (very important) to 5 (unimportant).

a. Protection of the dollar value of foreign assets.

very important 1 2 3 4 5 unimportant

b. Reduction of transaction-based foreign exchange losses to the lowest level possible.

very important 1 2 3 4 5 unimportant

c. Acceptance of additional foreign exchange risk in the short run if the potential for transaction-based foreign exchange gains exists.

very important 1 2 3 4 5 unimportant

d. Protection of the dollar value of future foreign currency cash flows.

very important 1 2 3 4 5 unimportant

e. Avoidance of the adverse impact of transaction-based, translation, and remeasurement-based gains and losses on price of firm's stock.

very important 1 2 3 4 5 unimportant

f. Reduction of remeasurement-based foreign exchange losses to the lowest level possible.

very important 1 2 3 4 5 unimportant

g. Reduction of the impact of exchange rate changes on the cumulative translation account in equity to the lowest level possible.

very important 1 2 3 4 5 unimportant

III. 8. e. Which of the following exposure measures do you develop for managerial use?

[ ] An economic exposure measure (describe) ____________

[ ] An accounting based exposure measure (describe) ____________

[ ] Operation's exposure in third currencies ____________

[ ] Other, please describe ____________

Source: Evans and Doupnik [1986, pp. 104-105, 111].

Figure 1. Evans and Doupnik's Questions Used To Infer Firm Objective

An MNC's inferred basic objective was regarded as *indeterminate,* and the firm was excluded from the sample, if: (1) the economic and accounting objectives were all rated "3" or lower; or (2) the economic objective was rated the highest, but the company did not calculate an economic exposure measure, while it did calculate an accounting exposure measure.

Sample Selection

Evidence of lobbying can be found in the letters of U.S.-based MNCs in response to the Exposure Draft of August 28, 1980, and the Revised Exposure Draft of June 30, 1981, which preceeded *SFAS 52.* The letters were examined to determine each firm's position on these drafts. Investigation of these letters indicated that corporate positions were usually clearly stated. The total number of MNCs lobbying and responding to the Evans and Doupnik questionnaire was 92. A review of the submission letters indicated that 29 MNCs responded to the Exposure Draft, 17 MNCs responded to the Revised Exposure Draft, and 46 MNCs responded to the Exposure Draft and the Revised Exposure Draft. The most recent position taken by MNCs which responded to both the Exposure Draft and the Revised Exposure Draft but shifted their position was used to determine their support for, or opposition to, *SFAS 52.* MNCs whose lobbying position could not be clearly determined were classified as ambiguous and were dropped from the sample.

From the total 92 MNCs, the basic objective, accounting or economic, could be inferred for 72; 37 were accounting-based, and 35 were economic-based. Determination of the lobbying position of these 72 firms indicated 45 for *SFAS 52* and 27 against. These 72 MNCs constituted the observations of this study.

METHODOLOGY TO TEST LOBBYING HYPOTHESES

Univariate analyses of each hypothesis were made to test its implications and multivariate analyses were made to test the overall discriminatory power of the entire set of discriminating variables.

Hypotheses 1 and 3 through 6 were tested by applying a chi-square test to the data of contingency tables. The level of significance was 0.10 unless otherwise specified.

Hypothesis 2 was tested by performing analysis of variance on ranks and certain rank scores of a response across a one-way classification.[2] To test Hypothesis 2, debt/equity was ranked by lobbying effort.

In addition to the above tests, multiple discriminant analysis was used to examine the overall discriminatory power of the entire set of variables. This was done because it was theorized that there exists a systematic relationship between the individual variables which would make it possible to differentiate (1) between MNCs with accounting-based and economic-based objectives, and (2) between MNCs which lobbied FASB in favor of, or opposition to, *SFAS 52.*

The model discriminated according to whether lobbying efforts were for, or against; it took the form:

$$D = B_0 + B_1\,BASICOBJ + B_2DTOE + B_3SALE83 + B_4NETIN83 + B_5NETASS83 + B_6MANCOMP$$

where:

D	=	discriminant score based on lobbying position	
B_0	=	constant term	
BASICOBJ	=	inferred FERM objective	0 = accounting-based 1 = economic-based
DTOE	=	debt/equity ratio	
SALE83	=	percentage of foreign annual sales to total sales (Evans' and Doupnik's question VII.3.a)	0 = below 20% 1 = between 20-40% 2 = above 40%
NETIN83	=	percentage of foreign net income to total net income (Evans' and Doupnik's question VII.3.b)	0 = below 20% 1 = between 20-40% 2 = above 40%
NETASS83	=	percentage of foreign net assets to total net assets (Evans' and Doupnik's question VII.3.c)	0 = below 20% 1 = between 20-40% 2 = above 40%
MANCOMP	=	presence of management compensation plan based on accounting data	0 = yes 1 = no

Each variable in the model was keyed to the above six lobbying hypotheses. Each variable was chosen for its hypothesized contribution to predicting MNC lobbying behavior.

Univariate Tests of Lobbying Hypotheses

The results of the univariate tests of Hypotheses 1 and 3 through 6 indicate that there were two statistically significant lobbying effort cross tabulations, *NETIN83* and *MANCOMP*. The remainder of the cross tabulations were not statistically significant at or below the cut-off level of 0.10 (see Table 1).

Note, however, that there was a relationship between basic objective, accounting-based or economic-based, and lobbying effort, pro or con, significant at the 0.161 level. Accounting-based firms (57.78%), as hypothesized, were more likely to lobby FASB in favor of *SFAS 52* than

Table 1. Lobbying Effort Cross Tabulation Results

Variable	*Hypothesis*	*Chi-square Value*	*Significance Probability*	*Accept (Reject) Null*
BASICOBJ	1	1.961	0.161	accept
SALE83	3	0.566	0.753	accept
NETIN83	4	6.508	0.039	(reject)
NETASS83	5	1.270	0.530	accept
MANCOMP	6	4.510	0.034	(reject)

Table 2. Lobbying by Basic Classification

	Basic Classification	
Lobbying Position	*Accounting-based*	*Economic-based*
For	26	19
Against	11	16

Significance probability: 0.161

Table 3. Lobbying by Foreign Net Income to Total Net Income

	Percent of Foreign Net Income to Total Net Income		
Lobbying	*< 20%*	*20-40%*	*> 40%*
For	23	11	9
Against	7	14	4

Frequency missing: 4
Significance probability: 0.039

economic-based firms (42.22%) (see Table 2). More than two-thirds of the accounting-based firms lobbied in favor of *SFAS 52;* while economic-based firms were nearly equally divided on the issue.

There was a statistically significant *inverse* relationship between lobbying effort and net income from foreign operations. Firms which lobbied the FASB in favor of *SFAS 52* were more likely to earn a smaller proportion of their net income from foreign operations (53.49% reported less than 20% from foreign operations) than firms which lobbied against *SFAS 52* (28.0%). This was opposite to the hypothesized direction (Hypothesis 4) (see Table 3).

Agency theory would suggest that the higher the net income from foreign operations the more likely the firm would have been to lobby on behalf of

Table 4. Lobbying by Management Compensation Scheme

	Management Compensation Scheme	
Lobbying	*Yes*	*No*
For	17	25
Against	18	9

Frequency missing = 3
Significance probability: 0.034

Table 5. Analysis of Ranks: Debt/Equity Ranked by Lobbying Effort

Lobbying	*Number*	*Mean Debt/Equity*
For	27	1.62
Against	46	1.07

Kruskal-Wallis chi-square approximation: 0.07
Degrees of freedom: 2
Significance probability: 0.7935

SFAS 52 since total net income would likewise be higher, ceteris paribus. Perhaps the income smoothing potential of *SFAS 52* was of greater concern to smaller firms than to firms with a larger proportionate share of foreign earnings to total net earnings. It may be that the larger firms had a relatively low cost hedging program in place compared to the smaller firms. Thus, revision of the prior *SFAS 8* may have been less attractive to them.

There was a statistically significant *inverse* relationship between lobbying effort and management compensation schemes. Proportionately more firms (73.53%) which had *no* management compensation scheme lobbied the FASB in favor of *SFAS 52* than those (48.57%) with a management compensation scheme. This was *not* in the hypothesized direction (Hypothesis 6) and does not conform with the earlier findings of Watts and Zimmerman [1978] and Dhaliwal [1982] (see Table 4). This phenomenon calls for an explanation. Perhaps firms without a management compensation scheme felt greater freedom to lobby FASB in favor of *SFAS 52*; the management of such firms could not easily have been accused of conflict of interest if they lobbied in favor of *SFAS 52*. Or, perhaps, the method for determining whether there was such a scheme by examining corporate financial reports and proxies was flawed; thus a number of firms might have been misclassified.

To test Hypothesis 2, debt/equity was ranked by lobbying effort, and a nonparametric one-way analysis of ranks was performed. As can be seen from Table 5, firms supporting *SFAS 52* had lower debt/equity ratios than those opposing it. This was *opposite* to the hypothesized direction. However, these results were not statistically significant. Thus, little support was given to Hypothesis 2.

Table 6. Lobbying Model Discriminated by Lobbying Effort Classification Summary for Holdout Sample (14 Firms)

Actual FASB Lobbying Position	Classified: For	Classified: Against
For	10	1
Against	0	3

(Percent correctly classified: 92.9%
PCC (Probability Chance Criterion):* 71.8%

Note: * Probability chance criterion = $P^2 + Q^2$
where:
P = proportion in group one
Q = proportion in group two

Table 7. MDA With Increasingly Larger Holdout Sample Model Discriminated by Lobbying Effort

Classification Sample Size	Holdout Sample Size	Correctly Classified: For N	For %	Against N	Against %	Percent of Probability Chance Criterion	Percent Correctly Classified
54	18	11	81.8	7	71.4	52.4	77.7
50	22	13	86.7	4	57.1	60.2	77.3
44	28	16	80.0	6	75.0	54.0	78.6

Multiple Discriminant Analyses of Lobbying Hypotheses

In addition to the above analyses, multiple discriminant analyses (MDAs) were made to evaluate total discriminating power of the variables. Priors were specified as proportional in this study.[3] In order to avoid upwardly biasing the prediction accuracy of the classification results, a holdout sample technique was employed. Fifty-eight classification observations were randomly chosen and used to develop a discriminant function. This function was saved and employed to classify the observations held out of the original data set.

In order to determine whether to employ a linear or a quadratic classification procedure, a test to determine if the respective groups had equal or unequal dispersions was made. The results of the test indicated unequal dispersion matrices. Therefore, the quadratic procedure was employed.

Of the holdout sample classified with the lobbying effort discriminant function, 1 MNC was misclassified out of 14: 1 for was classified against. The percentage of observations (or MNCs) correctly classified, was 92.9 percent compared to 71.8 percent expected by chance, which is given by the probability chance criterion (PCC) (see Table 6).[4]

To test whether the lobbying effort classification results (holdout sample size 14) were representative, a series of MDAs were made with different size holdout samples (see Table 7). The percentage correctly classified ranged from 77.3 percent to 78.6 percent, with an average of 78.0 percent, compared to 55.5 percent expected by chance, for an average improvement of 22.5 percentage points. Thus, the individual variables when combined in the discriminant model have moderate predictive power.

SUMMARY OF RESULTS

Univariate analyses of the individual variables in the lobbying models produced mixed results. There appears to be a weak relationship between basic classification and lobbying position.

Only two of the six variables hypothesized to effect lobbying behavior with regard to *SFAS 52* were found to be statistically significant, *NETIN83* and *MANCOMP,* at the 0.10 level. Agency theory suggests that management of firms with management compensation schemes might be expected to have lobbied heavily in support of the implementation of *SFAS 52* by FASB. However, the results of the present study indicate the opposite. Firms with management compensation schemes lobbied FASB in favor of *SFAS 52* proportionately less than those without a management compensation scheme.

Agency theory would suggest that the higher the net income from foreign operations the more likely the firm would have been to lobby on behalf of *SFAS 52* since total net income would likewise be higher, ceteris paribus. However, the results of this study show a statistically significant inverse relationship between lobbying position and net income from foreign operations.

Multiple discriminant analysis did indicate that it was possible to discriminate between firms which lobbied for or against *SFAS 52* using the variables hypothesized to be systematically related. The six variable model had moderate predictive power when tested on the holdout samples. It averaged 22.5 percentage points above what would have been expected purely by chance.

The validity of the results from this study may be subject to the following limitations. *SFAS 52* lobbying effort patterns may not be generalizable to other accounting policy interventions. The method employed to classify firms as accounting-based or economic-based may have resulted in some misclassifications. Important relevant variables may have been omitted from the discriminant model. Since the sample was non-random, results may not be generalizable to other MNCs.

CONCLUSIONS

The results of the present study contradict agency theory and previously published agency theory results. Contrary to expectations and previous agency theory literature, the presence of a management compensation scheme did not serve as a predictor of pro firm lobbying support for an accounting standard (*SFAS 52*) which, due to its clear impact on consolidated corporate net income, should have been seen by management as a direct index of their stewardship. *SFAS 52's* income smoothing potential could hardly have escaped their attention. Yet, firms which had no management compensation scheme lobbied in favor of *SFAS 52*.

A finite set of hypothetical variables cannot discriminate very well between accounting-based and economic-based firms and between pro and con lobbying positions. Apparently lobbying is a function of some other variables which have not yet been discussed in the literature. This suggests that there is need for a new theory to explain why firms lobby the FASB over proposed financial accounting standards.

NOTES

1. The following classification scheme is adapted from McMath [1985].
2. This is a nonparametric procedure for testing that the distribution of a variable has the same location parameter across different groups.
3. Eisenbeis and Avery [1972] have demonstrated that the assessment of the classification rules' performance depends heavily upon the proper selection of the a priori probabilities as well as upon the sample to be classified. Setting priors proportional to sample proportions involves making the assumptions that the sample proportions are similar to the population proportions, and that the proportions of observations in each group reflect the 'true' a priori probabilities in the total population.
4. The probability chance criterion is a term used to describe the classification results to be expected merely by chance. It is calculated by summing the squared proportions of the relevant groups in the classification matrix.

REFERENCES

Dhaliwal, D.S., "Some Economic Determinants of Management Lobbying for Alternative Methods of Accounting: Evidence from the Accounting for Interest Case" *Journal of Business, Finance and Accounting* 9, 2 [1982], pp. 255-265.

Easton, D. *A Systems Analysis of Political Life* [University of Chicago Press, 1979].

Eisenbeis, R.A., and R.B. Avery, *Discriminant Analysis and Classification Procedures: Theory and Applications* [Lexington Books, 1972].

Evans, T.G., and T.S. Doupnik, *Research Report: Foreign Exchange Risk Management under Statement 52* [FASB, 1986].

Fama, E.F. "Agency Problems and the Theory of the Firm," *Journal of Political Economy* 88, [April 1980], pp. 288-307.

Financial Accounting Standards Board, *Statement of Financial Accountant Standards No. 8,* "Accounting for the Translation of Foreign Currency Transactions and Foreign Currency Financial Statements" [FASB, October 1975].

________, *Exposure Draft,* "Foreign Currency Translation" [FASB, August 28, 1980].

________, *Exposure Draft (Revised),* "Foreign Currency Translation" [FASB, June 30, 1981].

________, *Statement of Financial Accounting Standards No. 52,* "Foreign Currency Translation" [FASB, December 1981].

Fortune [May 2, 1983].

Hair, J.F., Jr. et al., *Multivariate Data Analysis: With Readings* [Macmillan, 1984].

Jensen, M.C., and W.H. Meckling, "Theory of the Firm: Managerial Behavior, Agency Costs and Ownership Structure," *Journal of Financial Economics* 3 [1976], pp. 305-60.

Johnson, R.A., and D.W. Wichern, *Applied Multivariate Statistical Analysis* [Prentice-Hall, 1982].

Kirsch, R.J., *SFAS No. 52, An Accounting Policy Intervention: U.S. -Based Multinational Corporate Pre-Enactment Lobbying Behavior and Post-Enactment Reaction,* Ph.D. dissertation, University of South Carolina [1986].

Lambert, R.A., "Income Smoothing as Rational Equilibrium Behavior" *The Accounting Review* 59, 4 [October 1984], pp. 604-618.

McMath, H.K. *The Impact of Mandated Accounting Changes on Management Decisions: The Statement No 8 Episode,* Ph.D. dissertation, University of South Carolina [1985].

Robock, S.H., and K. Simmonds, *International Business and Multinational Enterprises* [Irwin, 1983].

Siegel, M.H., *Foreign Exchange Risk and Direct Foreign Investment* [UMI Research Press, 1983].

Watts, R.L., and J.L. Zimmerman, "Towards a Positive Theory of the Determination of Accounting Standards" *The Accounting Review* 53, 1 [January 1978], pp. 112-134.

EARNINGS VOLATILITY AND THE CORPORATE ADOPTION DECISION ON FASB STATEMENT NO. 52:

AN EMPIRICAL ANALYSIS

Gordian A. Ndubizu

ABSTRACT

This paper examines the relationship between firm-specific variables and decision to adopt FASB *Statement No. 52*. The results indicate that early adopters of *SFAS 52* are systematically different from late adopters in size, pre-adoption earnings growth, dividend per dollar of unrestricted retained earnings and changes in earnings volatility. However, changes in earnings volatility were the primary factors that appear to have motivated the corporate adoption decision of *SFAS 52*.

INTRODUCTION

The objective of this study is to examine the impact of earnings volatility on the decision to adopt FASB *Statement No. 52* (*SFAS 52*). Ndubizu [1987, 1989]

Advances in International Accounting, Vol. 3, pages 173-187.

ISBN: 1-55938-078-0

has surveyed multinational executives and found that earnings volatility was the primary foreign currency accounting concern of managers. These studies showed that managers want to avoid foreign currency standards which increase earnings volatility. Managers' concern over earnings variability might have been motivated by the perception that their performance evaluations are a decreasing function of earnings variability.[1] Beaver and Maneghold [1974] and Givoly and Lakonishok [1983] have shown that earnings volatility is associated with security market volatility. This finding suggests that earnings volatility increases market measure of risk, which in turn decreases firms' stock prices. The decrease in stock value would reduce managers' wealth through its effect on their stock ownership and human capital.[2]

Despite the importance of earnings volatility, previous studies of managers' motivation for voluntary adoption of *SFAS 52* have ignored this factor [Ayres, 1986a, 1986b; Gray, 1984]. Such an omission would result in a misspecification of the multivariate logistic model used in Ayres [1986a]. The misspecification would lead to biased and inefficient estimators of the independent variables, especially if the variables are correlated with earnings volatility.[3]

The remainder of the paper is organized as follows: (1) the research hypotheses are discussed, (2) the sample selection criteria are discussed, (3) the results are reported, and (4) some concluding remarks.

RESEARCH HYPOTHESES

Accounting research has used a number of hypotheses to identify firm-specific variables that explain accounting choice: the bonus plan hypothesis, the debt covenant hypothesis, the political cost hypothesis, the firm control hypothesis, and the earnings volatility hypothesis. Empirical studies can be divided into three categories. The first are studies that explain management lobbying behavior. Examples of such studies are Kelly [1982] and Watts and Zimmerman [1978]. The second group of studies examine corporate choice of accounting principles: Hunt [1985], for example, investigates the relationship between firm specific variables and the choice of inventory accounting methods, a choice which, once made, cannot be changed unilaterally. The third group examined voluntary early adoption of a mandated accounting method. Ayres [1986] provides a good example of such studies.

The current study falls within the third group, which differs from the second group in two respects. First, studies of early adoption explain managers' timing behavior. They also provide evidence on the motives management may have in selecting an accounting principle from the set of permissible alternatives. Second, early adoption is a one time decision. Once the standard is adopted it cannot be changed unless replaced by the FASB.

This study examines these hypotheses in order to explain managers' timing behavior, for example, early/late adoption of *SFAS 52*. The results of this study might provide insight on whether the same phenomena that explain the choice of accounting methods and lobbying behavior explain managers' timing behavior.

Bonus Plan Hypothesis

Corporate bonus schemes and performance plans are often a function of some earnings based measure of performance. Watts and Zimmerman [1978], Hagerman and Zmijewski [1979], Holthausen [1981], Zmijewski and Hagerman [1981], Collins, Rozeff, and Dhaliwal [1981], and Bowen, Noreen, and Lacey [1981] have tested the relationship between earnings based compensation schemes and managers' choice of accounting policy. The results of these studies are conflicting. These studies have several problems, among which was the use of the existence of a bonus plan as a determinant of accounting choice.[4] For example, the companies employed in this study have some sort of bonus plan. The implication of these findings is that bonus plan would not explain the motivation to adopt *SAFS 52*.

An alternative version of the bonus plan hypothesis appears in Ayres [1986a] and Healy [1985]. These studies argue that management has an incentive to attain a target level of earnings growth, which is an increasing function of prior years' earnings. Managers of companies with earnings below the target level of growth may be motivated to adopt an income-increasing accounting method. Ayres [1986a,b], Gray [1984], Bettner [1981], and Mathur and Loy [1981] indicate that the net effect of the change to *SFAS 52* was higher income for early adopters. This finding suggests that most early adopters may have earnings growth below the targetted level. The hypothesis tested is as follows:

H$_1$. Early adopters of *SFAS 52* have a smaller earnings growth rate in pre-adoption period than late adopters.

Debt Covenant Hypothesis

Holthausen and Leftwich [1983], Jensen and Meckling [1976], Smith and Warner [1979], Kelly [1983], and Hunt [1985] suggested that constraints in the debt covenant denominated in accounting numbers explain accounting choices of managers. Violation of a firm's debt agreement places the company in technical default. Default on debt covenant may decrease the value of managers' stock ownership and human capital via its effect on stock prices. Leftwich [1983] reported that most debt agreements limit dividend payment to unrestricted retained earnings. Early adoption of *SFAS 52* would increase unrestricted earnings and hence would relax the dividend payment restriction. The hypothesis tested is as follows:

H₂. Early adopters of *SFAS 52* had higher ratios of dividends to unrestricted retained earnings than late adopters.

Bowen et al. [1981] and Daley and Vigeland [1983] argue that interest coverage ratios motivate managers' choice of accounting methods. This motivation exists because firms with lower interest coverage ratios are likely to default on debt covenants and/or may have more difficulty in obtaining additional financing. *SFAS 52* increased earnings of most early adopters and therefore their interest coverage ratios. Ayres [1986] argues that a firm with a small proportion of debt financing may achieve a high coverage ratio with much lower income than a higher debt firm. To deal with this problem, the sample is divided into two groups based on the mean level of long-term debt to total assets (LEV). Firms with LEV greater or equal to the mean LEV were classified as high debt, and were assigned dummy variable 1, while other firms were classified as low-debt with dummy variable 0. The multiplicative function of dummy variable and interest coverage ratio was examined. This variable was highly correlated with interest coverage ratio (see variance inflation factor in Table 2). Consequently, the multiplicative dummy variable (INT) was eliminated from the multivariate analysis. The hypothesis is as follows:

H₃. Early adopters of *SFAS 52* had lower interest coverage ratios than later adopters.

Political Cost Hypothesis

Watts and Zimmerman [1978] have shown that managers of large firms have less incentive to adopt voluntarily the income increasing accounting methods. This is because the board of directors would discount earnings associated to mere accounting changes in evaluating managers. The politician, on the other hand, would not discount the cosmetic earnings associated to accounting changes in formulating and implementing anti-trust law, FIC regulations, tax law, etc. As a result of the accounting change, the future cash flow of the firms may decrease. The decrease would reduce the market value of the companies and managers' wealth. Since most early adopters have higher income, firms size is argued to be inversely related to the probability of early adoption [see Ayres 1986a]. The hypothesis tested is as follows:

H₄. Early adopters of *SFAS 52* are smaller in size than late adopters.

Firm Control Hypothesis

Dhaliwal et al. [1982] and Ayres [1986a] found that the control of a firm explains corporate choice of accounting methods. Manager-controlled firms are more likely than owner-controlled companies to adopt income increasing accounting methods. The reasoning here is that non-owner managers are more sensitive to short-run performance measures such as earnings trends than owner managers. The owner-managers, on the other hand, have a greater incentive to avoid an income increasing accounting method that does not increase cash flow. The percentage of stock that directors and officers own as a group is used to measure the extent of owner/manager control. Ayres points out that the higher the percentage of stock held by directors and officers, the more owner-controlled the firm, while a lower percentage signals more managerial control. The hypothesis tested is as follows:

H_5. Early adopters of *SFAS 52* have a lower percentage of stock owned by directors and officers than later adopters.

Earnings Volatility Hypothesis

Evans et al. [1978], Dukes [1978], Shank et al. [1979], Ijiri [1983], Griffin [1982], and Ndubizu [1987] have shown that earnings volatility was the primary problem managers wanted to resolve in foreign currency accounting. In response to pressure from managers, the Financial Accounting Standards Board (FASB) issued *SFAS 52* to reduce the impact of translation adjustments on earnings volatility. The requirements of *SFAS 52* might not reduce earnings volatility in all circumstances. For example, companies whose foreign subsidiaries' functional currency is the U.S. dollar are required to continue to apply the provisions of the previous FASB standard of *SFAS 8*. For companies translating foreign functional currencies, the behavior of earnings volatility and foreign currency adjustments in a post *SFAS 52* period would depend in part on the future exchange rate. For example, if the foreign currency strengthens significantly against the U.S. dollar, the translated amount of depreciation and cost of sales would be substantially greater than the amount translated under *SFAS 8*.

Ndubizu [1987] again surveyed multinational managers and found that earnings volatility was the primary consideration for early adoption of *SFAS 52*. Most early adopters expected *SFAS 52* to reduce earnings volatility or have an immaterial effect on earnings variability. There are economic reasons why managers would be concerned with earnings volatility. Evidence from the accounting literature suggests that earnings volatility increases market measures of risk, in which in turn decreases stock prices. Lower stock prices reduce managers' wealth through their effect on the value of managers' stock ownership and managers' human capital. Given the complexity of *SFAS 52* and the difficulty of predicting its effect on post-adoption period earnings volatility, early adopters are more likely to be firms that have relatively lower earnings variability in the pre-adoption period and are less likely to have significant changes in future earnings volatility. On the other hand, late adopters are expected to have higher pre-adoption earnings volatility and more changes in post-adoption earnings volatility. The hypotheses tested are as follows:

- **H_6.** Early adopters of *SFAS 52* have less earnings volatility in the pre *SFAS 52* period than late adopters.
- **H_7.** Early adopters of *SFAS 52* have less changes in post *SFAS 52* periods earnings volatility than late adopters.

The earnings volatility hypothesis is not without support in the literature. Lee and Hsieh [1985]and Dhaliwal [1980] have argued that earnings variability may influence managers' choice of accounting methods. Despite this evidence and the importance of earnings volatility to *SFAS 52,* previous studies of corporate adoption decisions of *SFAS 52* ignored earnings volatility. The omission of a relevant variable from the true model yields a biased and inconsistent parameter estimate.[5] The present study examines the impact of earnings volatility on the decision to adopt *SFAS 52.* The data and the sample used are discussed below.

SAMPLE SELECTION

The sample includes firms listed in the 1981-1983 volumes of the AICPA's *Accounting Trends,* and *Accounting Issues* [Bear Stearns, January 29, 1982], that meet the following criteria:

1. Financial data available on the Compustat Annual Industrial Tape and quarterly tape from 1976 to 1982. Proxy statement and annual report available on the National Databank Microfiche file for the year of adoption.
2. Quarterly foreign currency adjustments included in earnings available on the quarterly commercial Compustat tape from 1976 to 1980. Correlation between foreign currency adjustments and earnings was estimated. Firms with a correlation estimate below the mean correlation of thirty percent were eliminated from the sample. This selection criterion helps eliminate firms whose earnings volatility is not associated with foreign currency adjustments.

Table 1. Industry Membership of Sample Firms

SIC	Industry	SFAS 52 Adoption Years		Total Sample
		1981 Early Adopters	*1982 + 1983 Late Adopters*	
13	Crude Petroleum and National Gas	—	1	1
16	Construction Other Than Building	—	2	2
20	Food and Kindred	2	6	8
21	Tobacco	1	1	2
23	Apparel and Fabrics Products	—	1	1
24	Lumber and Wood	—	1	1
26	Paper	6	5	11
27	Printing and Publishing	—	2	2
28	Chemicals	12	19	31
29	Petroleum Refining	1	6	7
30	Rubber	2	1	3
32	Stone, Clay, Glass, Concrete	3	3	6
33	Primary Metal	—	4	4
34	Fabricated Metal	5	2	7
35	Machinery	6	14	20
36	Electrical Equipment	5	8	13
37	Transportation Equipment	5	7	12
38	Scientific Instruments	4	3	6
48	Communication	—	1	1
49	Electric, Gas, Sanitary Service	—	1	1
50	Wholesale Trade: Durable Goods	—	1	1
58	Eating and Drinking Places	—	2	2
89	Misc. Services	—	1	1
	Total	52	92	144

3. December 31 fiscal year end. This requirement guarantees that the estimation of earnings volatility for each firm is based on the same time periods.

These selection criteria provided a sample of 52 early adopters and 92 late adopters. Table 1 provides the frequency distribution of the sample by industry. The sample is diversified across industries with concentration in SIC 28 (Chemical and Allied Products), SIC 35 (Machinery) and SIC 36 (Electrical Equipment).

The firm-specific variables derived from the hypotheses discussed previously were computed as follows:

$$\text{EVOT}_i = \frac{\left[\sum_{t=1}^{T} (E_{it} - \bar{E}_i)^2 / T-1 \right]^{1/2}}{\bar{E}}$$

where:

E	=	quarterly earnings from 1976 to 1981 for pre-*SFAS 52* and 1983 to 1986 for post-*SFAS 52*.
COVINT	=	income before extraordinary items and discontinued operations minus income effect of adoption of *SFAS 52*/ interest expense.
DIVURE	=	[(preferred dividend and common dividend)/unrestricted retained earnings] × 100.
SIZE	=	total assets in book value.
DO	=	percentage of stock held by directors and officers as a group.
DIFF	=	|post-*EVOT* − pre-*EVOT*|.[6]
CEPS	=	([EPS_{1981} − CPS − EPS_{1980}]/|EPS_{1980}|) × 100, where EPS_T = primary earnings per share excluding extraordinary items and discontinued operations for year T, and CPS = the per share effect of adoption of *SFAS 52* for 1981 adopters; for late adopters CPS = 0 in 1981.
DUMMY	=	1 for higher (Long-Term Debt/Total Assets) and 0 otherwise.
INT	=	*COVINT* * *DUMMY*

ANALYSIS AND RESULTS

Univariate Analysis

Table 2 presents the results of the comparison of early and late adopters of *SFAS 52* based on the firm-specific variables derived from Hypotheses 1 to 7. In every case, the mean differences are in the hypothesized direction. A Mann-Whitney two sample test and a Kruskal-Wallis two sample test were

Table 2. Univariate Tests of the Relation Between Explanatory Variables and Adoption Years of *SFAS 52*

		Year of Adoption Mean		*Mann-Whitney 2 Sample Test*		*Kruskal-Wallis Test*		*Correlation Test*
Variables	*Hypotheses*	*Early (1)*	*Late (2)*	*Z-Value*	*1-Tailed Prob.*	*CHISQ*	*1-Tailed Prob.*	*Variance Inflation Factors (VIF)*
CEPS	(1) < (2)	-54.66	-13.29	-2.929	0.003*	8.59	0.003*	1.061
COVINT	(1) ≤ (2)	2.49	4.53	-0.078	0.937	0.01	0.936	28.392
INT	(1) ≤ (2)	2.00	4.03	-0.118	0.906	0.01	0.904	28.319
DIVURE	(1) > (2)	19.22	11.13	3.123	0.002*	9.77	0.002*	1.046
SIZE	(1) < (2)	22.75	52.16	-2.084	0.37*	4.35	0.037*	1.052
DO	(1) < (2)	5.18	6.25	-0.597	0.550	0.36	0.549	1.172
EVOT-Pre	(1) < (2)	48.95	59.24	-1.308	0.197	1.72	0.190	3.819
DIFF	(1) < (2)	15.66	27.08	1.797	0.072*	3.34	0.071*	3.401

Notes: VIF measures the interrelationship between the independent variables. According to Marquardt [1970], multicollinearity is troublesome only when it exceeds 10.00.
* Statistically significant at the 0.05 level.

applied to provide a univariate test of the hypotheses. The variables *CEPS, DIVURE,* and *SIZE* are significantly different for the two groups at the 0.05 level. *DIFF* is significant at the 0.07 level. *COVINT, DO,* and *EVOT* did not differ significantly between early and late adopters.

The results of the comparison of *CEPS* among early and late adopters of *SFAS 52* are consistent with Hypothesis 1. The mean *CEPS* for early adopters is -54.66 and -13.29 for late adopters. These results show that early adopters have smaller growth rate in pre-adoption earnings than late adopters. Thus early adoption might have been motivated by desire to achieve a higher earnings growth rate or targetted earnings rate.

The results of comparing *DIVURE* and *SIZE* among early and late adopters are consistent with Hypotheses 3 and 4, respectively. The mean *DIVURE* is 19.22 for early adopters and 11.13 for late adopters. These results show that early adopters have higher dividends per dollar of unrestricted retained earnings than late adopters. As for size, early adopters have smaller total assets on average than late adopters. The mean total assets is 22.75 for early adopters and 52.16 for late adopters. This result is consistent with the hypothesis that larger firms are less likely than smaller firms to adopt income increasing accounting methods.

DIFF is higher for late adopters than early adopters. This result suggests that larger firms have larger changes in earnings volatility following *SFAS 52* than smaller firms. The larger changes in earnings volatility might have motivated the later adoption of *SFAS 52.* This result is consistent with Ndubizu's [1987] finding that early adopters perceived *SFAS 52* to have less effect on earnings volatility than later adopters.

As for *EVOT,* no significant differences exist among early and late adopters. However, the two groups differ significantly in terms of *DIFF.* This result suggests that managers' adoption decisions are not only motivated by pre-adoption earnings volatility but, more importantly, their decisions were motivated by the expected changes in earnings volatility.

Table 2 also provides the variance inflation factors (VIF). The VIF measures the interrelationship between the independent variables. According to Marquardt [1970], multicollinearity is troublesome only when it exceeds 10.0. The result of VIF shows that *COVINT* and *INT* are highly correlated. Thus *INT* was eliminated from the multivariate logit model used to assess the joint effect of the independent variables on the decision to adopt *SFAS 52.* The logit model was used because the dependent variable is categorical, for example, early adopter (1) and late adopter (0).

Multivariate Analysis

Table 3 presents the results of the multivariate logistic model. In both Equations (1) and (2), *CEPS, COV,* and *DO* are not statistically significant at

Table 3. Logistic Model of SFAS 52 Adoption Decision: Early (1981) Versus Late (1982 + 1983) Adopters

	a	*CEPS*	*COV*	*DIVURE*	*SIZE*	*DO*	*EVOT*
Equation (1)							
Expected Sign		–	–	+	–	–	–
Coefficients	-0.056	-0.001	0.064	-0.067	0.021	0.017	-0.012
Chi-Square	-0.01	-0.05	2.68	-9.74	5.69	0.60	-3.33
P-Value	0.917	0.816	0.101	0.002*	0.017*	0.438	0.068
Likelihood Ratio 153.38							

	a	*CEPS*	*COV*	*DIVURE*	*SIZE*	*DO*	*DIFF*
Equation (2)							
Expected Sign		–	–	+	–	–	–
Coefficients	0.253	0.001	0.060	-0.068	0.022	0.020	-0.016
T-Value	0.29	0.11	2.54	10.14	5.44	0.78	-4.64
P-Value	0.588	0.737	0.110	0.001*	0.019*	0.376	0.031*
Likelihood Ratio 151.65							

Notes: Dependent Variable = 1 for early adopters; 0 for late adopters.
* Statistically significant at the 0.05 level.

the 0.05 level. These results suggest that these variables have no explanatory power once combined with other relevant variables. *SIZE, DIVURE,* and *DIFF* are significant at the 0.03 level. *EVOT* is significant at the 0.06 level. However, only *DIFF* and *EVOT* have the correct sign. The implication of this result is that the difference between pre-adoption earnings volatility and post-adoption (expected) volatility and pre-adoption earnings volatility had the greatest influence on managers' decisions to adopt *SFAS 52*. This result is consistent with the opinions expressed by managers regarding the primary motivation for early adoption of *SFAS 52*.

CONCLUSION

This study examined whether early adopters of *SFAS 52* differ from late adopters in terms of firm control, bonus plan, debt and dividend restrictions, size, and earnings volatility. The results show that early adopters (1) have lower pre-adoption earnings growth, (2) have smaller size, (3) have higher dividend per dollar of unrestricted retained earnings, and (4) have smaller changes in earnings volatility than late adopters. These results suggest that systematic differences exist between early and late adopters.

When firm control, bonus plan, interest and dividend restriction, size and changes in earnings volatility were jointly used to explain corporate choice of foreign currency standards, the results show that changes in earnings volatility were the primary factor motivating managers adoption decision of *SFAS 52*. Early adopters have relatively less changes in earnings volatility following *SFAS 52* adoption than late adopters. The results show that corporate decision to adopt *SFAS 52* was influenced jointly by pre-adoption earnings volatility and the expected changes in future earnings volatility.

ACKNOWLEDGMENTS

The author would like to thank Professors Bertrand Horwitz, Rohit Jain, and Augustine Arize for helpful comments on the earlier draft of this paper. Thanks also go to Graham Drake and Prakash Dheeiya for competent research assistance. Special thanks goes to Professor Ayres for allowing me to use her data bank on accounting choice.

NOTES

1. This view has been expressed in the smoothing literature [see Barefield and Comiskey, 1972; Gordon, 1964].
2. See Kelly [1983] for more discussion of managers' human capital.
3. Most economic variables are correlated [see *Econometric and Economic Forecasts and Model,* 1981, pp. 128-130]. Therefore, misspecification or specification error in econometric

modelling is likely to result in biased and inefficient estimators. The results in Table 2 show that earnings volatility is correlated with other independent variables.

4. Healy [1985] has shown that managers may decide to take a 'bath' in cases where adopting an income increasing technique would not help the firm to meet the targetted level of earnings (lower bound), specified in the bonus plan.

5. Multivariate models are based on the assumption that the models are correctly specified. Evidence of specification error should cast doubt on the validity of the multivariate estimate. For example if $ADD = a + b_1\ CEPS + b_2\ COVINT + b_3\ DIVURE + b_4\ SIZE + b_5\ DO + b_6\ EVOT$ is the correct specification while the incorrect specification is $ADD = a + g_1\ CEPS + g_2\ COVINT + g_3\ DIVURE + g_4\ SIZE + g_5\ DO$ then the estimated slope parameters of the misspecified model are:

$$E(g_1) = b_1 + b_6 \frac{COV(CEPS, EVOT)}{\text{Var}\ (CEPS)}$$

$$E(g_2) = b_2 + b_6 \frac{COV(COVINT, EVOT)}{\text{Var}\ (COVINT)}$$

$$E(g_3) = b_3 + b_6 \frac{COV(DIVURE, EVOT)}{\text{Var}\ (DIVURE)}$$

$$E(g_4) = b_4 + b_6 \frac{COV(SIZE, EVOT)}{\text{Var}\ (SIZE)}$$

$$E(g_5) = b_5 + b_6 \frac{COV(DO, EVOT)}{\text{Var}\ (DO)}$$

Since the second terms in the above equations are not expected to be zero (see variance inflation factors in Table 2), the least squares slope estimates of the misspecified model will yield a biased estimate of the true slope parameters b_i ($i = 1, \ldots, 5$).

6. The measurement of *DIFF* is based on the assumption that the expected future changes in earnings volatility are important variables for strategic planning. Given the difficulty of measuring/modelling management expectations, taking the difference between pre-adoption and post-adoption earnings volatility became an easy way out. The percentage difference is measured as follows:

$$DIFF\,\% = \left| \frac{\text{Post-}EVOT - \text{Pre-}EVOT}{\text{Pre-}EVOT} \right|$$

The results of 'percentage of *DIFF*' are not different from DIFF. Thus the percentage results were not reported.

REFERENCES

Ayres, R., "Characteristics of Firms Electing Early Adoption of SFAS No. 52," *Journal of Accounting and Economics* 8 [1986,a], pp. 143-158.

________, "A Comment on Corporate Preferences for Foreign Currency Accounting Standards," *Journal of Accounting Research* 24 [Spring 1986b], pp. 166-169.

Beaver, W., and J. Manegold, "The Association Between Market Determined and Accounting Determined Measure of Systematic Risk: Some Further Evidence," *Journal of Financial and Quantitative Analysis* [June 1875], pp. 231-284.

Bettner, J., "Major Accounting Rule Change Adopted Covering Foreign Currency Translation," *Wall Street Journal* [December 8, 1981], p. 8.

Bowen, R.E., E.W. Noreen, and J.M. Lacy, "Determinants of the Corporate Decision to Capitalize Interest," *Journal of Accounting and Economics* [August 1981], pp. 151-179.

Chow, C., "The Demand for External Auditing: Size, Debt, and Ownership Influences," *The Accounting Review* [April 1982], pp. 272-291.

Collins, O.W., M.S. Rozeff, and D.S. Dhaliwal, "The Economic Determinants of the Market Reaction to Proposed Mandatory Accounting Changes in the Oil and Gas Industry," *Journal of Accounting and Economics* [August 1981], pp. 37-71.

Daley, L.A., and R. Vigeland, "The Effects of Debt Covenants and Political Costs on the Choice of Accounting Methods: The Case of Accounting for R&D Costs," *Journal of Accounting and Economics 5* [1983], pp. 195-211.

Dhaliwal, D., G. Salamon, and E. Smith, "The Effect of Owner Versus Management Control on the Choice of Accounting Methods," *Journal of Accounting and Economics* [July 1982], pp. 41-53.

Dukes, R., *An Empirical Investigation of the Effects of Statement of Financial Accounting Standards No. 8 on Security Return Behavior* [FASB, 1978].

Evans, T.G., W.R. Folks, Jr., and M. Jilling, *The Impact of Statement of Financial Accounting Standards No. 8 on the Foreign Exchange Risk Management Practices of American Multinationals: An Economic Impact Study* [FASB, 1978].

Financial Accounting Standards Board, *Statement No. 52,* "Foreign Currency Translation" [FASB, December 1981].

Givoly, D., and J. Lakonishok, "Divergences of Earnings Expectations: The Effect on Market Response to Earnings Signals," Working Paper 768/83 [Faculty of Management, Tel Aviv University, February 1983].

Gray, D., "Corporation Preferences for Foreign Currency Accounting Standards," *Journal of Accounting Research 22* [Autumn 1984], pp. 760-764.

Griffin, P., "Foreign Exchange Gains and Losses: Impact on Reported Earnings," *ABACUS* 18 [1982], pp. 50-69.

Hagerman, R., and M. Zmijewski, "Some Economic Determinants of Accounting Policy Choice," *Journal of Accounting and Economics* [August 1979], pp. 141-161.

Healy, P.M., "The Effects of Bonus Schemes on Accounting Decisions," *Journal of Accounting and Economics* 7 [1985], pp. 85-107.

Holthausen, R.W., and R.W. Leftwich, "The Economic Consequences of Accounting Choice: Implications of Costly Contracting and Monitoring," *Journal of Accounting and Economics* [August 1982], pp. 77-118.

Hunt, H., III, "Potential Determinants of Corporate Inventory Accounting Decision," *Journal of Accounting Research* 23 [Autumn 1985], pp. 448-467.

Ijiri, Y., "Foreign Currency Accounting and Its Transition," in *Managing Foreign Exchange Risk* edited by R.J. Herring [Cambridge University Press, 1873], pp. 181-212.

Jensen, M., and W.H. Meckling, "Theory of the Firm: Managerial Behavior, Agency Costs and Ownership Structure," *Journal of Financial Economics* 3 [1976], pp. 305-360.

Kelly, L., "Corporate Lobbying and Changes in Financial or Operating Activities in Reaction to SFAS No. 8," *Journal of Accounting and Public Policy* [Winter 1982], pp. 153-173.

———, "The Development of a Positive Theory of Corporate Managements' Role in External Financial Reporting," *Journal of Accounting Literature* [Spring 1983], pp. 111-150.

Lee, C., and D.A. Hsieh, "Choice of Inventory Accounting Methods: Comparative Analysis of Alternative Hypotheses," *Journal of Accounting Research* 23 [Autumn 1985], pp. 468-485.

Leftwich, R., "Accounting Information in Private Markets: Evidence from Private Lending Agreements," *The Accounting Review* [January 1983], pp. 23-42.

Mathur, I., and D. Loy, "Foreign Currency Translation: Survey of Corporate Treasurers," *Management Accounting* (NAA) 63 [1981], pp. 31-38.

Moses, D., "Income Smoothing and Incentives: Empirical Tests Using Accounting Changes," *The Accounting Review* [April 1987], pp. 358-377.

Ndubizu, G., "An Empirical Investigation of the Security Market Reaction to Multinational Accounting Changes," Ph.D. Dissertation, Temple University [1985].

________, "Management Preferences Over Foreign Currency Standards: An Empirical Analysis,'" *International Journal of Accounting* [1987], pp. 115-129.

________, "Analysis of Economic Consequences of Foreign Currency Standards," *Advances in International Accounting* [1988], pp. 183-200.

Pindyck, R., and D. Rubinfeld, *Econometric and Models Economic Forecasts* [McGraw-Hill, 1981].

Shank, J.K., J.F. Dilliard, and R.J. Murdock, *Assessing the Economic Impact of the SFAS No. 8* [Financial Executives Research Foundation, 1979].

Smith, C., and J. Warner, "Financial Contracting: An Analysis of Bond Covenants," *Journal of Financial Economics* 7 [1979], pp. 117-162.

Watts, R., and J. Zimmerman: "Towards a Positive Theory of the Determination of Accounting Standards," *The Accounting Review* [January 1978], pp. 112-134.

Zmijewski, M., and R.L. Hagerman: "An Income Strategy Approach to the Positive Theory of Accounting Standard Setting/Choice," *Journal of Accounting and Economics* [August 1981], pp. 129-149.

THE IMPACT OF FASB STATEMENT NO. 52 ON FOREIGN EXCHANGE CONTRACTS:

AN EMPIRICAL EVALUATION

Hossein Shalchi and Ahmad Hosseini

ABSTRACT

Statement of Financial Accounting Standards No. 8 (*SFAS 8*) required U.S. multinational corporations (MNCs) to use the temporal method of foreign curency translation and to report all translation gains and losses in the income statement. *SFAS 8* was strongly criticized on the grounds of failure to reflect the underlying economic realities of foreign operations, heightened volatility in earnings, and its impetus for costly hedging activities. In view of the alleged problems and inconsistencies, the Financial Accounting Standards Board (FASB) rescinded *SFAS 8* and issued *SFAS 52* in December 1981. It has been asserted that the new requirements under *SFAS 52* will reduce the pressure on MNCs to undertake unnecessary hedging activities in order to offset potential earnings variabilities caused by exchange rate fluctuations. This study provides an empirical investigation of this assertion.

Advances in International Accounting, Vol. 3, pages 189-201.

ISBN: 1-55938-078-0

INTRODUCTION

Previous research in this area is generally descriptive in nature and has not attempted to empirically test for the direction and magnitude of the possible effects of *SFAS 52* on the actual utilization of foreign exchange hedging instruments, especially forward exchange contracts and their perceived usefulness for hedging against translation exposure [e.g., see Wilner, 1982; Evans and Doupnik, 1986; Houston and Mueller, 1988]. The motivation of the current study is to assess and test these assertions and effects in an empirical setting. To this end, the primary research objectives of this study are: (1) to empirically investigate whether the adoption of *SFAS 52* reduced the use of hedging activities as a measure of protection from foreign currency translation and earnings volatility, (2) to determine the effect of the functional currency dichotomy on the volume of MNC's hedgings against foreign exchange translation exposure, and (3) to examine the MNC's ratings of the relative usefulness of various hedging techniques under the dichotomy of functional currency set forth in *SFAS 52*.

The remainder of this paper is organized as follows. The next section provides a chronology of events and concerns leading to the adoption of *SFAS 52* as well as a discussion on the hypotheses derived. The third section presents the sample selection procedure. Section four reports the research methodology and findings. The last section provides a summary and suggestions for future research.

OVERVIEW OF THE PROBLEM

The issue of accounting for foreign currency translation has been continually debated in accounting literature, leading to a number of attempts by the accounting standards-setting bodies to resolve the problem. In 1975, FASB issued *SFAS 8* to alleviate the problems associated wtih the diverse foreign currency translation methods used by multinational corporations. *SFAS 8* standardized accounting for foreign subsidiaries of U.S. companies and required that all translation gains and losses be fully recognized in current income and that foreign currency items be translated using the temporal method. Under the temporal method, monetary items and current values are remeasured at current rates, while other items are translated at applicable historical rates. The temporal method prescribed by *SFAS 8,* coupled with the immediate recognition of translation gains and losses due to changes in foreign currency exchange rates, caused increased volatility in reported earnings [Massaro, 1978; Largay, 1983; Selling and Sorter, 1983]. It was further alleged that this heightened volatility in reported earnings frequently contradicted the underlying economic realities of foreign operations and the changes in exchange rates resulting in distorted and misleading financial statements. Consequently, many MNCs engaged in costly hedging activities to minimize their translation exposure (as opposed to transaction exposure) due to changes in foreign exchange rates. For example, empirical evidence provided by Evans, Folks, and Jilling [1978], Shank, Dillard, and Murdock [1979], and Wilner [1982] supports the contention that foreign exchange risk management practices changed measurably after the issuance of *SFAS 8*. More specifically, management undertook costly and unnecessary hedging activities to hedge the firm's accounting exposure to reduce earnings variability that resulted from currency swings [e.g., see Mauer, 1983; Griffith, 1983; Ziebart and Kim, 1987].

To correct these perceived distortions and costly hedging activities, the FASB issued *SFAS 52* in December 1981, replacing *SFAS 8*. Unlike its predecessor, *SFAS 52* permits different translation methods for different underlying economic circumstances. The main thrust of the new rules is the determination of the entity's functional currency, "the currency of the primary environment in which the entity operates and generates net cash flows" [*SFAS 52,* Par. 51]. More specifically, *SFAS 52* distinguishes between those subsidiaries that operate autonomously in foreign countries and those that are an integral part of the U.S. parent's operations or are operating in highly inflationary economies. In the former situation, the entity's functional currency is the local currency and its accounts as measured in that currency are translated into dollars by the current method. Under the current method, all assets and liabilities are translated at the current exchange rate. Moreover, when the current rate is used, the translation adjustment related to the foreign net assets are reported in the cumulative translation adjustment account in the stockholders' equity section. In the latter case, the functional currency would be the U.S. dollar. Accordingly, *SFAS 52* requires that the subsidiary's accounts be translated (technically remeasured) into dollars by the temporal method embodied in *SFAS 8*. It is also important to mention that whereas under *SFAS 8* accounting exposure generally consisted of net monetary assets (liabilities), accounting exposure under the current rate method is defined as net assets. Consequently, for foreign entities using the current rate method a weakening dollar will produce a translation gain instead of a translation loss under *SFAS 8* [for more details, see Largay, 1983]. In contrast, for foreign entities with the dollar as the functional currency, accounting exposure remains almost equivalent to that under *SFAS 8*. Given this dichotomy, it is asserted that when the functional currency is the local currency, the translations adjustment bypasses the income statement and will lead to smaller fluctuations in net income, thus significantly reducing the need for costly hedging practices of MNCs to offset potential adverse movements in foreign exchange rates [e.g., see Bender, 1982].

SFAS 52 also distinguishes between forward contracts that are speculative and those that are for hedging. If the hedged commitment is a firm's net foreign investment, then gains or losses on forward contract is reported as a separate component of stockholders' equity. In contrast, if the hedged commitment is an identifiable foreign currency transaction, then net gains or losses are recognized currently or deferred depending on whether the transaction has been consummated or not. Fekrat [1987] elaborated these different treatments and concluded that the *SFAS 52* provision that "a gain or loss on a forward contract or other foreign currency transaction that is intended to hedge an identifiable foreign currency commitment...shall be deferred and included in the measurement of the related foreign currency transaction" [*SFAS 52,* Par. 21] seems to be misleading and contradictory to the very idea of hedging [Fekrat, 1987, p. 252]. In view of these arguments and assertions, one would expect to observe a decline in the actual use and usefulness of hedging instruments after the *SFAS 52* adoption.

DEVELOPMENT OF RESEARCH HYPOTHESES

As previously stated, one major criticism of *SFAS 8* was that it forced unnecessary hedging activities, therefore it is desirable to determine if *SFAS 52* has reduced the MNCs' foreign currency exposure risk hedging practices. Accordingly, it is hypothesized that the adoption of *SFAS 52* reduced the need for costly hedging activities to offset gains and losses resulting from foreign currency translation exposures. The first hypothesis tested in this study addresses this issue:

H_1. There are no differences in the volume of MNCs' foreign currency exposure hedging activities before and after adoption of *SFAS 52*.

Rejection of the first null hypothesis would imply that the volume of MNCs' hedging practices have decreased. Such a result would strongly support the assertion that the adoption of *SFAS 52* would reduce the MNCs' need to undertake costly and unnecessary hedging activities. The question would naturally be raised as to whether the functional currency dichotomy—local currency versus dollar—has had any effect on the volume of MNCs' hedgings. As previously discussed, it has been asserted that when the functional currency is the local currency, the need for hedgings would be measurably reduced. The second hypothesis explicitly tests this assertion:

H_2. There are no differences in the volume of foreign currency translation hedging activities of firms designating local currency and those designating the dollar as their functional currency.

Rejection of H_2 would imply that functional currency designation has significant effect on the actual use of hedgings. More specifically, in situations where the functional currency is the local currency, hedging activities have measurably been reduced.

Given the argument that *SFAS 52* treatment of gain or loss on some foreign currency transactions is contradictory to the basic idea of hedging [Fekrat, 1987], combined with the assertion that when local currency is designated as the functional currency management's need for hedging will be reduced, one can expect to see a shift in the manager's attitudes toward the usefulness of hedging. This contention can also be supported from the agency theory perspective. That is, since most executive compensation schemes depend directly on accounting-based measures of earnings, changes in foreign currency reporting requirements can affect the managers' wealth and hence their attitudes toward certain actions, including hedging practices. Under *SFAS 8*, unexpected currency translation losses affected the reported income leading to lower managers' compensations. This uncertainty in turn would have induced managers to consider hedgings as useful tools for smoothing the reported income and thus their own compensations. The issuance of *SFAS 52* and the "situational" concept of functional currency determination should have reduced the usefulness of hedging techniques. The reason for this change is twofold: (1) when the functional currency is the local currency, translation exposure gains and losses do not effect current income, and (2) hedging is a very costly practice which management would avoid it if did not increase the value of their compensation package.

Therefore, it is desirable to empirically investigate managers' assessed usefulness of various hedging instruments and the effect of the functional currency dichotomy on the relative usefulness of each technique. It is hypothesized that significant differences among the relative usefulness of various foreign currency hedging instruments exist and moreover, the usefulness of hedging depends on the functional currency designation. The first step for examining these issues is to identify the most widely used hedging instruments. Aggarwal [1984], among others, provides such a subset. In addition, a recent study by Evans and Doupnik [1986] gives descriptive statistics on the actual usage and the opinions of respondents concerning the relative usefulness of various exchange risk hedging techniques. The ten most widely used/useful hedging techniques were: forward exchange contracts; borrowing in local currency; accelerate/decelerate dividend payment; reschedule intercompany debt payments; accelerate/delay intercompany receivables; adjust sales prices; delay/accelerate payables; delay/accelerate receivables; foreign currency options; and alter credit terms [Evans and Doupnik, 1986, pp. 88-90]. Moreover, as a result of the literature survey and discussions with corporate executives in charge of foreign operations during the questionnaire development stage of the study, two more hedging instruments were included in the study: back-to-back loans, and currency swaps. Accordingly, a total of twelve hedging techniques are included to test the next two null hypotheses:

H_3. There are no differences in the relative usefulness of the hedging techniques under the same functional currency situation.

H_4. There are no differences in the relative usefulness of the hedging techniques between the firms designating the local currency versus those using the dollar as their functional currency.

SAMPLE SELECTION

The sample selection procedure for this study began by drawing a sample of 400 firms with substantial foreign operations from the *Fortune* 1000 list. This was achieved by selecting those Fortune 1000 firms which appeared in the *Dun and Bradstreet Directory of International Companies* list. Two other goals guided the initial sample selection process: (1) the desire to obtain representative firms of different sizes, and (2) the desire to maximize the number of industries included in the sample. Next, a questionnaire was developed, pilot-tested, and administered. The questionnaire was designed in consultation with, and pre-tested by, five corporate executives involved in foreign currency operations, six university professors, and one banker. Questionnaires were mailed to each firm's executive in charge of international operations. The cover letter explained the nature of the survey as well as assuring complete anonymity to respondents in order to avoid possible bias in their responses. To increase the response rate, follow-up letters were sent as needed approximately one month after the questionnaire was originally mailed. Only firms which were subject to the requirements of both *SFAS 8* and *SFAS 52* were considered for the final sample. There were 133 questionnaires returned, of which 108 were usable. This yielded a response rate of approximately 27 percent. Although the final sample is not random, it includes firms of different sizes from various industries.

Table 1 portrays some characteristics of the sample firms. The sales volumes reported in Table 1 indicate that the sample companies were relatively large firms with substantial foreign activities. In fact, 74 percent of the firms reported annual sales in excess of $500 million while 76.9 percent of companies had foreign sales which accounted for more than 10 percent of their annual sales.

ANALYSIS OF RESULTS

Since accounting exposure is significantly different under *SFAS 52* from what it was under *SFAS 8,* foreign exchange hedging activities and their usefulness

Table 1. Summary Descriptive Statistics for Sample Firms

Dimensions	*n*	%
Annual Sales Volume:		
Below $500 million	28	26.0
$500 million-$1 billion	20	18.5
$1 billion-$5 billion	47	43.5
More than $5 billion	13	12.0
Total	108	100.0
Foreign Sales as Percentage of Total Sales		
Below 10%	25	23.1
10%-25%	42	38.9
25%-40%	28	26.0
Above 40%	13	12.0
Total	108	100.0

may shift considerably. Specifically, for a foreign entity with local currency as the functional currency, it is expected that corporate foreign exchange hedging practices, borrowing strategies, and other matters related to managing foreign exchange risk be scaled back. To address these questions, the questionnaire contained a section on the actual volume of foreign exchange contracts before and after the adoption of the revised set of accounting rules embodied in *SFAS 52* as well as the volume of hedging activities as a function of the functional currency situations.

The hypothesis that the volume of hedging activities of MNCs pre-*SFAS 52* was greater than their post-*SFAS 52* hedgings (**H**$_1$) was tested using paired *t*-test and Chi-square test. The *t*-statistic was -7.46 with 107 degrees of freedom. Both statistics are significant at the 0.005 level, indicating that the actual volume of foreign exchange translation hedgings after the adoption of *SFAS 52* has declined significantly. This result shows that the *SFAS 52* requirements have measurably reduced the pressure on MNCs to undertake unnecessary hedgings to offset potential earnings variabilities caused by foreign exchange translation exposure.

For testing **H**$_2$, it is first necessary to control for the effect of size differences across firms in the two groups. Failure to consider this effect can result in the drawing of erroneous inferences. Moreover, firm size captures numerous aspects of a firm's attitudes and subsequent economic behaviors. In the foreign currency context, for example, it can be argued that larger firms are more likely to be invested internationally and thus their foreign currency hedging activities are expected to be higher than smaller firms. Total assets and foreign sales are two measures that can be used to control for the effect of size differences

Table 2. Total Assets and Foreign Sales Comparisons

	Local Currency Group	*Test Statistic*	*U.S. Dollar Group*
Number of Firms	73		24
Mean Total Assets (in thousands)	$2,854,435		$3,069,260
t-statistic		-.21	
Mann-Whitney U-Statistic		762	
Kilmogorov-Smirnov Z-Statistic		.745	
Mean Foreign Sales (in thousands)	$902,048		$861,243
t-statistic		.14	
Mann-Whitney U-Statistic		835	
Kilmogorov-Smirnov Z-Statistic		.432	

across firms or over time. The mean and median of the total assets and foreign sales for the two groups along with the statistics employed to test for any signficiant differences in the size of the two groups are presented in Table 2. The *t*-test, the Kilmogorov-Smirnov two-sample test, and the Mann-Whitney U-test results indicate that there is no difference between the firms designating the dollar and those using the local currency as their functional currency.

The second hypothesis (**H**$_2$) explicitly tests for the effect of the functional currency designation on the actual usage of hedging techniques. The reason for this possible effect is due to the fact that the designation of the dollar as a functional currency would require MNCs to recognize foreign currency translation gains or losses in the income statement. Accordingly, it is expected that hedging activities be utilized more frequently by entities using the dollar as the functional currency as opposed to those for which the local currency is the functional currency. The volumes of the hedging activities by two subgroups, each exclusively using either the local currency or the dollar as the functional currency were computed and tested. Because of the small and uneven sample sizes, the Chi-square statistic and the Mann-Whitney U-test were employed. The median test and the Mann-Whitney U-tests are non parametric tests for testing the equality of the medians. Using both statistics, the **H**$_2$ was rejected at the .01 level of significance revealing that entities designating the dollar as the functional currency use hedging activities more extensively than firms for which the local currency is being treated as the functional currency. The Chi-square of the difference is significant at the 0.01 level and the Fisher exact test probability is 0.0055 indicating the validity of the results for the sample sizes used. This finding supports the FASB's assertion that the new rules on the functional currency dichotomy and the resulting current method set forth in *SFAS 52* would reduce the MNCs' need to undertake costly hedging activities.

Table 3. Results of Two-Factor Analysis of Variance

Source	*Mean Square*	*F Statistic*	*P-Value*	*Test of*
Hedging Method (HM)	31.930	28.799	.0001	$\mathbf{H}_{03}$
Functional Currency (FC)	18.249	16.460	.0001	$\mathbf{H}_{04}$
Interaction (FC x HM)	1.470	1.331	.140	

The second motive of this paper is to compare the usefulness of forward exchange contracts with other hedging practices in reducing foreign translation exposures. Accordingly, the participants were asked to rank the 12 hedging methods based on their relative usefulness. Moreover, to assess the usefulness of these hedging techniques in different operational settings, three different translation exposure environments were specified in the questionnaire: overall foreign exchange operations, operations for which the local currency is the functional currency, and situations in which the dollar is considered to be the functional currency. This distinction helps to identify the possible effects of *SFAS 52* on the hedging practices as a result of the "situational" concept of the functional currency set forth in *SFAS 52*. Of the 108 firms in the full sample, 73 companies used only the local currency as the functional currency, 24 companies reported using only the U.S. dollar as their functional currency, and 11 reported using the local currency for some subsidiaries and U.S. currency as the functional currency in other foreign subsidiaries.

Hypotheses $\mathbf{H}_3$ and $\mathbf{H}_4$ were tested using a two-stage statistical procedure. The first stage comprised a two-factor analysis of variance approach. In addition to information about the effect of each factor (functional currency designation and hedging method) on the usefulness ratings, this two-factor design permits the evaluation of the combined effects of functional currency selection and hedging method. In the second stage of statistical testing, pairwise tests were conducted to determine if the forward exchange contracts were rated significantly more useful by the respondents. Table 3 presents the results of the two-factor analysis of variance on the perceived usefulness of the hedging methods in reducing translation exposure.

The observed significance level associated with the interaction between functional currency designation and hedging method is approximately 0.14. Therefore, it appears that there is no interaction between the two factors. Given no significant interaction, the effect of the two factors on the usefulness ratings can be tested separately. Notice that a null hypothesis of no difference among usefulness ratings of hedging methods is rejected as evidence by *p*-values of less than 0.001. The results obtained also indicate that both functional currency selection and hedging method selection affect the perceived usefulness of foreign currency hedging techniques. In particular, the evidence provided is

Table 4. Test Statistics for Comparison of Perceived Usefulness of Alternative Hedging Strategies

	Overall: Sample Size = 108 Friedman Test = 215.214[a]			*Local Currency: Sample Size = 73 Friedman Test = 157.118*[a]			*U.S. Dollar: Sample Size = 24 Friedman Test = 28.143*[a]		
Hedging Strategy	*Mean Rank*	*Rank*	*Wilcoxon Statistic*	*Mean Rank*	*Rank*	*Wilcoxon Statistic*	*Mean Rank*	*Mean Rank*	*Wilcoxon Statistic*
Forward Exchange Contract	8.90	1	—	8.47	1	—	8.67	1	—
Tighten Credit	6.93	6	3.86[a]	8.29	6	2.51[a]	6.85	6	0.83
Delay/Accelerate Receivables	5.84	9	6.09[a]	5.72	9	4.27[a]	4.94	12	3.21[a]
Borrowing	8.44	2	.91	8.29	2	.23	8.06	2	0.53
Reschedule Company Debt	6.13	7	5.44[a]	6.09	7	4.05[a]	6.17	7	2.04[b]
Accelerate/Delay Dividend Payments	7.11	5	3.49[a]	7.52	5	1.49[c]	5.90	8	1.81[b]
Accelerate/Delay Settlement of A/P	7.81	3	2.16[b]	8.19	3	.15	7.50	3	0.10
Accelerate/Delay Collection of A/R	7.42	4	2.94[a]	7.79	4	.84	7.13	4	0.31
Foreign Currency Options	4.26	12	7.67[a]	4.06	12	5.94[a]	5.52	10	1.68[b]
Back-to-Back Loans	4.72	10	6.70[a]	4.56	10	5.49[a]	5.63	9	2.06[b]
Currency Swaps	4.44	11	7.11[a]	4.38	11	5.51[a]	5.10	11	1.35
Increasing Sale Prices	6.00	8	5.25[a]	6.06	8	3.57[a]	6.54	6	1.21

Notes: [a] Significant at the 0.01 level.
[b] Significant at the 0.05 level.
[c] Significant at the 0.10 level.
[d] Each Wilcoxon test statistic entered in the table results from comparing the hedging method on the side with the forward exchange contract.

consistent with the contention that hedging is more useful when the functional currency is the U.S. dollar rather than when the local currency is the designated functional currency. The results pertaining to the hedging methods usefulness rankings under the three different operational situations are reported in Table 4. As expected, regardless of the functional currency position, forward exchange contracts received the highest importance ranking with borrowing as the second important hedging strategy. Options trading was ranked the least important hedging tool on the overall and local currency situations and was ranked 10th when the dollar is designated as the functional currency. Despite these differences in the importance ratings, further statistical analysis is needed before any conclusions on the effects of functional currency designation on the relative usefulness of the hedging methods in reducing foreign currency exposure risk can be made.

The second stage of the statistical analysis was to determine which hedging methods were rated differently under the three functional currency situations. This issue was addressed by performing a series of paired Wilcoxon signed-ranks tests for each of the three functional currency groups. Moreover, for each group the Friedman test, based on two-way analysis of variance by ranks, was performed to retest $\mathbf{H}_3$. These nonparametric statistical procedures are independent of the assumptions on the distributional properties of the data and are robust, insensitive to the sample size, and, therefore, are appropriate for this stage of statistical testing [Conover, 1971]. Table 4 reports the results of the two-stage statistical analysis, the Friedman test and paired tests, for each of the three functional currency situations (overall, local currency, and the U.S. dollar).

For the overall situation, where respondents were required to rate the importance of the different hedging methods, regardless of the functional currency selection, the null hypothesis of no difference in importance ratings is rejected at the 0.01 level. As mentioned before, forward exchange contract is ranked the highest in importance among the hedging methods. Using Wilcoxon test statistics, importance ratings for forward exchange contracts are statistically superior to 10 of the 11 other hedging methods.

With respect to companies that designated the local currency as their functional currency, the Friedman statistic is highly significant when the 12 methods are tested as a group; that is, the null hypothesis of identically distributed importance ratings is rejected at the 0.01 level. The statistics computed to test for the paired comparisons of forward exchange contracts versus other hedging methods are also presented. The differences in the importance ratings of forward exchange contracts against seven of the methods is statistically significant. The evidence, thus, supports the notion that forward exchange contracts are being considered as the best tool in hedging translation exposures when the local currency is designated as the functional currency.

The Friedman test statistic as well as paired Wilcoxon statistics for the firms using the U.S. dollar as the functional currency are presented in the last three columns of Table 4. The Friedman test statistic is once again significant at the 0.01 level when the hedging methods are tested as a group. The pairwise comparisons reveal that while the forward exchange contract is still rated the highest in terms of its importance, it is only superior to one method (delay collection of receivables denominated in foreign currency) at the 0.01 level of significance and rated higher than four other methods at the 0.05 level. Therefore, it seems safe to conclude that the findings presented here suggest that when the dollar is the designated functional currency, the differences between the rate importance of the forward exchange contracts and other hedging approaches narrow.

CONCLUDING REMARKS

Little research effort has been directed toward investigating whether the actual use and importance of the foreign exchange contracts has been affected by the issuance of *SFAS 52*. If the assertion that *SFAS 52* would bring a reduction in unnecessary and costly hedging activities were true, then (ignoring any externalities) one would expect to observe a change in the perceived usefulness and actual use of various hedging methods. This study empirically examined the effect of the adoption of *SFAS 52* and the functional currency dichotomy on the actual volume and relative usefulness of various hedgings against foreign exchange translation exposure. The findings of the study were: (1) the actual volume of MNCs' hedging activities decreased after the adoption of *SFAS 52,* (2) the functional currency designation has had a significant effect on the volume of MNCs' hedgings, (3) the relative usefulness of various hedgings are different, and (4) the relative usefulness of hedgings is a function of the functional currency designation.

The findings and conclusions of this research are subject to some inherent limitations. First, the study is based on a group of firms which may not be representative of the total population of MNCs. Another inherent limitation is that there might exist a potential response bias if those firms that completed the questionnaire did so because they experience a small (large) effect of compliance with the *SFAS 52*. Finally, in the light of the importance of accounting for foreign currency translation and forward exchange contracts, more research using different approaches and samples is warranted.

ACKNOWLEDGMENT

The authors appreciate the helpful comments of Kenneth Most and the anonymous referees on the earlier drafts of this article.

REFERENCES

Aggarwal, R., *Financial Policies for Multinational Companies* [Praeger, 1976]

Beaver, W., and M. Wolfson, "Foreign Currency Translation Gains and Losses: What Effect Do They Have and What Do They Mean?," *Financial Analysts Journal* [March-April 1984], pp. 28-36.

Bender, D.E., "Foreign Currency Translation—FASB 52—Part III," *CPA Journal* 52, 8 [August 1982], pp. 40-43.

Brown, B.C., and J.T. Brandi, "Security Reaction to Changes in Foreign Currency Translation Standards," *Journal of Accounting, Auditing and Finance* [1986], pp. 185-205.

Conover, W.J., *Practical Nonparametric Statistics* [Wiley, 1971].

Evans, T.G., and T.S. Doupnik, *Foreign Exchange Risk Management Under Statement 52* [FASB, 1986].

Evans, T.G., W.R. Folks, Jr., and M. Jilling, *The Impact of Financial Accounting Standards No. 8 on the Foreign Exchange Risk Management Practices of American Multinationals: An Economic Impact Study* [FASB, 1978].

Fekrat, M.A., "Accounting for Forward Exchange Contracts: Theory and Implications for Practice," *Advances in International Accouting* 1 [1987], pp. 249-262.

Financial Accounting Standards Board, *Statement of Financial Accounting Standards No. 8,* "Accounting for the Translation of Foreign Currency Transactions and Foreign Currency Financial Statements" [FASB, October 1975].

________, *Statement of Financial Accounting Standards No. 52,* "Foreign Currency Translation" [FASB, December 1981].

Griffin, P.A., "Management's Preferences for FASB Statement No. 52: Predictive Ability Results," *Abacus* 9, 2 [1983], pp. 130-138.

Houston, C.O. and G.G. Mueller, "Foreign Exchange Rate Hedging and SFAS No. 52 - Relatives or Strangers?," *Accounting Horizons* [December 1988], pp. 50-57.

Largay, J.A., "SFAS No. 52: Expediency or Principle?," *Journal of Accounting, Auditing and Finance* [Fall 1983], pp. 44-53.

Massaro, V.G., "Corporate Experience with FASB Statement No. 52," *Conference Board Information Bulletin, No. 40* [Fall 1983], pp. 44-53.

Mauer, L.J., "MNCs Gain New Freedom Under FASB 52 Flexibility," *Management Accounting* [December 1983], pp. 30-33.

Selling, T.I., and G.H. Sorter, "FASB Statement No. 52 and Its Implications for Financial Statement Analysis," *Financial Analysts Journal* [May-June 1983], pp. 64-69.

Shank, J.K., J.F. Dillard, and R.J. Murdock, *Assessing the Impact of FASB 8: A Research Study* [Financial Executives Research Foundation, 1979].

Smith, E.W., Jr., and R.M. Stulz, "The Determinants of Firms' Hedging Policies," *Journal of Financial and Quantitative Analysis* 20 [December 1985], pp. 391-405.

Wilner, N.A., "SFAS 8 and Information Inductance: An Experiment," *Accounting Organizations and Society* 7, 1 [1982], pp. 43-52.

Ziebart, D.A. and D.H. Kim, "An Examination of the Market Reactions Associated with SFAS No. 8 and SFAS No. 52," *The Accounting Review* [April 1987], pp. 343-357.

PART IV

CROSS-CULTURAL STUDIES

MANAGERIAL, ACADEMIC AND PROFESSIONAL INFLUENCES, AND DISCLOSURE ADEQUACY: AN EMPIRICAL INVESTIGATION

Ahmed Belkaoui

ABSTRACT

This paper examines the international differences in disclosure adequacy and relates these differences to the extent of managerial, academic, and accounting profession influences. The results are significant. The implications of these findings are discussed with a call for (a) a study of the professional value systems of accounting academicians internationally and (b) a study of the lobbying behavior of professionals and managers for accounting standards internationally.

INTRODUCTION

Despite international efforts of harmonization, accounting objectives, standards, policies, and techniques continue to differ among countries. Various attempts have been made to identify the environmental conditions likely to

Advances in International Accounting, Vol. 3, pages 205-214.

ISBN: 1-55938-078-0

affect the determination of accounting principles [Previts, 1975; Radebaugh, 1975; American Accounting Association, 1977; Da Costa et al., 1978; Frank, 1979; Nair and Frank, 1980; Belkaoui, 1983; Belkaoui and Maksy, 1985]. However, these studies assumed that the economic, political, and social factors were the only factors that explain the differences in accounting principles and techniques between the various countries. The results were mixed. Also, an important factor that affects accounting development was not included in these studies; namely the extent of managerial, academic, and professional influences on accounting development. Consequently, the objective of this study is to examine the international differences in disclosure adequacy and to relate these differences to the extent of managerial, academic, and professional influences on accounting development in each country.

DETERMINANTS OF THE DEVELOPMENT OF ACCOUNTING

To identify the determinants of the development of accounting, a disclosure index is used as one of the representatives of the state of accounting development in a given country [Belkaoui, 1983; Belkaoui and Maksy, 1985]. If this disclosure index is viewed as an expression of a social behavior, we may hypothesize that the index is a direct product of its environment based on a well-accepted thesis in sociology that social structure determines social behavior.[1] This index, as shown in Figure 1, may then be represented as being influenced by the extent of academic, professional, and managerial influences on accounting development.

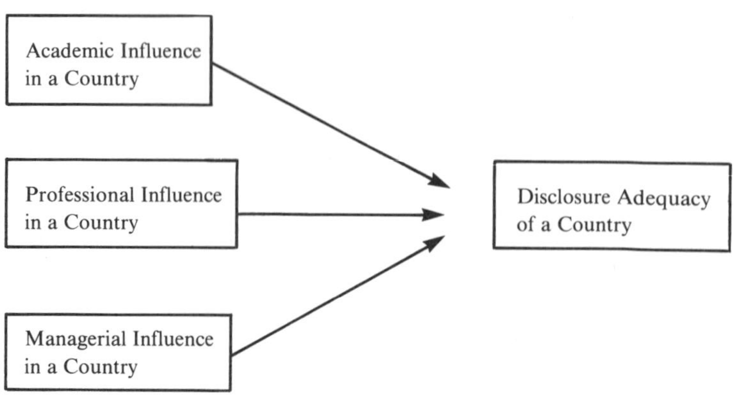

Figure 1. Model of Accounting Development

Managerial Influence

The managerial class of a given country is of particular importance to the development of accounting in general and financial disclosure. When managers do not exert any influence on accounting development they are less likely to be supportive of its standards of reporting and disclosure. An increase in their influence and their participation generates a willingness to abide by its rules and improve the disclosure adequacy of accounting reports. There is likely to be a positive relationship between disclosure adequacy and managerial influence because managers feel bound to abide by the disclosure rules they helped shape. While these propositions may be perceived as intuitive, the objective of this study is to empirically test their validity.

Academic Influence

The academic class of a given country is also important to the development of accounting in general and financial disclosure in particular. When academicians are not asked to participate in standard setting, there is less of a likelihood that important research findings will be incorporated in those standards; consequently, their usefulness and credibility may suffer. Academicians asked to participate and exert some influence lend more credibility to the disclosure standards, especially if the same standards have been subjected to intense research scrutiny. There is likely to be a positive relationship between disclosure adequacy and academic influence as academicians bring a "cultural" capital, crucial to the soundness of the standards [Peasnell and Williams, 1986].

Professional Influence

The professional accountant class of a given country is also important to the development of accounting in general and financial disclosure in particular. Not only its existence but its active participation in standard setting is crucial to the development and successful implementation of objectives of accounting [Buckley and Buckley, 1975; Carey, 1969]. Without the participation and influence of this professional accountant class, accounting development may suffer as its technical and demanding requirements may be misunderstood, or misapplied by an "alienated" profession. Its participation and influence on accounting development, however, will generate a more solid commitment to its goals and a desire to improve its image. In such a case there is likely to be a positive relationship between disclosure adequacy and professional influence on accounting development. For the professional influence to be unconstrained the profession needs to be a large extent self-regulated.

On the basis of these a priori analyses, the following hypothesis is proposed.

H_0. The disclosure adequacy will differ with differences in the academic, professional and managerial influences on accounting development.

PROCEDURES

Methodology and Sample

The dependent variable in this study is a disclosure adequacy index. Independent variables are the: (1) academic influence on accounting development, (2) professional influence on accounting development, and (3) managerial influence on accounting development. First, each of these variables is explained and measured. Second, a regression model is run to identify the significant determinants of the development of accounting internationally.

To be included in our sample a country must have available data to measure both the dependent and independent variables. Thirty countries met this test. They are shown in Table 1.

Disclosure Adequacy Index

Most studies investigating the determinants of disclosure adequacy have relied on the data base in the Price Waterhouse *International Survey of Accounting Principles and Reporting Practices* [1975]. The data relates to 1978. This study relied instead on a more recent data base which relates to 1982 and was produced by the University of Glasgow in collaboration with Deloitte Haskins

Table 1. Countries Included in the Study

Argentina	Japan
Australia	Malaysia
Belgium	Mexico
Brazil	New Zealand
Channel Islands	Philippines
Chile	Portugal
Colombia	South Africa
Denmark	Spain
Finland	Switzerland
France	Thailand
Germany	United Kingdom
Hong Kong	United States
Indonesia	Uruguay
Ireland	Zambia
Italy	Zimbabwe

and Sells International [Gray, Campbell, and Shaw, 1984]. Unlike Price Waterhouse's data, the Gray et al. data distinguishes between measurement and disclosure. First, as this study is concerned with the *regulation* of disclosure adequacy only the disclosure items were considered in the measurement of the index. Second, unlike Belkaoui's [1983] study which included all the propositions on a subject which refers to the same item, this study included the proposition yielding the highest score. These two transformations resulted in the reduction of the disclosure variables in the Gray et al. data to 107. Their data base indicates for each of the 107 variables the extent of application in each country in terms of a fivefold classification: (1) required, (2) recommended, (3) permitted, (4) not applicable, and (5) nonpermitted. In this study each of the five classifications are coded as:

Classification	Scale for the Extent of Application
1. required	4
2. recommended	3
3. permitted	2
4. not applicable	0
5. nonpermitted	-1

The scale for the extent of application of each of the 107 variables constituted a separate observation for each of the 30 countries. The sum of these observations per country is used as the actual disclosure adequacy index.

A high score on the "actual disclosure adequacy index" indicates a willingness by the given country to adhere to and enforce 107 disclosure practices deemed necessary for enhancing the quality of accounting disclosure and encourage international harmonization [Gray et al., 1984]. Where differences in disclosure practices exist, this either reflects the degrees of professional, academic and managerial influences on accounting development, or indicates that a different measure of disclosure adequacy is considered appropriate. This study favors the former interpretation, which is (1) that the conformity with each of the 107 disclosure practices is a desired goal for each of the countries in the study, and (2) that the degree of conformity depends on the extent of academic, professional and managerial influences on accounting development. That conformity is the desired goal is evident in the efforts of the various international standard setting bodies. That the degree of conformity is a reflection of the extent of academic, professional and managerial influences on accounting development is the subject of this study.

Academic, Professional, and Managerial Influences

The first chapter of Gray et al. [1984] included questions on influences on accounting development. Three of the questions and answers were used for the measurement of the extent of academic, professional and managerial influences on accounting development.

A. The managerial influence was determined by the following question: "What is the attitude of business management to information disclosure and accounting standards?" The answer was determined in terms of the fivefold classification: (1) strongly against, (2) moderately against, (3) indifferent, (4) moderately support, and (5) strongly support. For the purposes of this study each of the several classifications are coded as follows:

Classification	Scale for the Extent of Application
1. Strongly against	-2
2. Moderately against	-1
3. Indifferent	0
4. Moderately support	1
5. Strongly support	2

B. The professional influence was determined by the following question: "To what extent can it be said that the government keeps its intervention to a minimum, relying instead of self regulation within the financial country (based on professional standards, training, and a high standard of ethical behavior)?" The answer was threefold: (1) low professional self-regulation, (2) medium professional self-regulation, and (3) high professional self-regulation. For the purposes of this study each of the three classifications are coded as follows:

Classification	Scale for the Extent of Application
1. Low professional self-regulation	1
2. Medium professional self-regulation	2
3. High professional self-regulation	3

C. The academic influence was determined by the following question: "Does the academic side of the profession influence the setting of standards relating to externalfinancial reporting?" The answer was either a yes or no, coded respectively as 1 or 0.

Table 2. Regression Results

Independent	*Intercept*	*Managerial Influence*	*Academic Influence*	*Professional Influence*
Coefficients	2.272	0.1076	0.1553	0.1648
T-Statistic	14.18	2.15**	2.05***	2.63*
R^2	38.91			
F	5.52*			
n	30			

Notes: * Significant at $\alpha = 0.01$.
** Significant at $\alpha = 0.05$.
*** Significant at $\alpha = 0.10$.

RESULTS: DETERMINANTS OF FINANCIAL DISCLOSURE ADEQUACY

A multiple regression analysis was used to determine the association between the extent of academic, professional, and managerial influences on accounting development and the actual disclosure adequacy of each country in the sample. Table 2 presents the results of the regression. The three independent variables of academic, professional and managerial influences appear to be significant. They are positively related to actual disclosure adequacy. The overall regression was also significant (F significant at $\alpha = 0.01$) and the three independent variables explain 38.9% of the variations in the dependent variable of actual disclosure adequacy: This indicates that while academic, professional, and managerial influences are important to the financial disclosure adequacy in a given country, other factors are also important and need to be included in the model. Future research may inquire into the nature of the variables which need to be added to the model to increase its explanatory power. In any case, the results show the crucial role of academicians, managers, and professional accountants in promoting accounting development and improving financial disclosure adequacy in the process.

DISCUSSION

The significant findings that academic, professional, and managerial inputs into the financial reporting process determine the disclosure adequacy internationally have serious implications.

The first question that needs to be asked relates to whether disclosure is more or less adequate where the academics have inputs into the financial reporting process internationally? The answer rests on solving whether academicians are *ersatz* academics as suggested by Watts and Zimmerman [1979] or scholar saints as suggested by Peasnell and Williams [1986]. Watts and Zimmerman make the assumption that individuals act to maximize their wealth and perquisites (including creative fulfillment, prestige, and leisure). Two conclusions are made: (1) sectional interest will "demand" accounting theories that will provide excuses for the policies they prefer and (2) incentives exist to ensure a "supply" of such theories. This close relationship to a policymaker, whether it is a standard setting agency or another, makes the accounting academicians, like all other academicians, "bureaucratic" intellectuals who exercise advisory and technical functions within a bureaucracy as opposed to those intellectuals who elect to stay unattached to a bureaucracy [Merton, 1968, pp. 256-226; Nettle, 1965, pp. 15-32]. The bureaucratic intellectual is reduced to being an "ideologue" because he subordinates the search for a universally comprehensive understanding of social, cultural, and physical reality in favor of an immediately instrumental arbitration of competing policies or courses of action [Barrow, 1987, p. 423]. Such a role is unfortunate if one subscribes to the prevailing assumption that a "particularization" of intellectual activity which links or constrains academic inquiry to specific social interests or needs leads to a fall from the "sacred" and a descent into the dishonorable realm of "ideology" [Ashcraft, 1980; Mannheim, 1971, pp. 116-131, 1986, pp. 265-266].

Peasnell and Williams [1986] disagree with this view of academicians and suggests that the academic reward system in the leading universities does not encourage the *ersatz* academics. One way of solving this problem is to determine the value systems of accounting academics internationally. A first attempt at studying the professional value systems of academic accountants found them not to be clearly defined, and personal and professional values not to be easily separated [Belkaoui and Chan, 1988].

The second question that needs to be asked relates to whether professional and managerial influences on accounting disclosure are inevitably restrictive. The professional influence may be restrictive as public accountants favor regulation that may benefit them in three ways: (1) barriers to entry, (2) increased demand for auditing services, and (3) reduction in negative externalities from freeriders [Benston 1985, p. 53]. The managerial influence is central to the determination of standards internationally. Moonitz [1974] supports this view:

> Management is central to any discussion of financial reporting, whether at the statutory or regulatory level, or at the level of official pronouncements of accounting bodies [p. 64].

But that role is inevitably restrictive with the evidence from the beginnings of a positive theory of accounting that explores those factors influencing management's attitudes on accounting standards which are likely to affect corporate lobbying on accounting standards [Watts and Zimmerman, 1978]. Managers' position is a function of the proposed standard's effect on the firm's value and on earnings used in compensation plans. "Ceteris paribus managers are more likely to oppose standards that restrict accounting procedures used in contracts (increasing agency costs) and reduce reported earnings than standards that do not restrict accounting procedures used in contracts and/ or do not reduce reported earnings" [Watts and Zimmerman, 1986, p. 333]. The evidence of the restrictive nature of managerial and professional influence is, for the time being, restricted to the U.S. context. Evidence in other national contexts is needed for a better evaluation of those influences on accounting disclosure adequacy internationally.

SUMMARY AND CONCLUSIONS

This study examined the international differences in financial disclosure adequacy and relates these differences to the extent of academic, managerial, and professional influences on accounting development. The results indicate that the financial disclosure adequacy in terms of conformity to 107 disclosure practices is likely to differ with differences in the extent of academic, professional, and managerial influences on accounting development. The main conclusion to be derived from these results is that for a country to improve its financial disclosure adequacy the supportive role of its academicians, managers, and professional accountants is crucial. For the developing countries the results suggest a reinforcing of the institutions and enactment of laws to allow the academicians, managers, and professionals to have an active and constructive role in accounting development.

The implications of these findings are that these influences can be restrictive. Evidence is needed on (a) the professional value systems of accounting academicians internationally and (b) the lobbying behavior of managers and professionals internationally.

NOTE

1. This thesis results from the sociological paradigm of structural functionalism which holds that structural determinants—social facts—constitute the primary methodological foci for explanation of social behavior. The classical statement of this method can be traced to Durkheim [1893, 1895], and more recently to Parsons [1971] and Ritzer [1975].

REFERENCES

American Accounting Association, "Report of the 1975-76 Committee on International Accounting Operations and Education," *The Accounting Review* 11 [1977], Supplement, pp. 65-132.

Ashcroft, R., "Political Theory and The Problem of Ideology," *Journal of Politics* [August 1980], pp. 687-705.

Barrow, C.W., "Intellectuals in Contemporary Social Theory: A Radical Critique," *Sociological Inquiry*.

Belkaoui, A., "Economic, Political and Civil Indicators and Reporting and Disclosure Adequacy: Empirical Investigation," *Journal of Accounting and Public Policy* [Fall 1983], pp. 207-219.

Belkaoui, A. and J. Chan, "Professional Value System of Academic Accountants," *Advances in Public Interest Accounting* [Spring 1988].

Belkaoui, A. and M. Maksy, "Welfare of the Common Man and Accounting Disclosure Adequacy: An Empirical Investigation," *The International Journal of Accounting Education and Research* [Spring 1985], pp. 81-94.

Benston, G.J., "The Market for Public Accounting Services: Demand, Supply and Regulation," *Journal of Accounting and Public Policy* [Spring 1985], pp. 33-80.

Buckley, J.W. and M.H. Buckley, *The Accounting Profession* [Melville, 1975].

Carey, J.L., *The Rise of the Accounting Profession,* Vols. 1, 2 [AICPA, 1969].

Da Costa, R.C., J.C. Bourgeois, and W.M. Lawson, "A Classification of International Financial Accounting Practices," *The International Journal of Accounting Education and Research* [Spring 1978], pp. 73-85.

Durkheim, E., *The Division of Labor in Society,* translated by G. Simpson [MacMillan, 1933].

Durkheim, E., *The Rules of Sociological Method,* translated by S.S. Solovay and J.H. Mueller, edited by G.E.G. Cathin [Free Press, 1964].

Frank, W.G., "An Empirical Analysis of International Accounting Principles," *Journal of Accounting Research* [Spring 1979], pp. 593-605.

Gray, S.J., L.G. Campbell, and J.C. Shaw, eds., *International Financial Reporting* [*A Comparative International Survey of Accounting Requirements and Practices in 30 Countries*] [Macmillan, 1984].

Merton, R.K., *Social Theory and Social Structure* [Free Press, 1968].

Moonitz, M., *Obtaining Agreements on Standards,* Studies in Accounting Research No. 8 [ARA, 1974].

Nair, R.D. and W.G. Frank, "The Impact of Disclosure and Measurement Practices on International Accounting Classification," *The Accounting Review* [July 1980], pp. 426-450.

Nettle, J.P., "Power and the Intellectuals," in C.C. O'Brien and W.D. Vanech, eds., *Power and Consciousness* [New York University Press, 1969], pp. 53-125.

Parsons, T., *The System of Modern Societies* [Prentice-Hall, 1971].

Peasnell, K.V. and D.J. Williams, "Ersatz Academics and Scholar Saints: The Supply of Financial Accounting Research," *ABACUS* [September 1986], pp. 121-135.

Previts, G.J., "On the Subject of Methodology and Models for International Accountancy," *International Journal of Accounting Education and Research* [Spring 1975], pp. 1-12.

Radebaugh, L.H., "Environmental Factors Influencing the Development of Accounting Objectives, Standards and Practices in Peru," *The International Journal of Accounting Education and Research* [Fall 1975], pp. 39-56.

Ritzer, G., *Sociology: A Multiple Paradigm Science* [Allyn & Bacon, 1975].

Watts, R.L. and J.L. Zimmerman, "Towards a Positive Theory of the Determination of Accounting Standards," *The Accounting Review* [January 1978], pp. 112-134.

Watts, R.L. and J.L. Zimmerman, "The Demand for and Supply of Accounting Theories: The Market for Excuses," *The Accounting Review* [April 1979], pp. 273-305.

Watts, R.L. and J.L. Zimmerman, *Positive Accounting Theory* [Prentice-Hall, 1986].

THE CULTURAL RELATIVITY OF ACCOUNTING AND INTERNATIONAL PATTERNS OF SOCIAL ACCOUNTING

M.H.B. Perera and M.R. Mathews

ABSTRACT

This article considers the impact of culture on accounting and specifically on social accounting developments. The study of culture and cultural structures by Hofstede is reviewed, together with the application of these ideas to accounting, particularly in the work of Gray. Explanations were sought of differences in accounting practices in Anglo-American and Continental European countries within the literature on culture and accounting. The area of social accounting, specifically employee and environmental impact reports, is considered. Anglo-American accounting systems are found to be considerably less concerned with the development of employee reporting than those of Continental European countries. The opposite was found to be the case when consideration was given to the dislosure of environmental impact in annual reports. Differences in approaches are at least partly explained by the analysis of cultural effects on accounting. This paper suggests that there is evidence of the need to make allowances for these cultural effects when conducting any type of research into social accounting.

Advances in International Accounting, Vol. 3, pages 215-251.

ISBN: 1-55938-078-0

INTRODUCTION

This paper deals with the relationship between culture and accounting, and particularly with the effects of culture on the emerging field of social accounting. Social accounting is an area of growing significance but at the same time is relatively poorly defined. The aspect of social accounting that attracts most attention has been referred to as social responsibility accounting [Mathews, 1984], corporate social reporting [Abbott and Monsen, 1979; Alexander and Bucholz, 1978; Gray, Owen, and Maunders, 1987], corporate social responsibility [Bowman and Haire, 1975; Corson and Steiner, 1974], and corporate social accounting and reporting [Ramanathan and Schreuder 1982], as well as other numerous possible alternatives. The disclosures include employment related information, environmental measures, value added statements, additional segmented information, product related information, and statements of future prospects. The type of reporting envisaged here is aimed at a number of user groups including shareholders, governmental organizations at the national, regional, and institutional level, employees and trade unions, and other groups such as consumers organizations [Lee, 1981; Schreuder, 1981; Schoenfield 1978; Ernst and Ernst, 1972-78; Guthrie and Mathews, 1985]. There are many unresolved issues in this area including the validity of user demands, measurement problems involved, and the criteria for evaluating social costs and benefits [Benston, 1982, 1984; Schreuder and Ramanathan, 1984] where externalities are brought into focus. The term *social reporting* is sometimes used to represent reporting to society as a whole and yet at other times it is used to represent reporting on social matters to employees of the corporation.

Recent research in the social accounting area has included market studies, philosophical considerations, radical theory, and attempts to develop a structured organization of the area. Little consideration has been given so far to the effects which national and regional cultures and subcultures may have on the development of social accounting.

Market studies have attempted to show that disclosures of socially related information (of one type or another) have an effect on share prices and market returns [Belkaoui, 1976; Spicer, 1978; Ingram, 1978; Stevens, 1982; Shane and Spicer, 1983; Mahapatra, 1984; Freedman and Stagliano, 1984]. The results have been mixed and appear to be strongly influenced by the samples available and the statistical tests employed. Overall, it may be argued that these additional disclosures do have information content for shareholders, as reflected in changes in share prices.

Philosophical considerations include the social contract of business with society [Donaldson, 1982] and organizational legitimacy [Lindblom, 1983]. Externalities have provided the opportunity for a debate which has its origins in value positions [Ramanathan, 1976; Benston, 1982a, 1982b, 1984; Schreuder and Ramanathan, 1984a, 1984b]. The philosophical-based literature extends financial reporting to encompass parties other than shareholders who might have a "right to know," such as *The Corporate Report* [ICAEW, 1975].

Critical (radical) theorists have offered alternative and competing views of social accounting as part of an approach to a Marxist restructuring of the decision-making and accountability functions in society [Tinker, Merino, and Niemark 1982; Merino and Neimark, 1982; Cooper and Sherer, 1984; Tinker, 1984]. Much of this literature is intolerant of current social accounting research which is viewed as supportive of the status quo in society (with limited modifications). Critical theorists want to avoid the use of the market mechanism for the allocation of resources, in favor of an administrative solution.

In addition to these attempts to argue why the area of social accounting is important to one or other group of users of accounting reports, a limited amount of research has been carried out on the various dimensions of social accounting. This paper closely defines or delineates the nature of social accounting and thereby provides a structure to be addressed. Attempts to provide structures have included Ramanathan [1976], Mathews [1984], Burke [1984], and Tinker [1984]. The *Corporate Report* [ICAEW, 1975] also has a number of structural implications.

Although a large volume of published material has argued the case for additional disclosures, provided classifications and structures, and reported on the state of the art [Ernst and Ernst, 1972-78; Guthrie and Mathews, 1985], the rate of development of social accounting has been relatively slow. A number of factors may influence the acceptance of the new ideas that are contained in the various types of accounting which comprise social accounting. These include economic and political conditions, the strength or weakness of the influence of marginal economic values [Tinker, 1984], the influence of the capitalist system and its social reproduction, lethargy, inertia, and the resistance to change often exhibited by the accounting profession. These factors, and many others, comprise the culture of a given country or region or are manifestations of that culture.

It has been demonstrated that the effects of culture may be used to group countries in order to study their accounting systems [Gray, 1985]. International accounting has been marked by attempts at harmonizing accounting techniques and standards and the resistance to harmonization has only recently been identified as culturally related [Perera, 1985]. Although a relatively recent hypothesis, the culture-accounting interrelationship has provided some interesting results. This paper attempts to apply some of these ideas and developments to social accounting. Social accounting researchers can perhaps learn from the experiences of others in the area of effects of culture on accounting.

This paper consists of an examination of the evidence for the influence of culture on financial accounting, and an extension to the field of social accounting. A number of specific examples show how culture may be an unspecified factor in reported research results.

THE IMPACT OF CULTURE ON ACCOUNTING

Introduction

There is a growing amount of research on national systems of accounting focused particularly on the Anglo-American countries—United States, Canada, United Kingdom, Australia, and New Zealand—and continental Europe [Zeff, 1972; Lafferty, 1975; Benston, 1982; Oldham, 1981; Nobes and Parker, 1981; Holzer, 1984]. In the middle 1970s, subsequent to the entry of the United Kingdom into the European Economic Community (EEC) accounting in Continental Europe became a significant research issue, and subsequently a number of relatively detailed studies of individual countries became available. These included Germany [Beeny, 1975] and France [Beeny and Chastney, 1978]. In addition, there were several comparative studies, relatively comprehensive in scope, which covered a wide range of countries: AICPA [1975], covering 30 countries; Price Waterhouse [1973, 1975, 1979], covering 38, 46 and 64 countries respectively; OECD [1980], covering 20 countries; Choi and Bavishi [1982], covering 100 companies in 24 countries; Cairns, Lafferty, and Mantile [1984], covering 250 companies in 33 countries; and Gray, Campbell, and Shaw [1984], covering 20-50 companies in each of the 30 countries concerned. The findings of these studies confirmed the existence of world-wide diversity of accounting requirements and practices and this diversity has been attributed to a variety of environmental factors under which accountants work.

Classification of National Systems of Accounting

As national differences in accounting systems and practices became known to researchers, attempts were made to identify patterns and to classify countries on the basis of those patterns. Two alternative approaches have been taken. The first involves the identification of relevant environmental factors and links them to national accounting practices [Mueller, 1967, 1968; Zeff, 1972; Radebaugh, 1975; Nobes, 1983, 1984]. The second classifies accounting practices using statistical analysis and then attempts to explain the patterns discovered by reference to environmental factors [AAA, 1977; Frank, 1979; Nair and Frank, 1980; Da Costa et al. 1980; Goodrich, 1982; Belkaoui, 1983].

It is interesting to note that many of the classifications developed through these approaches suggest, inter alia, significant differences between Anglo-American countries and continental European countries in terms of their patterns of accounting development. For example, Mueller [1967] identified four categories of accounting in western capitalist countries: (1) accounting in a macro framework, where enterprise accounting is closely linked with national economic policies (Germany, Sweden); (2) accounting based on microeconomic factors, where accounting is regarded as part of business economics (Netherlands); (3) accounting as an independent discipline, where accounting is regarded as a separate service function in business practice (United Kingdom, United States); and (4) uniform accounting, where accounting is viewed as a regulatory device (France). Nobes [1983, 1984] adopted Mueller's analysis as the basis of a classification which divided western capitalist countries and their accounting systems into two broad categories: micro-based systems and macro-uniform systems. Subclassifications were also identified. Micro-based systems were divided into business economics based (Netherlands) and business practice based systems. The macrouniform systems were divided into Continental and government economic-based systems (Sweden). Nobes went on to divide the business practice based group into systems under U.K. influence (Australia, New Zealand, United Kingdom, Ireland) and under U.S. influence (Canada, United States), and the Continental group into tax based systems (Belgium, France, Spain, Italy), and law based systems (Germany).

It can be seen that the Anglo-American countries are grouped as micro-business practice based systems, whereas the European countries, with the exception of the Netherlands, are grouped together as macrouniform systems. The classifications put forward by Mueller and Nobes are shown in Figures 1 and 2. The data on which these classifications were based have been criticized as being defective; however, such criticisms do not materially affect the relevance of those classifications to the present discussion.

1	2	3	4
Accounting in a macro framework:	Microeconomic factors:	Service function in business practice:	Uniform accounting:
Germany Sweden	The Netherlands	United Kingdom United States	France

Figure 1. Mueller 1967

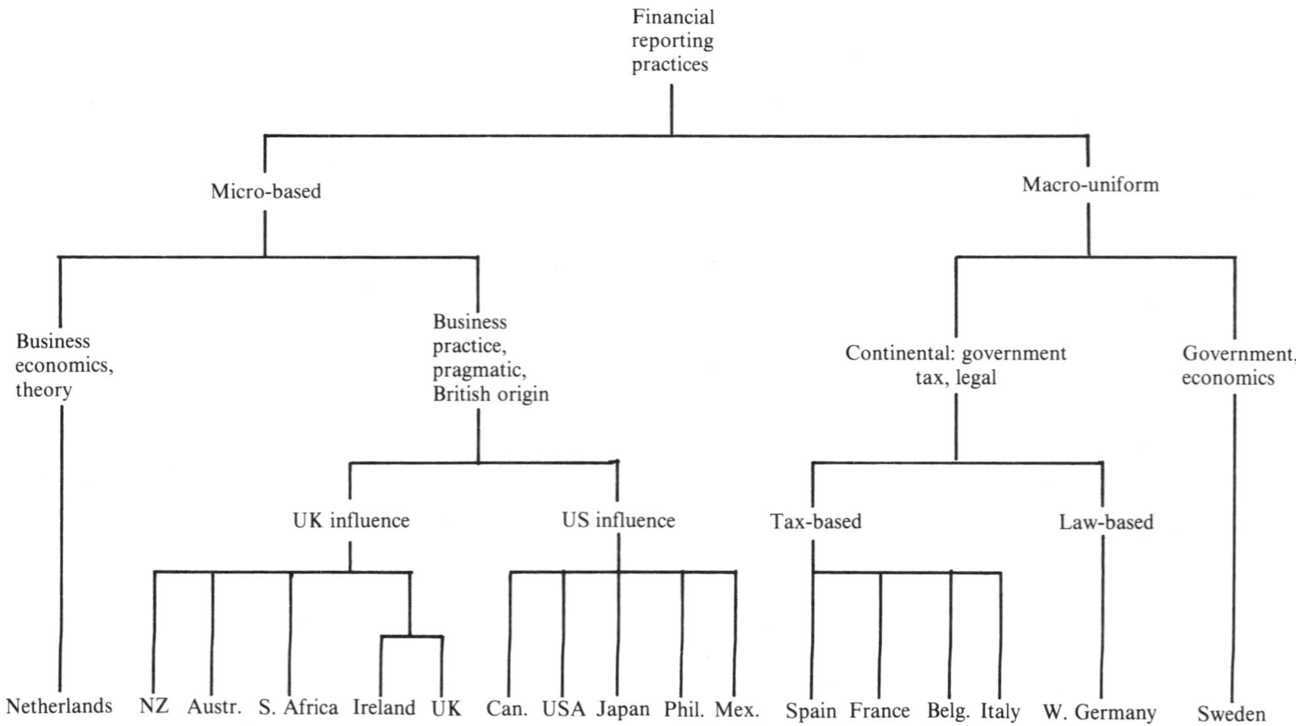

Figure 2. Nobes 1983-1984

One of the significant outcomes of research endeavors in the comparative analysis of accounting in different countries has been an enhanced awareness of the importance of environmental factors in moulding a country's accounting system. This in turn has led to serious attempts at identifying both the relevant environmental factors and the mechanism by which such factors influence accounting.

Only recently, particularly since the early eighties, has culture been considered as a significant environmental factor influencing accounting. The argument here is that because accounting is a sociotechnical activity it involves dealing with both human and nonhuman resources or techniques as well as with the interaction between the two. Although the technical aspect of accounting is less culture-dependent than the human aspect, since the two interact, accounting cannot be culture-free. It has also been argued that accounting is in fact culturally determined [Violet, 1983]. The relationship between accounting and culture was the theme of at least three recent international conferences: Workshop on Accounting and Culture (Amsterdam, June 1985), AAA Annual Conference (New York, August 1986) [Cushing 1987], and Workshop on Accounting and Culture (Brussels, December 1987).

ASPECTS OF CULTURE

"Culture" is not a monolithic concept. It has been defined as: "the total way of life of a people"; "the social legacy the individual acquires from his [her] group"; "a way of thinking, feeling and believing"; "an abstraction from behavior"; "a theory on the part of Anthropologists about the way in which a group of people in fact behave"; "a storehouse of pooled learning"; "a set of standardised orientations to recurrent problems"; "learned behaviour"; "a mechanism for the normative regulation of behaviour"; "a precipitate of history" [1973]. In view of the diffusion demonstrated, any attempt to provide an all-encompassing definition would be nonproductive. Culture is to a human collectivity what personality is to an individual.

National culture is the sum of the shared values of members of a nation. However, this does not mean that every individual within that culture behaves in the same way. Culture produces an average pattern of behavior, yet within a national culture, there are also a large number of subcultures. For example organizational culture is identified by the values shared by the members of an organization, and occupational culture consists of the values of those belonging to a distinct occupation such as accounting. We can also identify a generation culture, a class culture, and so on. However, in general, reference is often made to the fact that members of a given culture tend to share social meanings, understandings, values, beliefs, and symbols [Takatera and Yamamoto, 1987]. That is, they subconsciously assign similar interpretations to events, and think, react, and perceive events in a consistent fashion. This is similar to Hofstede's [1980] definition of culture: "The collective programming of the mind which distinguishes the members of one human group from another" [p. 25].

Hofstede [1983c] observed how the cultural differences between nations, which often appear to share similar frameworks of meanings, values, and symbols, manifest themselves in behavior. For example, the British will form a neat queue whenever they have to wait but the French will not; the Dutch will, as a rule, greet strangers when they enter a small enclosed space (railway compartment, doctor's waiting room, lift) but not the Belgians; Austrians will wait at a red pedestrian traffic light even where there is no traffic but not the Dutch; the Swiss tend to become very angry when somebody, say a foreigner, makes a mistake in traffic, but the Swedes do not. Hofstede concluded that all these manifestations are part of an invisble set of mental programs which constitute these countries' national cultures.

Culture-based behavior patterns, as demonstrated by individuals, are difficult to change unless s(he) is detached from his/her culture. Within a nation culture changes only slowly, particularly because what is in the minds of the people generally enters the institutional arrangements such as government, legal and educational systems, industrial relations, family structures, religious organizations, sports clubs, settlement patterns, literature, architecture, and even scientific theories. All these reflect traditions and common thinking patterns, which, rooted in one culture, may be different in another [Hofstede 1983a].

Prior to 1970, most attempts to understand the determinants of human behavior had a distinctly ethnocentric bias [Triandis, 1980]. Recently there has been an increased interest in cross-cultural research, primarily due to the desire to test the universality of Euro-American psychological theories [Berry, 1975]. Research findings have resulted in the realization that not all the key elements of contemporary psychological theories, such as motivation theory, may be universal. This has led to efforts to determine which aspects of psychological theorizing are truly universal, and which may be valid only in a particular culture area.

A major difficulty in cross-cultural research has centered on the contrast between emic and etic considerations. The emic concept is that cultures can only be understood in their own contexts. Individual features of different cultures have different "cultural meanings," and, hence, they are not comparable. On the other hand, the etic concept considers behavior across many cultures from a universal perspective. As such, etics present culture-free aspects that must operate in at least more than one culture. A potential pitfall is the tendency to use the emic concepts of one culture to explain characteristics of another. Triandis [1980, p. 35] pointed out that this was the case in most cross-cultural research prior to the 1970s.

The study of culture is characterized by another problem arising from the infinite nature of its components. It is essential, therefore, that in analysing the impact of culture on the behavior of the members of any particular subculture, a researcher must select the cultural components or dimensions most pertinent to the particular facet of behavior being studied.

ACCOUNTING AND CULTURE

Recently there has been an increase in interest in applying behavioral ideas to accounting. This has, no doubt, enriched the field and contributed significantly to changing the status of accounting as a purely technical discipline. Research in this area has ranged from consideration of the psychological factors which influence the preparers of accounting statements, to sociopolitical consideration of the role of accounting in organizations and societies. The most recent social science area to be applied to accounting, is cultural anthropology.

A social science orientation of accounting research has led to the realization that some behavior patterns of accountants as well as users of accounting reports were likely to be moulded by culture. For example, Jaggi [1975] attempted to identify the impact of culture on the disclosure of financial information. He argued that the values of managers are an important factor influencing their disclosure decisions, and that such value orientations of individuals in society are, to a great extent, the product of the cultural environment of that society. Jaggi used concepts developed by Parsons and Shils [1950] to identify the different patterns of value orientations of individuals in different countries; "Universalism," representing a value orientation toward institutionalized obligation to society, and "Particularism," representing a value orientation toward institutionalized obligation to friendship.

In an attempt to classify countries on the basis of the value orientation of individuals, Jaggi identified countries which possess complex technology, emphasize individual freedom and mobility, and appreciate competition and achieved status as predominantly universalistic. Those countries that are less technical, less scientific, and less urban were identified as predominantly particularistic value oriented. Accordingly, the economically developed countries are categorized under the former group, and the developing countries under the latter. Extending this classification to work situations, individuals in universalistic societies are expected to be impersonal in their relations with other individuals, loyal to the firm, and honor their obligations to society. In the work situation of particularistic societies, individuals are assessed by others primarily in terms of their relations with them, and evaluation in an impersonal and objective manner is rare. Jaggi noted that this kind of impersonal association is also extended to the adult's entire social world, which influences perceptions of social situations and close personal bonds. He draws support for the argument from management literature [for example, Harbison and Myers, 1959; Haire, Ghiselli, and Porter, 1966]. With regard to information disclosure, it can be argued that managers with universalistic value orientations are likely to be committed to disclosing relatively reliable information compared to those with particularistic value orientations, who are not likely to accept obligations to outsiders or to society. The obligations of the particularistic value oriented managers will be related to family members owning and managing firms with external reporting practices designed to meet legal and customary requirements. This may result in relatively low reliability of information disclosed in financial statements because these statements are not central to the family interests.

Beazley [1968] stated that cultural differences and similarities between countries are likely to explain why people behave differently and that different is not necessarily synonymous with inferior. McComb [1979] expressed a similar view: it is important to try and understand the cultural and structural reasons for the existence of national differences in accounting principles and practices. AlHashim [1973] drew attention to the study of cultural factors as important in determining the attitudes of preparers and users of accounting statements, which are significantly influenced by the environments in which they operate. With regard to corporate disclosure in India, Singvi [1967] and Das Gupta [1977] expressed similar views and both referred to the reluctance of managers to disclose certain information for economic and cultural reasons. Frank [1979] and Nair and Frank [1980] attempted to establish that a close association existed between economic and cultural variables and the classification of countries into groups based on their accounting practices. They concluded that due to economic and cultural differences it may be more difficult for policymakers to achieve harmonization of practices than was previously realized.

In an examination of the suitability of U.S. management accounting concepts to other cultural environments, Seidler [1969] pointed out that American management accounting techniques and concepts, such as responsibility accounting, are based on the assumption that attempts to increase both individual discretion and responsibility in large organizations will be acceptable to both management and employees. He then argued that such techniques and concepts may be both unacceptable and unworkable in many developing countries where drive for achievement and advancement is not strong and employees may not desire additional, or indeed any, responsibility at the price of possible failure.

The implications of motivation theory for accounting have also attracted the attention of accounting researchers. An understanding of the motivational effects of accounting systems and reports is vital for (at least) the following reasons: (1) a major purpose of managerial planning and control systems is to motivate performance; (2) organizational goals and accomplishments are often stated in accounting terms; and (3) individual performance is often evaluated by accounting measures. However, cross-cultural research has revealed that the problem of motivating people differs from one society to another and, therefore, not all of the key elements of contemporary motivation theory may be universal [Tannenbaum, 1980].

Culture has featured prominently in more recent discussions of the factors influencing the accounting development of a country [Nobes and Parker, 1981; Bromwich and Hopwood, 1983; Choi and Mueller, 1984; Arpan and Radebaugh, 1985; Perera, 1985]. It has also been argued that the lack of consensus on what represents good accounting is because its purpose is cultural not technical. The content of financial reports depends on local history and convention [Hofstede, 1985]. This is probably why the product of accounting—financial statements and reports—sometimes has a shareholder orientation, other times a creditor orientation, and occasionally serves the interests of national planners or public administrators [Mueller, 1985].

It is clear that cross-cultural behavioral research in accounting is likely to provide some explanations about why there are differences in accounting techniques and practices between countries and to answer the question whether the first findings of researchers in one culture can be transferred without modification for effective use in another culture. However, most of what has been written on this subject so far consists of ex cathedra propositions lacking analysis, or of nongeneralizable case studies. Therefore, research efforts should be directed toward developing a theoretical framework to be used in analyzing the issues involved. In this context, research findings on similar issues in other related fields may be helpful. For example, in the field of management, Hofstede has sought to analyze differences in work-related values across cultures. His study was based on data collected through an employee attitude survey in a multinational corporation. The survey took place twice between 1968 and 1973, involving different subsidiaries in 64 countries, and 116,000 questionnaires in 20 languages [Hofstede, 1983a].

Hofstede's Model

In an attempt to develop a commonly acceptable, well-defined, and empirically-based terminology to describe cultures, Hofstede identified four distinct dimensions which he considered reflected the cultural orientation of a country: (1) Individualism versus Collectivism, (2) Large versus Small Power Distance, (3) Strong versus Weak Uncertainty Avoidance, and (4) Masculinity versus Femininity. The main features of each of the dimensions is discussed, followed by a consideration of their implications for accounting.

Individualism versus Collectivism

This dimension relates to the degree of integration a society maintains among its members, or the relationship between an individual and his/her fellow individuals. Individualism represents a preference for a loosely knit social framework in society, wherein individuals are supposed to take care of themselves and their immediate families only; similar to Jaggi's notion of Universalism. On the other hand, Collectivism represents a preference for a tightly knit social framework in which individuals can expect their relatives or other in-group to look after them in exchange for unquestioning loyalty, similar to Jaggi's Particularism.

The identified characteristics of this dimension tend to raise some questions in regard to established theories which have a bearing on management thought in general—for example, the validity of economic theories based on self-interest, and of psychological theories based on self-actualization—because in a collectivist society, preference is given to collective interest and achievement. Some other issues that are likely to become important under this dimension include the nature of the employer-employee relationship, and the priority given in business. In an individualist society, employer-employee relationships tend to be calculative, whereas in a collectivist society, such relationships tend to be morally based. On the other hand, in an individualist society, priority in business is given to task rather than to the relationship as in the case of a collectivist society. Hofstede [1983c, p. 80] concluded that the degree of individualism in a country is statistically related to that country's wealth. Accordingly, wealthy countries tend to be more individualist oriented, whereas poor countries tend to be more collectivist oriented. Japan represents an unique situation in that, although it is certainly among the wealthy countries of the world, it is given a ranking of 29-30 on Hofstede's Individualism vs. Collectivism scale, indicating a much lower degree of individualism as compared to that of the United States or United Kingdom. However, the Individualism/ Collectivism dimension would seem to indicate an aspect of clear difference in societal values that exist between countries (see Appendix 1).

Large versus Small Power Distance

This dimension relates to the extent to which the members of a society accept that power in institutions and organizations is distributed unequally. For example, in large power distance societies, people tend to accept a hierarchical order in which everybody has a place which needs no further justification, whereas in small power distance societies, people tend to strive for power equalization and demand justification for those power inequalities that do exist.

The identified characteristics of this dimension tend to draw attention to issues such as whether subordinate consultation is necessary or paternalistic management is accepted. In a large power distance society, subordinate consultation may not be as important as in a small power distance society, because there is a tendency for its members to accept paternalistic management. The degree of inequality in a society is measured by the extent of power distance. The level of power distance is related to the degree of centralization of authority and the degree of autocratic leadership. Societies in which power tends to be distributed unequally can remain so because this situation satisfies the psychological need for dependence of the people without power. In other words, the value systems of the two groups are complementary. Hofstede [1983c, p. 82] identified a global relationship between power distance and collectivism. Collectivist countries always show large power distance, although individualist countries do not always show small power distance. It is interesting to note that all poor countries are collectivist with large power distance (see Appendix 1).

Strong versus Weak Uncertainty Avoidance

This dimension relates to the degree to which the members of a society feel uncomfortable with uncertainty and ambiguity. The fundamental issue involved here is how a society reacts to the fact that the future is unknown-whether it tries to control the future or to let it happen. In the weak uncertainty avoidance societies people have a natural tendency to feel relatively secure, whereas in strong uncertainty avoidance societies people tend to try and beat the future because the future remains essentially unpredictable and there will be a higher level of anxiety. In such societies, there will also be institutions that try to create security and avoid risk. One important way of creating security is through the law and other formal rules and institutions, whereby protection is provided against the unpredictability of human behavior. The existence of a relatively high degree of planning of economic activities in strong uncertainty avoidance societies could also be explained in terms of this value dimension. Religion is another way of creating a feeling of security. All religions attempt to create in the minds of people an expectation of something which is certain.

The identified characteristics of this dimension tend to draw attention, among other things, to the existence of an emotional need for formal and informal rules to guide behavior, the degree of formalization, standardization, and ritualization of organizations, the extent of tolerance for deviant ideas and behavior, and willingness to take risks. There are different patterns of relationship between the degree of uncertainty avoidance and power distance (see Appendix 1).

Masculinity versus Femininity

This dimension relates to the division of the roles between the sexes in society. Masculinity represents a societal preference for showing off, achievement, heroism, assertiveness, making money or enjoying material success, thinking big, and so on. Femininity represents a preference for putting relationships with people before money, helping others and caring for the weaker, the quality of life, preservation of the environment, "small is beautiful," and so on.

The characteristics identified by this dimension tend to draw attention to the existence within society of competitiveness as against solidarity, equity as against equality, and achievement motivation as against relationship motivation. Career expectations and the acceptability of macho manager behavior are some of the issues raised by this dimension. On this dimension there is no identifiable pattern between countries (see Appendix 1).

Gray's Adaptation of the Model

Arpan and Radebaugh [1985] identified a set of cultural factors which are considered to influence accounting practices: conservatism, secrecy, attitudes toward business, and attitudes toward the accounting profession. They did not, however, provide any systematic analysis of the relationships between these factors and accounting practices. Gray [1985] attempted to develop such a model by identifying the mechanism by which societal values are related to the accounting subculture which directly influences accounting practices. Gray employed Hofstede's culture-based societal value dimensions as the basis for his analysis. Furthermore, he identified four value dimensions of the accounting subculture which are also related to societal values: professionalism, uniformity, conservatism, and secrecy. Professionalism thrives where there is a preference for the exercise of individual professional judgment and the maintenance of self-regulation as opposed to compliance with legal requirements and statutory control. Uniformity exists where there is a preference for the maintenance of uniform accounting practices between companies and for the consistent use of such practices over time as opposed to flexibility to suit the perceived needs of individual companies. Conservatism exists where there is support for a prudent and cautious approach to measurement so as to cope with the uncertainty of future events. Secrecy occurs where there is support for confidentiality and the restriction of information about the business to only those closely involved with management and financing functions.

Using Gray's analysis, it is possible to identify certain direct associations between the values of the accounting subculture and the societal dimensions of individualism and uncertainty avoidance (Table 1). By extending his analysis, Gray also classified accounting systems on the basis of each of the four accounting values (Appendix 2).

Values of the accounting subculture are likely to influence certain aspects of accounting practice, namely (a) the authority of accounting, (b) its force of application, (c) the measurement practices used, and (d) the amount of information disclosed [Gray, 1985]. In particular, the degree of professionalism preferred in an accounting subculture would influence the nature of authority

Table 1. Direct Associations Between Societal and Accounting Values

Values of Accounting Subculture	*Relationship with Societal Values*	
	Positive	*Negative*
Professionalism	Individualism	Uncertainty Avoidance
Uniformity	Uncertainty Avoidance	Individualism
Conservatism	Uncertainty Avoidance	Individualism
Secrecy	Uncertainty Avoidance	Individualism

Table 2. Relationship Between Societal Values and Accounting Practice

Societal Values Managerial/Work-Related Values →	*Accounting Values* →	*Accounting Practice*
Individualism vs. Collectivism	Professionalism	Authority
Large vs. Small Power Distance	Uniformity	Application
Strong vs. Weak Uncertainty Avoidance	Conservatism	Measurement
Masculinity vs. Femininity	Secrecy	Disclosure

for accounting. The higher the degree of professionalism the greater the degree of professional self-regulation and the lower the need for government intervention. The degree of uniformity preferred in an accounting subculture would have an effect on the manner in which accounting is used. The higher the degree of uniformity the lower the extent of professional judgment and the stronger the force applying accounting rules and procedures. The amount of conservatism preferred in an accounting subculture would influence the measurement practices used. The higher the degree of conservatism the stronger the ties with traditional measurement practices. The degree of secrecy preferred in an accounting subculture would influence the extent of the information disclosed in accounting reports. The higher the degree of secrecy, the lower the extent of disclosure. These associations between culture based societal values and accounting systems are shown in Table 2.

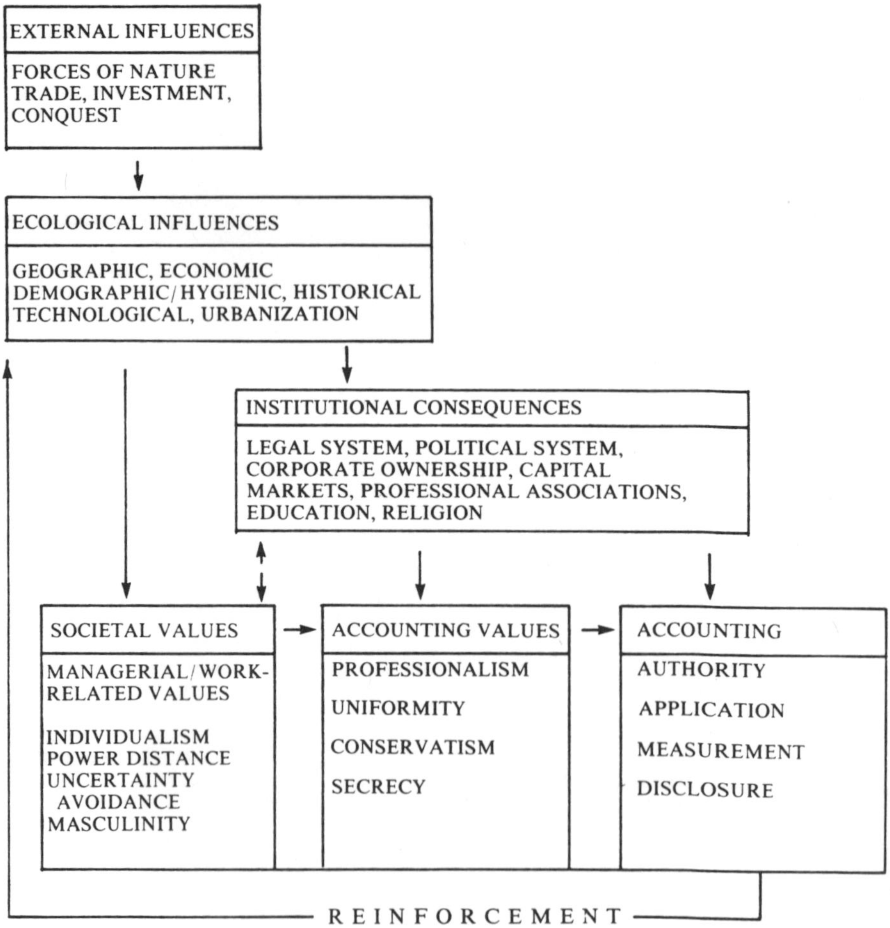

Figure 3. Accounting and Culture

However, any given aspect of accounting practice may be influenced by more than one accounting value. For example, the extent of disclosure is likely to be influenced not only by the degree of secrecy, but also by the degrees of conservatism, uniformity and professionalism preferred in an accounting subculture. The higher the degree of conservatism the more prudence will be preferred to disclosure; the higher the degree of uniformity (or the lower the degree of professionalism) the more emphasis placed on compliance rather than disclosure. Therefore, the extent of disclosure in financial reports would seem to differ between countries in line with differences in the value orientations of the preparers of those reports.

On a broader perspective, societal values are affected by ecological influences through geographic, economic, demographic, historical, technological, and urbanization factors, which in turn are influenced by external factors, such as the forces of nature, trade, investment, and conquest. On the other hand, both ecological factors and societal values influence a society's institutional arrangements with regard to the legal and political systems, corporate ownership, capital market, professional associations, education, religion, and so on, which impact upon accounting values and accounting practices. These relationships are shown in Figure 3.

The foregoing analysis suggests some associations between societal values and accounting values (hence accounting itself). Understandably the associations are complex. Tables 1 and 2 and Figure 3 incorporate Hofstede's four variables concerning culture-based societal values:

- Individualism v. Collectivism
- Large v. Small Power Distance
- Strong v. Weak Uncertainty Avoidance
- Masculinity v. Feminity

and Gray's four values of an accounting subculture:

- Professionalism
- Uniformity
- Conservatism
- Secrecy.

Focusing on the relationships between societal values and the accounting subculture (and disregarding for the moment the link between the accounting subculture and accounting), Table 3 could be used to formulate the following specific propositions about those relationships.

Proposition 1. The greater the Individualism and the smaller the Uncertainty Avoidance within a society *then* the greater the Professionalism (or the smaller the Uniformity) exhibited within an accounting subculture.

Corollary. The less the Individualism and the greater the Uncertainty Avoidance within a society *then* the less the Professionalism (or the greater the Uniformity) exhibited within an accounting subculture.

Proposition 2. The greater the Uncertainty Avoidance and the less the Individualism within a society then the greater the Conservatism exhibited within an accounting system.

Table 3. Frequency of Publication of Corporate Social Responsibility Information

	United[a] Kingdom 1982/83	United States[b] 1978
A. Environment		
1. Pollution control	10	133
2. Prevention or repair of environmental damage	7	15
3. Conservation of natural resources	—	39
4. Other environmental disclosures	—	46
B. Energy		
5. Conservation	16	126
6. Energy efficiency of products	10	45
7. Other energy related disclosures	2	29
C. Firm Business Practices		
8. Employment of minorities	1	52
9. Advancement of minorities	26	47
10. Employment of women	6	49
11. Advancement of women	—	142
12. Employment of other special interest groups	11	18
13. Support for minority businesses	—	18
14. Socially responsible practices abroad	15	43
15. Other statements on fair business practices	1	104
D. Human resources		
16. Employee health and safety	46	69
17. Employee training	53	80
18. Other human resource disclosures	75	32
E. Community involvement		
19. Community activities	13	56
20. Health and related activities	5	35
21. Education and the arts	11	70
22. Other community activity disclosures	7	56
F. Products		
23. Safety	11	42
24. Reducing pollution from product use	—	22
25. Other product related disclosures	14	46
G. Other social responsibilities disclosed		
26. Other disclosures	11	56
27. Additional information	49	16

Notes: [a] Analysis of sample of 300 reports used for Financial Reporting 1983-84.
[b] Adjusted from sample size of 500 pro rata to 300 to provide comparison with United Kingdom [Ernst & Ernst, 1978].

Source: Gray, Owen, and Maunders [1986, p. 60].

Corollary. The smaller the Uncertainty Avoidance and greater the Individualism within a society *then* the smaller the Conservatism exhibited within an accounting system.

Proposition 3. The greater the Uncertainty Avoidance and the less the Individualism within a society *then* the greater the Secrecy exhibited within an accounting subculture.

Corollary. The smaller thc Uncertainty Avoidance and greater the Individualism within a society *then* the smaller the Secrecy exhibited within an accounting suculture.

As previously stated, these hypotheses were developed from Hofstede's observations and classifications of circumstances in 1968-73. This would seem to suggest an excellent project for further research in this area. For example, under such a project, it would be possible to replicate the above analysis by remeasuring variables to see whether the relationships hypothesized from 1968-73 data still hold in 1990s.

CULTURAL INFLUENCES ON SOCIETAL ACCOUNTING DISCLOSURES

The distinctive nature of the culture of a particular people implies that its programmes may represent alternative solutions to common problems. This may be relevant to an understanding of the wide range of national differences which exist in social accounting disclosure patterns and also in formulating strategies to promote international social accounting disclosures.

Different Cultural Environments: Anglo-American versus Continental European

That the ideas developed in any society are a product of the socio-politico-economic environment can be illustrated by a number of specific examples. The growth of economic activity in the United Kingdom took place in an atmosphere of classifical liberalism with a broadly laissez faire approach to government. This was also true of the economic growth that began to gain momentum in the United States in the middle of the nineteenth century. In such a highly individualist atmosphere, the promotion of investment, by trying to interest people with uncommitted funds in various investment projects, became an important activity. Once prospective investors began to assess investment opportunities on the basis of their expected earnings, financial statements that included some kind of earnings figure became a necessity for the functioning of the entire system [Abel, 1971]. This was the background for the development of capital market activity which is the main source of funds for investment in both countries. The activities of these markets have resulted in continuous pressure being exerted for the provision of financial information for investors, making investors the most important recipients of accounting reports from companies [AICPA, 1973; FASB, 1978]. The pressure for disclosure had a significant effect on the development of accounting principles and practices in these countries and the requirements of the capital markets became a major influencing factor in their disclosure patterns. Furthermore, financial reporting and capital market activity were so closely related that they became interdependent [Barrett, 1977]. Similar developments took place in other Anglo-American accounting countries such as Australia, Canada, and New Zealand. It was assumed that these developments should be implemented by accountants, independent of legal direction or government intervention.

The position in much of Continental Europe is quite different from that already outlined. There has been a tradition of state intervention in economic affairs in both France and Germany. Unlike the position in the United Kingdom and the United States the influence of the classical economists was far more limited in Continental Europe. Instead, there have been a succession of economic theories with a common thread of anti-individualism. Financial accounting in France since World War II is generally influenced by legislation, due mainly to the determination of the French Government to obtain data for macro-accounting purposes. The 1947 *Plan Comptable Général* (uniform chart of accounts), which has been adopted by virtually all French enterprises, contains a detailed chart of accounts and a series of model financial and statistical reports which are considered necessary for the micro- and macro-accounting purposes. The French plan makes it clear that among its objectives in seeking data on an enterprise are, (a) the promotion of more reliable national economic policies, (b) the minimization of social misunderstandings, (c) ensuring the availability of data for government studies of market trends, and (d) assistance to the government authorities in exercising control over the economy. Furthermore, French companies have traditionally relied much less on an active new issue market as a source of long-term funds than have U.K. and U.S. companies. This has resulted in a lower emphasis being given to the investor-oriented corporate financial reporting and to the audit function as a safeguard for investors. Therefore, the primary influence on the development of accounting principles and practices in France has been the uniform chart of accounts, rather than the pronouncements of the accounting profession. Similarly, in Germany, as demand for industrial capital increased during the second half of the nineteenth century, strong banks, rather than individuals organized by a promoter, emerged as suppliers of a significant portion of that capital.

These environmental differences are reflected in the different approaches taken in those countries with regard to accounting issues. For example, it is widely held that accounting reports should be oriented toward the user's needs on the assumption that the public interest will be best served by a user orientation. In industrialized countries, the public interest is taken to be synonymous with the interest of the main group that provides capital. However, this group varies from one country to another; in the United States, it is the private investors [Nobes and Parker, 1981, p. 64]; in the United Kingdom, it is the institutional investors such as pension funds and building societies [Lee and Tweedie, 1977, p. 4]; in France, it is the family holdings and the state; and, in Germany, it is the banks [Hopwood and Schreuder, 1984]. The social and cultural differences between these countries can also be seen in the paths they have taken toward the development of social reporting.

Social Reporting: International Pressures for More Disclosure and National Disclosure Patterns

There has been considerable pressure at an international level, particularly from the UN and the EEC, for greater disclosure with special reference to information which is relevant to employee interests. The 1977 UN proposals highlighted the need to extend the scope of required disclosures beyond purely financial reporting [UN, 1977]. These proposals, although not specifically recommended, favored the production of separate social reports. Areas identified for disclosure were: labor and employment, production, investment programs, organizational structure, and environmental measures.

The fifth EEC directive on employee information and consultation, and the Vredeling proposals for giving information rights to employees of "large" companies (issued in 1980 and revised in 1983) were even more extensive in scope. They required the disclosure of information relating to corporate organizational structure, employment, the economic and financial situation, probable developments in production, sales and employment, production and investment programs, rationalization plans, and plans for new working methods or other methods that could have "a substantial effect" on employee interests. The OECD [1976] also required the disclosure of the average number of employees, categorized by function, together with employment costs showing social security costs and pensions. However, despite these pressures at an international level, for a well chosen program for promoting greater disclosure in social reporting, the extent of regulation at national level tends to be minimal [Gray, McSweeny, and Shaw, 1984] with the notable exception of France, where employee reports are required by law. Since 1977, large corporations in France have been required by law to publish a separate social report (*Bilan Social*). Detailed information must be disclosed about a wide range of matters including: employment; wages, salaries, and social security payments; hygiene and safety conditions of work; training; and trade union activities. The emphasis is on the impact of the corporation on employees. The extent of voluntary disclosure is significant and growing in other European countries such as Germany, the Netherlands, and Sweden, where additional special employee reports are often provided [Schoenfeld, 1978; Schreuder, 1979, 1981]. Information relating to employees is also required to be disclosed by U.S. and U.K. companies but the instances are fewer and the required disclosures are relatively minimal.

Some Specific Examples of Differences in Reporting Practices

Employee Reporting

The Continental European countries seem to be much more advanced in regard to "social" or "employee" reporting, at both institutional and practical levels than the Anglo-American countries. This can be explained to some extent in terms of their different cultural environments. Systems usually develop unique characteristics as a result of both internal and external pressures. Pressure groups and institutional influences which are active in developing social disclosures in industrialized countries generally include employees and trade unions, shareholders, community leaders, environmentalists, comsumerists, idealists and moralists, professional guidelines and pronouncements, and legislation and regulation. In a given country some of these will be more prominent than the others, and the emergence of pressure groups and institutional arrangements is likely to be influenced by its cultural background. As clearly demonstrated elsewhere by historical development and also by Hofstede's analysis of culture, the United Kingdom and United States are both oriented toward individualism, whereas France and Germany are relatively less individualist and more collectivist oriented (see Appendix 1 for specific data). It is interesting to see how the pressures for social disclosures have varied between these two groups of countries. Employees have been a powerful force in France and Germany whereas consumerists and environmentalists have been predominant in the United States and the United Kingdom, although recent changes in the relationship between the United Kingdom and Europe may be expected to affect these positions in the longer term.

Industrial Democracy

In the collectivist oriented cultures of Continental Europe, industrial democracy or worker representation on boards of directors has provided a co-determination framework for corporate performance and disclosures. As a result, employees have been a powerful force [Gray, Owen, and Maunders, 1987]. By contrast, in individualist cultures, the relationship between the employer and employee is a business relationship based on the assumption of mutual advantage. Either party can terminate the relationship in favor of a better deal elsewhere. In classical economic theory which was largely responsible for moulding the individualist cultural thinking, employees are "labour," a "factor of production," and "part of a labour market." They are not regarded as important contributors to decision making by the organization management. This is why employee and union pressure in North America has been relatively insignificant in terms of claims for additional disclosures. For example, when top-ranking officials of each of the 20 largest Canadian unions were surveyed in 1984 about industrial democracy, they did not agree that workers should be represented on boards of directors and doubted that this would become widespread by 1994 [Brooks, 1986]. Therefore, contrary to the European experience, social disclosure developments in the United States and Canada have developed from other forces such as environmentalists, consumerists, and idealists. Also, in the United Kingdom, the issue of expanded social reporting has not met with rapid acceptance, partly due to the current value accounting debate which has tended to retain the forefront of disclosure proposals and partly the result of political shifts following the 1979 election [Gray, Owen, and Maunders 1987].

The situation in Japan is different. Although Japan scores as the most collectivist amongst the industrialized countries (see Appendix 1), the relationship between employee and employer has a moral component. On the side of the employer, protection of the employee is maintained, almost regardless of the latter's performance in the workplace. In return, the employee is loyal to the employer to the point where changing employers is often socially disapproved. Under these circumstances, because companies' have traditionally assumed a protective role toward employees, they are not pressing for more information [Estes, 1977, p. 2]. Therefore, unlike the position in Europe, the collectivist orientation of Japanese culture has exerted a negative effect on employee reporting. On the other hand, as Triandis [1980] points out, achievement and affiliation in workplaces tend to be negatively correlated in the western industrialized countries, but positively correlated in Japan. Futhermore, the attitude toward culture itself is dependent on culture. For example, the collectivist environments find culture a natural control approach, thereby reinforcing existing relationships, while in strong individualist environments such as the United States, culture's importance and efficacy are underplayed leading to a resistance towards research demonstrating the importance of culture as a variable.

Environmental Disclosures

In contrast to the position on employee reporting there is some evidence of a greater concern for environmental matters in North America. Tinker [1984] has referred to the Love Canal scandal, Wiseman [1982] and Rockness [1985] have examined the veracity of corporate disclosures on environmental matters, and the Ernst and Ernst [1972-1978] studies of disclosures by Fortune 500 companies showed that considerable attention was given to environmental matters. A summary of the 1978 survey is shown in Table 3, which also incorporates similar data from U.K. studies.

The categories provided show a wide range of disclosures, in contrast with Continental European reports which emphasize employee matters almost exclusively [for example, Deutsche Shell as reported by Schreuder, 1979]. Although the Ernst and Ernst studies show some human resource disclosures, in additon to those connected with the employment and advancement of minorities and women, they are proportionately underrepresented in comparison with categories such as environment, energy, and community involvement. The later U.K. study carried out by Gray, Owen, and Maunders shows that compared with the United States, U.K. companies have a higher proportion of disclosures relating to employees; nevertheless, there are disclosures in all the categories other than Human Resources.

Brooks [1986] provided a useful analysis of the issues addressed in corporate social reports. The results, presented in Table 4, show the different emphasis which has already been noted. Studies of corporate social reports originating in West Germany, Austria, and Switzerland show an overwhelming concern for the human resources category of disclosure compared to those from the United States. Human resources related material in U.S. reports has been divided into different categories by Brooks [1986, p. 213] and the nonmonetary verbal disclosures do not appear in the table. Australian company disclosures are divided between most of the categories used.

A number of attempts have been made to link the provision of environmental information, whether supplied by the reporting organization or an outside body such as the Council for Economic Priorities (CEP), with changes in the market price of shares [Stevens, 1982; Spicer, 1978; Shane and Spicer, 1983]. This work follows the general trend of the individualist, market related cultural features, to which we have already shown in Table 2.

Conversely, the discussion of the measurement and valuation of externalities has been contested by several academics [Benston, 1982, is probably the best known example] on the grounds that shareholders would be forced to pay for additional information which they would not want. The same view would be put forward in relation to other social disclosures.

Institutional Requirements and Uncertainty Avoidance

It is also clear that European companies are much more subject to institutional requirements for social disclosure than are their North American counterparts. This may also have a cultural basis because the extent to which people feel that behavior should follow fixed rules differs from one culture to another. It is important to note here that the Continental European

Table 4. Issues Addressed in Corporate Social Reports

	Two-Year Period			One-Year Period			
	West Germany ($n = 16$ X 2)	*Austria* ($n = 6$ X 2)	*Switzerland* ($n = 9$ X 2)	*Japan* ($n = 29$)	*U.S. Monetary*[a] (($n = 500$)	*U.S.* *$*	*Australia* ($n = 50$)
Human Resources							
General personnel policy	12	4	14	3	30	89	65
Size of workforce, distribution, changes	10	5	7	2			
Employment of foreigners	3	1	2				
Labor costs	11	6	6	2			
Working conditions	10	1	2	2			
Training and development	15	6	12	2			
Fringe benefits—general	19	10	10	1			
Employee health services	9		1				
Company pension plans	8	5	4				
Company housing	9	2	3	1			
Employee ownership of property	4		1				
Labor representation	5		2	2			
Communication with employees	7		3				
Communication involvement	NA	NA	NA	NA	54	71	8
Environment	19	1	10	10	161	61	6
Energy	NA	NA	NA	NA	39	107	1
Product related matters	NA	NA	NA	10	1	7	0
Research and development	9	4	7	NA	NA[b]	NA[b]	
Miscellaneous	7	2	8	12	1	1	5
Stockholder relations	6			4	NA	NA	
Fair business practice	NA	NA	NA	NA	19	70	

Notes: NA = not available.

[a] U.S. statistics do not include 180 companies with only nonmonetary verbal disclosures.

[b] Subsequent to the survey date, the FASB required research and development disclosure.

Source: Brooks [1986], p. 213.

countries—in particular France and Germany—are high on the Uncertainty Avoidance scale, whereas Anglo-American countries are relatively low on the same scale (Appendix 1). The characteristics of the Uncertainty Avoidance dimension reveals that in cultures which are high on the scale, behavior tends to be more rigidly prescribed, either by written rules or by unwritten social codes; the presence of these rules satisfies people's emotional needs for order and predictability in society, and people feel uncomfortable in situations where specific rules are absent. Although there will be written and unwritten rules, people are able to live comfortably in situations where specific rules are absent in cultures low on the scale. Therefore, in general, one can expect more formalization and institutionalization of procedures in strong uncertainty avoidance societies than in weak uncertainty avoidance societies.

Figure 3 shows some direct association between societal values and accounting values. Accordingly, a high level of individualism in a society will have a positive effect on the degree of professionalism and negative effect on the degrees of uniformity, conservatism, and secrecy preferred in the accounting subculture. A strong uncertainty avoidance in a society will have a negative effect on the degree of professionalism and positive effects on the degrees of uniformity, conservatism, and secrecy preferred in its accounting subculture. The former represents the situation in Anglo-American countries while the latter conditions apply in continental European countries, particularly France and Germany. For example, as described elsewhere, there is a preference for the exercise of individual professional judgment, the maintenance of professional self-regulation, and flexibility in accordance with the perceived circumstances of individual companies in the accounting subcultures of Anglo-American countries. On the other hand there is a preference for compliance with prescriptive legal requirements and statutory control, the maintenance of uniform accounting practices between companies, and the consistent application of such practices over time, in the accounting subcultures of continental Europe. Also, there is more support in the former group for a prudent and cautious approach to measurement to cope with the uncertainty of future events and the confidentiality of the information by restricting disclosures to only those involved with the management and financing of the organization. These characteristics in turn tend to influence the degree of disclosure expected in the respective accounting systems or practices. For example, in France and Germany, where the level of professionalism is relatively low and the preference for conservatism and secrecy is relatively high, the combined effect on the degree of disclosure will be negative. On the other hand, the collectivist or nonindividualist values of the society require business enterprises to be accountable to society by way of providing information, therefore, it becomes necessary for the government to intervene and lay down certain disclosure requirements, including those in regard to social accounting, in particular employee reporting. Furthermore, this situation is not likely to be rejected by the accounting profession, because as discussed earlier, there is a preference for compliance with prescriptive legal regulation and statutory control in the accounting subculture. By comparison, in the United States and United Kingdom, although the relatively high level of professionalism and the low level of preference for conservatism and secrecy tend to have a positive combined effect on the degree of disclosure in accounting practices, the individualistic values of the society are more concerned with the provision of information to shareholders or investors than with those issues involving accountability to society at large. The fate of the recommendations in The Corporate Report would support this position.

CONCLUDING COMMENTS

This paper has explored the recent work on the effects of culture on accounting and the implications for social accounting, as a developing area within the accounting discipline. Social accounting has been the subject of a number of examinations in the recent past including empirical studies about disclosures which demonstrate changes over time within the one social system (Ernst and Ernst) and differences between different social systems at the same time [Brooks 1986].

The study of the impact of culture on accounting has a relatively short history and has not yet been extended to the developing area of social accounting. This paper is a first attempt and deals only with macro groupings on a limited basis, namely Anglo-American accounting and that practiced in Continental Europe, particularly in the area of employee reporting and environmental disclosures. No attempt has been made at this stage to consider differences within the major groups such as those between the United States and Canada and the extent to which the United Kingdom approach is moving toward that of Continental Europe as a result of that country's entry to the EEC.

The application of the work of Hofstede [1983] and others to the field of international accounting differences [Gray, 1985] is worthy of a further extension to the social accounting field and should not be ignored by social accountants working in both empirical and normative-deductive domains.

(Appendices follow)

APPENDIX 1

Value of the Indices for Fifty Countries (With Rank Numbers) and Three Regions

	Power Distance		Uncertainty Avoidance		Individualism		Masculinity	
Country	*Index*	*Rank*	*Index*	*Rank*	*Index*	*Rank*	*Index*	*Rank*
Argentina	49	18-19	86	36-41	46	28-29	56	30-31
Australia	36	13	51	17	90	49	61	35
Austria	11	1	70	26-27	55	33	79	49
Belgium	65	33	94	45-46	75	43	54	29
Brazil	69	39	76	29-30	18	25	49	25
Canada	39	15	48	12-13	60	46-47	52	28
Chile	63	29-30	86	36-41	23	15	28	8
Colombia	67	36	80	31	13	5	64	39-40
Costa Rica*	35	10-12	86	36-41	15	8	21	5-6
Denmark	18	3	23	3	74	42	16	4
Equador*	78	43-44	67	24	8	2	63	37-38
Finland	33	8	59	20-21	63	34	26	7
France	68	37-38	86	36-41	71	40-41	43	17-18
Germany (F.R.)	35	10-12	65	23	67	36	66	41-42
Great Britain	35	10-12	35	6-7	89	48	66	41-42
Greece	60	26-27	112	50	35	22	57	32-33
Guatemala*	95	48-49	101	43	6	1	37	11
Hong Kong	68	37-38	29	4-5	25	16	57	32-33
Indonesia*	78	43-44	48	12-13	14	6-7	46	22
India	77	42	40	9	43	30	56	30-31
Iran	58	24-25	59	20-21	41	27	43	17-18
Ireland	28	5	35	6-7	70	39	68	43-44
Israel	13	2	81	32	51	32	47	23
Italy	50	20	75	28	76	44	70	46-47

Jamaica*	45	17	13	2	39	26	68	43-44
Japan	54	21	92	44	46	28-29	95	50
Korea (S)*	60	26-27	85	34-35	10	11	39	13
Malaysia*	104	50	36	8	26	17	50	26-27
Mexico	81	45-46	82	33	30	20	69	45
Netherlands	38	14	53	18	30	46-47	14	3
Norway	31	6-7	50	16	59	38	8	2
New Zealand	22	4	49	14-15	19	45	58	34
Pakistan	55	22	70	26-27	14	6-7	50	26-27
Panama*	95	48-49	86	36-41	11	3	44	19
Peru	64	31-32	87	42	16	9	42	15-16
Philippines	94	47	44	10	32	21	64	39-40
Portugal	63	29-30	104	49	27	18-19	31	9
South Africa	49	18-19	49	14-15	65	35	63	37-38
Salvador*	66	34-35	94	45-46	29	12	40	14
Singapore	74	40	8	1	20	13-14	48	24
Spain	57	23	86	36-41	51	32	42	15-16
Sweden	31	6-7	29	4-5	71	40-41	5	1
Switzerland	34	9	58	19	68	37	70	46-47
Taiwan	58	24-25	69	25	17	10	45	20-21
Thailand	64	31-32	64	22	10	13-14	34	10
Turkey	66	34-35	85	34-35	17	24	45	20-21
Uruguay*	61	28	100	47	16	23	38	12
United States	40	16	46	11	91	50	62	36
Venezuela	81	45-46	76	29-30	12	4	71	48
Yugoslavia	76	41	83	43	27	18-19	21	5-6
Regions:								
East Africa*	64	(31-32)	52	(17-18)	27	(18-19)	41	(14-15)
West Africa*	77	(42)	54	(18-19)	20	(13-14)	46	(22)
Arab Centers*	80	(44-45)	68	(24-25)	39	(25)	53	(28-29)

Note: * New data.
Source: Hofstede [1983a].

APPENDIX 2

Classification of Accounting System on the Basis of Accounting Values

A. Professionalism Groupings

I High	II Medium	III Low
Australia	Austria	Japan
Canada	Israel	—
New Zealand	—	Argentina
United Kingdom	Germany	Brazil
United States	Switzerland	—
—	—	—
Netherlands	Denmark	Colombia
	Finland	Mexico
	Norway	Venezuela
	Sweden	—
	—	Iran
	Ireland	Pakistan
		Taiwan
		Thailand
		—
		Chile
		Peru
	Belgium	Portugal
	France	—
	Italy	Greece
	Spain	—
	South Africa	India
		Philippines
		—
		Hong Kong
		Singapore

B. Uniformity Groupings

I Strong	II Medium to Strong	III Weak to Medium	IV Weak
Belgium	Germany	India	Netherlands
France	Switzerland	Philippines	Norway
—	—	—	—
Argentina	Austria	Hong Kong	Australia
Brazil	Israel	Singapore	Canada
Italy	—		New Zealand
Spain	Finland		South Africa
—			United States
Colombia			
Mexico			
Venezuela			
—			Denmark
Chile			Sweden
Peru			—
Portugal			Ireland
—			United Kingdom
Greece			
Japan			
Iran			
Pakistan			
Taiwan			
Thailand			

C. Conservatism Groupings

I Strong	II Medium to Strong	III Weak to Medium	IV Weak
Belgium	Germany	India	Netherlands
France	Switzerland	Malaysia	Norway
		Philippines	—
—	—	—	Australia
Argentina	Austria	Hong Kong	Canada
Brazil	Israel	Singapore	New Zealand
Italy	—		South Africa
Spain	Finland		United States
Colombia			
Mexico			
Venezuela			
—			Denmark
Chile			Sweden
Peru			—
Portugal			Ireland
—			United Kingdom
Greece			
Japan			
Iran			
Pakistan			
Taiwan			
Thailand			

D. Secrecy Groupings

I High	II Medium to High	III Low to Medium	IV Low
Greece	Chile	Denmark	Australia
	Portugal	Finland	Canada
Argentina	—	Netherlands	Ireland
—	Yugoslavia	Norway	New Zealand
Belgium		Sweden	South Africa
Italy			United Kingdom
Colombia			United States
Mexico	France		—
Venezuela	—		India
—	Brazil		Philippines
Italy	Spain		
	—		
	Peru		
Japan	Turkey		Hong Kong
	—		Singapore
	Israel		
Austria			
Germany	Iran		
	—		
	Pakistan		
Switzerland	Taiwan		
	Thailand		

Source: Gray [1985].

REFERENCES

Abbott, W.F. and R.J. Monsen, "On the Measurement of Corporate Social Responsibility: Self Reported Disclosures as a Method of Measuring Corporate Social Involvement," *Academy of Management Journal* 22(3) [1979].

Abel, R., "The Impact of Environment on Accounting Practices: Germany in the Thirties," *International Journal of Accounting Education and Research* [Fall 1971].

Accounting Standards Steering Committee, *The Corporate Report* [ICAEW, 1975].

Alexander, J.J. and R.A. Bucholz, "Corporate Social Responsibility and Stock Market Performance," *Academy of Management Journal* 21 [1978].

AlHashim, D., "Accounting Control through Purposive Uniformity," *International Journal of Accounting Education and Research* [Spring 1973].

American Institute of Certified Public Accountants, *Professional Accounting in Twenty Five Countries* [AICPA, 1964].

American Institue of Certified Public Accountants, *Objectives of Financial Statements* [AICPA, 1973].

American Institute of Certified Public Accountants, *Professional Accounting in Thirty Countries* [AICPA, 1975].

Arpan, J.S. and L.H. Radebaugh, "An International Implication for Accounting," in *International Accounting and Multinational Enterprises* [Wiley 1985].

Barrett, V.M.E., "The Extent of Disclosure in Annual Reports of Large Companies in Seven Countries," *International Journal of Accounting Education and Research* [Spring 1977].

Beazley, G.F., "An International Implication for Accounting," *International Journal of Accounting Education and Research* [Spring 1968].

Beeny, J.H., *European Financial Reporting—West Germany* [ICAEW, 1975].

Beeny, J.H., *European Financial Reporting—France* [ICAEW, 1976].

Beeny, J.H. and J.G. Chastney, *European Financial Reporting—Netherlands* [ICAEW, 1978].

Belkaoui, A., "The Impact of the Disclosure of the Environmental Effects of Organizational Behaviour on the Market," *Financial Management* [Winter 1976].

Belkaoui, A., "Economic, Political and Civil Indicators and Reporting and Disclosure Adequacy: Empirical Investigation," *Journal of Accounting and Public Policy* [Fall 1983].

Benston, G.J., "Accounting and Corporate Accountability," *Accounting, Organizations and Society* 7(2) [1982a].

Benston, G.J., "An Analysis of the Role of Accounting Standards for Enhancing Corporate Governance and Social Responsibility," *Journal of Accounting and Public Policy* [Fall 1982b].

Benston, G.J., "Rejoinder to Accounting and Corporate Accountability: An Extended Comment," *Accounting, Organizations and Society* 9(3/4) [1984].

Berry, J., "An Ecological Approach to Cross-cultural Psychology," *Netherlands Journal of Psychology* 30 [1975].

Bowman, E.H. and M. Haire, "Social Impact Disclosures and Corporate Annual Reports," *Accounting, Organizations and Society* 1(1) [1976].

Bromwich, M. and A.G. Hopwood, *Accounting Standard Setting: An International Perspective* [Pitman, 1983].

Brooks, L.J., *Canadian Corporate Social Performance* [Society of Management Accountants of Canada, 1986].

Burke, R.C., *Decision Making in Complex Times: The Contribution of a Social Accounting Information System* [Society of Management Accountants of Canada, December 1984].

Cairns, D., M. Lafferty, and P. Mantile, *Survey of Accounts and Accountants 1983-1984* [Lafferty Publications, 1984].

Corson, J.J. and G.A. Steiner, *Measuring Businesses Social Performance: The Corporate Social Audit* [Committee for Economic Development, 1974].

Choi, F.D.S. and V.B. Bavishi, "Financial Accounting Standards: A Multinational Synthesis and Policy Framework," *International Journal of Accounting Education and Research* [Fall 1982].

Choi, F.D.S. and G.G. Mueller, *International Accounting* [Prentice-Hall, 1984].

Commission of the European Communities, *Proposal for a Directive on Procedures for Informing and Consulting the Employers of Undertakings with Transactional Undertakings* [Brussels, 1980].

Cooper, D.J. and M.J. Sherer, "The Value of Corporate Accounting Reports: Arguments for a Political Economy of Accounting," *Accounting, Organizations and Society* 9(3/4) [1984].

Cushing, B.E., ed., *Accounting and Culture* Plenary Session Papers and Discussants' Comments from The 1986 Annual Meeting of The American Accounting Association [AAA, 1987].

Da Costa, R.C., J.C. Bourgeois, and W.M. Lawson, "A Classification of International Financial Accounting Practices," *International Journal of Accounting Education and Research* [Spring 1978].

Das Gupta, N., *Financial Reporting in India* [Sultan Chand, 1977].

Donaldson, T., *Corporate Morality* [Prentice-Hall, 1982].

Ernst and Ernst, *Social Responsibility Disclosures: Surveys of Fortune 500 Annual Reports* [Cleveland, OH, annually 1972-78].

Financial Accounting Standards Board, *Statement of Financial Accounting Concepts No. 1,* "Objectives of Financial Reporting by Business Enterprises" [FASB, 1978].

Frank, W.G., "An Empirical Analysis of International Accounting Principles," *Journal of Accounting Research* [Autumn 1979].

Freedman, M. and A.J. Stagliano, "The Market Impact of Social Information: Investor Reaction to Public Disclosure," *Proceedings* [AAA Mid-Atlantic Regional Meeting, Baltimore, April 1984].

Geertz, C., *The Interpretation of Cultures* [Basic Books, 1973].

Goodrich, P.S., "Accounting and Political Systems," Discussion Paper No. 109, School of Economic Studies, University of Leeds [1982].

Gray, R.H., D. Owen, and K.T. Maunders, *Corporate Social Reporting* [Prentice-Hall, 1987].

Gray, S.J., "Cultural Influences and the International Classification of Accounting Systems," Paper presented at EIASM Workshop on "Accounting and Culture," Amsterdam, June 1985.

Gray, S.J., L.G. Campbell, and J.C. Shaw, eds., *International Financial Reporting* [*A Comparative International Survey of Accounting Requirements and Practices in 30 Countries*] [Macmillan, 1984].

Gray, S.J., I.B. McSweeney, and J.C. Shaw, *Information Disclosure and The Multinational Corporation* [Wiley, 1984].

Guthrie, J.E. and M.R. Mathews, "Corporate Social Accounting in Australasia," in L.E. Preston, ed., *Research in Corporate Social Performance and Policy,* Vol. 7 [Fall 1985].

Haire, M., E. E. Ghiselli, and L.W. Porter, *Managerial Thinking: An International Study* [Wiley, 1966].

Harbison, F. and C.A. Myers, *Management in the Industrial World* [McGraw-Hill, 1959].

Hofstede, G., *Culture's Consequences* [Sage, 1980].

Hofstede, G., "Dimensions of National Cultures in Fifty Countries and Three Regions," in J.B. Deregowski, D. Dzuirawiec, and R.C. Annis, eds., *Explications in Cross-Cultural Psychology* [Swets and Zeitlinger, 1983a].

Hofstede, G., *Culture and Management Development* [International Labour Office, 1983b].

Hofstede, G., "The Cultural Relativity of Organizational Practices and Theories," *Journal of International Business Studies* [Fall 1983c].

Hofstede, G., 'Cultural Dimensions in Management and Planning," *Asia and Pacific Journal of Management* [January 1984a].

Hofstede, G., "National Cultures Revisited," *Asia and Pacific Journal of Management* [September 1984b].

Hofstede, G., "The Ritual Nature of Accounting Systems," paper presented at EIASM Workshop "Accounting and Culture" [Amsterdam, June 5-7, 1985].

Holzer, H.P., ed., *International Accounting* [Harper & Row, 1984].

Hopwood, A.G. and H. Schreuder, eds., *European Contributions to Accounting Research, The Achievements of the Last Decade* [Free University Press, 1984].

Ingram, R.W., "An Investigation of the Information Content of (certain) Social Responsibility Disclosures," *Journal of Accounting Research* 16(2) [1978].

Jaggi, B.L., "Impact of Cultural Environment on Financial Disclosure," *International Journal of Accounting Education and Research* [Spring 1983].

Lafferty, M., *Accounting in Europe* [Woodhead-Faulkner, 1975].

Lee, T.A., ed., *Developments in Financial Reporting* [Philip Allan, 1981].

Lee, T.A. and D.P. Tweedie, *The Private Shareholder and The Corporate Report* [ICAEW, 1977].

Lindblom, C.K., "The Concept of Organizational Legitimacy and its Implications for Corporate Social Responsibility Disclosure," Working Paper No. 7 [Public Interest Section, AAA, Fall 1983].

Oldham, K.M., *Accounting Systems and Practices in Europe* [Gower, 1981].

Organization for Economic Cooperation and Development, *International Investment and Multinational Enterprises* [OECD, 1976].

Organization for Economic Cooperation and Development, *Accouting Practices in OECD Member Countries* [OECD, 1980].

McComb, D., "International Harmonization of Accounting: A Cultural Dimension," *International Journal of Accounting Education and Research* [Spring 1979].

Mahapatra, S., "Investor Reaction to a Corporate Social Reporting," *Journal of Business Finance and Accounting* 11(1) [Spring 1984].

Mathews, M.R., "A Suggested Classification for Social Accounting Research," *Journal of Accounting and Public Policy* [Fall 1984].

Merino, B.D. and M.D. Neimark, "Disclosure Regulation and Public Policy: A Socio-Historical Appraisal," *Journal of Accounting and Public Policy* 1 [1982].

Mueller, G.G., *International Accounting* [McMillan 1967].

Mueller, G.G., "Accounting Principles Generally Accepted in the United States Versus Those Generally Accepted Elsewhere," *International Journal of Accounting Education and Research* [Spring 1968].

Mueller, G.G., "Is Accounting Culturally Determined," paper presented at EIASM Workshop "Accounting and Culture," [Amsterdam, June 1985].

Nair, R.D. and W.G. Frank, "The Impact of Disclosure and Measurement Practices on International Accounting Classification," *The Accounting Review* [July 1980].

Nobes, C.W., "A Judgemental International Classification of Financial Reporting Practices," *Journal of Business Finance and Accounting* [Spring 1983].

Nobes, C.W., *International Classification of Financial Reporting* [Croom Helm, 1984].

Nobes, C.W. and R.H. Parker, *Comparative International Accounting* [Philip Allan, 1981].

Parsons, T. and E.A. Shils, eds., *Towards a General Theory of Action* [Harvard University Press, 1950].

Perera, M.H.B. (1985), *The Relevance of International Accounting Standards to Developing Countries* (Research Monograph) [University of Glasgow, 1985].

Price Waterhouse International, *Accounting Principles and Reporting Practices: A Survey in 38 Countries* [ICAEW, 1973].

Price Waterhouse International, *Accounting Principles and Reporting Practices: A Survey in 38 Countries* [ICAEW, 1975].

Price Waterhouse International, *International Survey of Accounting Principles and Reporting Practices* [Butterworths, 1979].

Radebaugh, L.H., "Environmental Factors Influencing the Development of Accounting Objectives, Standards and Practices in Peru," *International Journal of Accounting Education and Research* [Fall 1975].

Ramanathan, K.V., "Toward a Theory of Corporate Social Accounting," *The Accounting Review* 51(3) [1976].

Ramanathan, K.V., and H. Schreuder, "The Case for Social Accounting and Reporting: A Macro Perspective," paper presented at a Workshop on "Accounting in a Changing Social and Political Environment," [Brussels, December 1982].

Renshall, M., "The International Transfer of Financial Accounting Standards," paper presented at EEA Annual Conference [University of Glasgow, 1983].

Rockness, J.W., "An Assessment of the Relationship Between U.S. Corporate Environmental performance and Disclosure," *Journal of Business Finance and Accounting* 12(3) [1985].

Schoenfeld, H.M., "The Status of Social Reporting in Selected Countries," *Contemporary Issues in International Accounting, Occasional Paper No. 1* [University of Illinois, 1978].

Schreuder, H., "Corporate Social Reporting in the Federal Republic of Germany—An Overview," *Accounting, Organizations and Society* 4(1/2) [1979].

Schreuder, H., "Employees and The Corporate Social Report: The Dutch Case," *The Acounting Decision* [April 1981].

Schreuder, H. and K.V. Ramanathan (1984), "Accounting and Corporate Accountability: An Extended Comment," *Accounting, Organizations and Society* 9(3/4) [1984].

Seidler, L.J., "Nationalism and the International Transfer of Accounting Skills," *International Journal of Accounting Education and Research* [Fall 1969].

Shane, P.B. and B.H. Spicer, "Market Response to Environmental Information Produced Outside the Firm," *The Accounting Review* 58(3) [July 1983].

Singhvi, S.S., "Characteristics and Implications of Inadequate Disclosure: A Case Study of India," *International Journal of Accounting Education and Research* [Spring 1978].

Spicer, B.H., "Accounting for Corporate Social Performance: Some Problems and Issues," *Journal of Contemporary Business* [Winter 1978].

Stevens, W.P., "Market Reaction to Corporate Environmental Performance," paper presented to the AAA Annual Conference [San Diego, 1982].

Stillwell, M.I., *European Financial Reporting–Italy* [ICAEW, 1977].

Takatera, S. and M. Yamamoto, "The Cultural Significance of Accounting in Japan," paper presented at Workshop on "Accounting and Culture," European Institute for Advanced Studies in Management [Brussels, December 1987].

Tannenbaum, A., "Organisational Psychology," in H. Triandis and W. Lambert, eds., *Handbook of Cross-Cultural Psychology* [Allyn & Bacon 1980].

Tinker, A.M., B.D. Merino, and M.D. Neimark, "The Normative Origins of Positive Theories: Ideology and Accounting Thought," *Accounting, Organizations and Society* 7(2) [1982].

Tinker, A.M., *Paper Prophets* [Praeger, 1984].

Triandis, H., "Reflections on Trends in Cross-Cultural Psychology," *Journal of Cross-Cultural Psychology* [March 1980].

United Nations, *International Standards of Accounting and Reporting for Transnational Corporations* [UN, 1977].

Violet, W.J., "The Development of International Accounting Standards: An Anthropological Perspective," *International Journal of Accounting Education and Research* [Spring 1983].

Wiseman, J., "An Evaluation of Environmental Disclosures Made in Corporate Annual Reports," *Accounting, Organizations and Society* 7(1) [1982].

Zeff, S.S., *Forging Accounting Principles in Five Countries: A History and an Analysis of Trends* [Stipes, 1972].

JAI PRESS

Advances in International Accounting

Edited by **Kenneth S. Most,** *College of Business Administration, Florida International University*

EDITORIAL BOARD: Harold E. Arnett, *University of Michigan.* **A.N. Dutta,** *Editor, The Management Accountant, The Institute of Cost Accountants of India.* **C.T. Heazlewood,** *Massey University, New Zealand.* **H. Peter Holzer,** *University of Illinois.* **Adonai Ibarra,** *University of Costa Rica.* **Nobuichiro Nakamura,** *Osaka University.* **L. Perridon,** *University of Augsberg.* **Robert H. Raymond,** *University of Nebraska.* **Norlin E. Rueschoff,** *University of Notre Dame.* **John R. Small,** *Heriot-Watt University.*

REVIEW: ". . . the articles form a nice compendium for researchers in the area. . . ."

- *The Accounting Review*

Volume 1, 1987, 404 pp. $63.50
ISBN 0-89232-693-X

CONTENTS: List of Contributors. Part I. INTERNATIONAL ACCOUNTING STANDARDS. Classification of Financial Accounting Practices, *Christopher W. Nobes, University of Strathclyde.* **The Intrinsic Uniformity of International Accounting,** *Norlin G. Rueschoff, University of Notre Dame.* **Part II. COUNTRY STUDIES. Financial Accountability in West German Government,** *Maureen H. Berry, University of Illinois.* **Aspects of Hungarian Accounting,** *G.D. Donaleavy, Hong Kong Polytechnic.* **The Brazilian System of Monetary Correction,** *Timothy S. Doupnik, University of South Carolina.* **The French Contribution to the Theory of Accounting,** *Vassilios P. Filos, University of Athens.* **Accounting Needs of Islamic Banking,** *Abdul Wassay Haqiqi, Formerly, Ministry of Finance, Afghanistan and Felix Pomeranz, Florida International University.* **Independence of External Auditors: A Canadian Perspective,** *Daryl Lindsay and Harold Silvester, University of Saskatchewan, Morina Rennie, and George Murphy, University of Regina.* **Accounting and Reporting in Belgium,** *Hilda Theunisse, University of Antwerp.* **Part III. TECHNICAL STUDIES. Accounting for Foward Exchange Contracts,** *M. Ali Fekrat, Georgetown University.* **A Discriminant Analysis of Soviet Decision-Making Behavior in Selecting United States Suppliers of Goods and Services,** *Ronald E. Hoyt, University of Ottawa annd Michael Legault, Lavel University.* **Price Adjusted Financial Information and Investment Returns in a Highly Inflationary Economy,** *Juan M. Rivera, University of*

Notre Dame. **Regulation of International Data Communications and the Effect Upon Multinational Corporations,** *Joseph L. Sardinas, University of Massachusetts and Susan Merrill, Systems and Computer Technology Corporation.* **Accounting Resource (Currency) Translation: A Comparative Analysis of Approaches,** *Pontus Troberg, European Institute of Business Administration.* **Part IV. ACCOUNTING EDUCATION. The Attitudes of the Members of Three Canadian Accounting Organizations Towards Continuing Education,** *I.M. Gordon, Simon Fraser University and M.R. Mathews-Massey, Univesity of New Zealand.* **A Comprehensive Model for Improving Accounting Education in Developing Countries,** *Manuel A. Tipgos, University of Kentucky.*

Volume 2, 1989, 310 pp. $63.50
ISBN 0-89232-694-8

CONTENTS: List of Contributors. Part I. INTERNATIONAL ACCOUNTING THEORY. Replacement Value Accounting Theory: The "Circular Flow" and the Circulation of Value, *Abram Mey, University of Amsterdam.* **Replacement Value Accounting: Theory and Practice,** *Dick H. Van Offeren, University of Amsterdam.* **Conceptual Systems of Accounting Theory Formation,** *Hiroshi Yoshida, Kobe University of Commerce.* **Part II. COUNTRY STUDIES. An Analysis of the Accounting Standard Setting Framework in Two European Countries: France and The Netherlands,** *Robert Bloom, John Carroll University and M. Ahmed Naciri, Concordia University.* **Economic Considerations in the Choice of Depreciation Methods: Some Additional Evidence from Nigeria,** *Ademola Ariyo, University of Ibadan.* **A Survey of Current Development in Chinese Accounting,** *Lin Zhijun, Xiamen University.* **Tax Accounting in Japan and Its International Aspects,** *Hiroji Takao, Kansai University.* **Recent Advances in European Accounting,** *Klaus Macharzina, Hohenheim University.* **A Comparative Income Statement Approach to Integrating International Topics in the Financial Accounting Curriculum,** *David E. Stout, Villanova University, Donald E. Wygal and James Volpi, Rider College.* **Part III. FOREIGN CURRENCY TRANSLATION. The Functional Currency Determination: A Strategy to Smooth Income,** *Timothy S. Doupnik, University of South Carolina and Thomas G. Evans, Bowling Green State University.* **Analysis of the Economic Consequences of Foreign Currency Standards: A Classification Issue,** *Gordian A. Ndubizu, Drexel University.* **Part IV. INTERNATIONAL GOVERNMENTAL ACCOUNTING. Research in Governmental Accounting and Auditing,** *Mortimer Dittenhofer, Florida International University.* **The Future of International Standards in Government Accounting,** *Adolf J.H. Enthoven, University of Texas at Dallas.* **Government Auditing Standards**

JAI PRESS

in Twenty-Five Countries, *Peter N. Dean, United Nations, New York.* **Court of Audit, A European Phenomenon: The Situation in The Netherlands,** *Frans G. Kordes, Court of Audit, The Netherlands.* **The Federal Government Reporting Study (Canada and the U.S.),** *Edward R. Rowe, Deputy Auditor General, Canada.* **The Concept of a National Comptroller (Accountant),** *J.A. MacDonald, Comptroller General, Treasury Board, Canada.* **Some Ideas Concerning the Need to Reforn Financial Management in the Public Sector of Developing Countries,** *Roberto Dominguez, Inter-American Development Bank.* **Converting the Recognized Needs of Municipal Financial Report Users into Responsive Accounting Systems,** *Rowan H. Jones, University of Birmingham and the University of Illinois at Chicago.* **The Use of Accounting for Municipal Management Purposes,** *David C. Jones, World Bank.* **Chinese Accounting Books Translation Project.**

Volume 3, 1990, 249 pp. $63.50
ISBN 1-55938-078-0

CONTENTS: List of Contributors. Introduction. PART I. INTERNATIONAL AUDITING STANDARDS. International Auditing Problems, *Kenneth S. Most, Florida International University.* **PART II. COUNTRY STUDIES. The Use of Corporate Financial Reports by Investors in Saudi Arabia,** *Mahmound Abdelsalam, King Saud University.* **Economic Consequences in Canadian Accounting Standard Setting: A Technical Tool,** *Robert Bloom, John Carroll University and M. Ahmed Naciri, University of Quebec at Montreal.* **Investment Decisions and Equity Accounting Standards: The Case of Singapore and Malaysia,** *Eugene E. Comiskey and Charles W. Mulford, Georgia Institute of Technology.* **An Investigation of the Impact of Contextual Factors on Canadian Bankers' Perceptions of Auditors' Ability to Resist Management Pressure,** *Daryl Lindsay, University of Saskatchewan.* **Accounting for Changing Prices in Dutch Annual Reports,** *Dick van Offeren, University of Amsterdam, The Netherlands.* **PART III. FOREIGN CURRENCY TRANSLATION. Financial and Managerial Effects of Translating Foreign Inventories,** *Kathleen Ranney Bindon, University of Alabama.* **The Special Drawing Right as a Reporting Currency,** *M. Ali Fekrat, Georgetown University.* **Impact of SFAS 52 On the Accuracy of Analysts' Earning Forecasts,** *Bikki Jaggi and Gurprit Chhatwal, Rutgers University.* **FSAB Statement 52, An Accounting Policy Intervention: U.S.—Based Multinational Corporate Preeenactment Lobbying Behavior,** *Robert J. Kirsch, Thomas G. Evans, Bowling Green State University, and Timothy S. Doupnik, University of South Carolina.* **Earnings Volatility and the Corporate Adoption Decision on FASB Statement No. 52: An Empricial Analysis,** *Gordian A. Ndubizu,*

Drexel University. **The Impact of Financial Accounting Standards Board Statement No. 52 on Foreign Exchange Contracts: An Empirical Evluation,** *Hossein Shalchi University of Michigan-Flint and Ahmad Hosseini, University of Detroit.* **PART IV. CROSS-CULTURAL STUDIES. Managerial, Academic and Professional Influences, and Disclosure Adequacy: An Empirical Investigation,** *Ahmed Belkaoui, University of Chicago-Illinois.* **The Cultural Relativity of Accounting and International Patterns of Social Accounting,** *M.H.B. Perera and M.R. Mathews, Massey University, New Zealand.*

J A I P R E S S

JAI PRESS INC.
55 Old Post Road - No. 2
P.O. Box 1678
Greenwich, Connecticut 06836-1678
Tel: 203-661-7602

Volume 2, 1987, 197 pp. $63.50
ISBN 0-89232-698-0

CONTENTS: List of Contributers. Preface. Professional Value System of Academic Accountants: An Empirical Inquiry, *Ahmed Belkaoui and James L. Chann, University of Illinois at Chicago.* **Of Gods and Demons, Science and Ideology,** *Wai Fong Chua, The University of New South Wales.* **Risk, Financial Self-Discipline and Commodity Relations: An Analysis of the Growth and Development of Life Insurance in Contemporary Capitalism,** *David Knights, University of Manchester Institute of Science and Technology.* **Accounting Ethics: Surviving Survival of the Fittest,** *Cheryl R. Lehman, Hofstra University.* **Directions for Social Accounting Research: A Survey of Potential Data Sources,** *Joanne W. Rockness, North Carolina State University and Paul Schlachter, Florida International University.* **Case Study Research in Accounting: Methodological Breakthrough or Ideological Weapon,** *Chris Smith, Aston University, Richard Whipp, University of Warwick and Hugh Willmott, Aston University.* **Waving Goodbye to the TWA Bus: "Paper Prophets" and the Sraffian Critique of Marginalism,** *Tony Tinker, Baruch College, The City University of New York.* **Towards a "Real" Value Accounting,** *James F. Becker, New York University.* **The Dingell Hearings and Related AICPA Initiatives,** *Thomas P. Kelley, American Institute of Certified Public Accountants.* **The Regan Administration, A New Issue with Warmed Over Ingredients,** *John E. Ullmann, Hofstra University.* **A Social Analysis of Corporate Polution Disclosures: A Comment,** *David J. Cooper, University of Manchester Institute of Technology.* **An Analysis of the Impact of Corporate Pollution Disclosures: A Comment,** *In-Mu Haw, Baruch College, The City University of New York and Byung T. Ro, Purdue University.* **An Analysis of the Impact of Corporate Pollution Disclosures: A Reply,** *Martin Freedman, The State University of New York at Binghamton and Bikki Jaggi, Rutgers University.*

Volume 3, 1990, 275 pp. $63.50
ISBN 0-89232-784-7

CONTENTS: Editorial. Intellectual Tyranny and the Public Interest: The Quest for the Grail and the Quality of Life, *Ed Arrington, University of Iowa.* **Talking About Accounting: A Comment on Arington's Paper,** *Paul F. Williams, North Carolina State University.* **Publica or Privatus: Pro Whose Bono?,** *Ralph Estes, Wichita State University.* **The Debate on Whether Client Management Should Negotiate Audit Contracts: Yuppiees Versus Puuppies Versus Guppies Versus Supplies,** *Robert E. Jensen, Trinity University.* **The Market For Poitive Theory: Deconstructing the Market for**

the ACCOUNTING REVIEW

Quarterly Journal
of the
American Accounting Association

VOL. 65 JANUARY 1990 No. 1